The Garden of Emuna

A practical guide to life

By

Rabbi Shalom Arush

Translated by

Rabbi Lazer Brody

New Enlarged Fourth Edition

Shvat, 5779

In all matters relating to this book, please contact:

Chut Shel Chessed Institutions

POB 50226, Jerusalem, Israel

972-2-5812210

ISBN : 9798387757730

Distribution:

Tel: 972-52-2240696

www.myemuna.com

The Garden of Emuna

A Practical Guide to a Life of Emuna
And to your own personal connection to Hashem

by

Rabbi Shalom Arush

Director of Chut Shel Chessed Institutions

Author of:

The Garden of Emuna

The Garden of Peace

The Garden of Yearning

In Forest Fields

Women's Wisdom

The Garden of Riches

The Garden of Gratitude

The Universal Garden of Emuna

The Garden of Wisdom

The Garden of Education

The Garden of Knowledge

The Garden of Purity

The Garden of Emuna for Young People

I Said Thank-You and I Saw Miracles

and other books

Translated by: Rabbi Lazer Brody

ב"ה

OVADIA YOSSEF
RISHON LEZION
AND PRESIDENT OF TORAH SAGES COUNSIL

עובדיה יוסף
הראשון לציון
ונשיא מועצת חכמי התורה

Jerusalem, Tammuz, 5767

Approbation

The manuscript of "The Garden of Emuna" has been brought before me. It is a lovely collection of teachings about emuna, filled with stories and the words of our sages, the work of a master, a cherished and loyal scion of his people, the esteemed righteous scholar Rabbi Shalom Arush shlit'a, a man of purity whose literary collection is pure, full of ethics and spiritual stimulation, organized and edited beautifully - may his strength continue in Torah.

My prayer is that this book shall rise above all others to enhance Torah and its prestige. May the author enjoy lengthy years in joy and pleasantry and rejoice in his offspring and may his light - the light of tzaddikim - be as bright as the noonday sunshine. In his days, may Judea and Israel live securely and see salvation with no fear or threat and may the world fill with knowledge of Hashem. May the Redeemer come to Zion and may Jacob rejoice and Israel be glad, and may the palace of justice, our Holy Temple, be rebuilt speedily in our days, amen.

David Chaim Stern

President of "Yeshivat Be'er Yisroel" and "Kollel Harav Mendel"

Bnei Brak

Letter of Blessing

With Hashem's help

Our sages tell of Aaron who loved peace and pursued peace, and who would make peace between man and fellow man and between husband and wife to gladden both G-d and man, teaching us that there is nothing greater than peace, for it is one of the Almighty's Names.

Abraham would convert the men and Sarah the women; that's why he was called "the father of many nations", so much so that the Torah testifies that his heart was loyal to his Creator and that he was the greatest of believers in the entire world in all generations.

I was delighted today, for this was the day I awaited, when the greatest of spiritual guides who brings the masses close to the Creator, a man with a holy spirit, a righteous scholar whose internal dimension is just as pure as his external dimension, one who beautifully practices what he preaches and brings hearts of sons back to their father in Heaven, the great luminary **Rabbi Shalom Arush shlit'a** head of "Chut Shel Chesed Institutions", who works tirelessly to spread emuna, has been privileged to come out with the wonderful book of wisdom, **"The Garden of Emuna"**, a salve for the soul and a delight for the eyes.

In the pages of this book, the author tastefully serves the principles of emuna on a silver platter, showing this generation how to deal with the difficult challenges of life every moment of the day, with proper instruction to avoid pitfalls and to succeed and attain true happiness with Hashem's will.

May the merit of our forefather Abraham and outreach to the masses stand in the credit of the author and may his fountains flow forth for many years to come, with health of body and Divine illumination with satisfaction and peace of mind.

May we soon merit in greeting our righteous Moshiach and seeing our rebuilt Holy Temple, speedily and in our days, amen!

Signed on behalf of Jewish outreach,

דוד חיים שטערן

David Chaim Stern

RABBI N. MOSKOWITZ
OF MELITZ
RECHOV HATSIVONY 7\14
ASHDOD, E. ISRAEL

נפתלי א. י. מאסקאוויטש
ממעליץ
רח' הצבעוני 7/14 טל. 08-8640028
אשדוד

בס"ד תמוז תשס"ה

With Hashem's help, Tammuz, 5765

I surely saw the manuscript all about emuna that my dear friend the righteous scholar and master of outreach Rabbi Shalom Arush shlit'a wrote, and it's full of spiritual stimulation and practical advice for strengthening emuna in daily life. It is solidly based on faithful sources that lead one on the path of holiness. I am pleased to recommend that this book should be distributed to everyone, for every individual will derive great benefit from it. There is no limit to the need of constantly learning and reviewing the lessons of emuna until they fully penetrate the heart. May the author shlit'a enjoy length of years and may his holy teachings be distributed far and wide. May emuna and the merit of the masses stand in the credit of his pure soul, to be blessed with everything good, amen.

וכעז באהבה
נפתלי מאסקאוויטש

Naftali Moskowitz

Melitzer Rebbe, Ashdod

Rabbi Shammai Kehat Hacohen Gross

Rabbi and Dayan of the "Machzikei Hadat Community" of Belz in the Land of Israel

7 Divrei Chaim Street, Kiryat Belz, Jerusalem

With Hashem's help, Iyar, 5769

I have been presented with the cherished books, more valuable than gems and pearls, "The Garden of Emuna" and "In Forest Fields", written by the righteous scholar and master of outreach Rabbi Shalom Arush shlit'a. They are written beautifully and tastefully, presenting the principles of pure and simple emuna in Hashem, all based on the firm foundations of our sages and the great tzaddikim, may their holy memory protect us. These books are very stimulating and inspiring, giving instruction for successfully coping with life's daily challenges and are a must for everyone, for they stimulate the love and fear of Hashem and the strengthening of Torah and prayer, instilling a person with awe of G-d, emuna and purity. I pray that the author's wellsprings shall flow forth to the credit of the masses.

Signed with blessings for the author,

Shammai Kehat Hacohen Gross

Yehuda Zev Leibowitz

Son of the holy scholar Yechiel Tzvi, may Hashem avenge his martyred blood

Author of "Or Levi Ziv Yehuda", "Minchat Yehuda" and other books

Bnei Brak. With Hashem's help, Tuesday, 3 Sivan, 5779

To the honorable and celebrated Rabbi

Who returns the hearts of sons to their Father

The righteous scholar Rabbi Shalom Arush shlit'a

Head of Chut Shel Chessed Institutions

With warmest regards, I hereby send my blessing in honor of the publication of the important books, "The Garden of Emuna", "The Garden of Yearning", "The Garden of Riches", "In Forest Fields" and "Women's Wisdom." May it be the will of the Almighty that the author's wellsprings flow forth to greatly increase soldiers in the service of the Almighty. These books should be in every Jewish home to strengthen the foundations of Judaism and the foundations of emuna. And in this month of the giving of the Torah, may the esteemed author merit in receiving the Torah both spiritually and physically.

From me with blessings,

Yehuda Zev Leibowitz

Contents

Foreword

This book has revitalized, strengthened and brought joy to countless people. People with terrible sicknesses have turned to it and found salvation in its pages. People who lost their joy in life discovered life again. Everyone who has read this book has testified that the mere reading of it has given them tranquility and that they couldn't put it down. Many Torah seminaries have devoted time to learn it. Intellectuals have testified that from the many books of spirituality that they have read, this is the only book that appealed to them. The simple truth in each of its concepts found its way to the hearts of readers. Some of the righteous spiritual leaders of this generation said that the Divine Presence shines from its pages, that it revitalizes souls and that publishing it is a great mitzvah.

In short, every level of society has received this book with love and eagerness, beyond any expectations. The book has stimulated many non-Jews to believe in the Creator! The explanation is that Divine will has ordained that this book spread worldwide to teach emuna, for the entire purpose of creation is to bring a person to emuna.

We had no idea of the profound effect that learning about emuna has on people. Every word that enhances a person's awareness of emuna is an elixir of life and a wonder cure that everyone needs and can derive limitless benefit from, as the reactions to this book bear witness.

Introduction to the Fourth Edition

More than a decade has passed since the first edition of "The Garden of Emuna" appeared, and with thanks to Hashem, the book has become a multi-million-copy bestseller that appears currently in some twelve languages, with more in planning.

One should know that this is not a mere pleasure book but a workbook. In other words, the reader should live the lessons of this book and work on internalizing them and applying them to daily life, virtually living and breathing the book. The Gaon of Vilna learned "Path of the Just" 101 times, even though he knew it by heart already after learning it the first time. Rebbe Nachman of Breslev learned the book "Reishit Chochma" 400 times.

Why did these tzaddikim take the trouble of reviewing what they already knew?

The answer is that knowledge alone is insufficient. Even after a person learns a subject thoroughly, he or she must still work hard to internalize it and make that knowledge second nature until they virtually live what they have learned. What's more, there are fine points that become more and more clarified every time a person learns the material again. And, especially with emuna, one must pray to be able to implement each idea and principle.

Don't be surprised, dear reader, when you see that we come out with a new enlarged and improved edition every few years. The reason is that the contents of this book are dynamic and alive. When we learn a better way to learn, acquire and apply emuna, we pass this on for everyone's benefit. As such, most of this edition is rewritten and explained with greater detail and clarity.

Even though many of the principles are the same, you certainly won't lose from learning this new edition. Here's why:

1. At any rate, reviewing emuna is vital.
2. There are new additions to this edition that are highly important.
3. Many of the principles are much more explained and expanded.

This book is called "The Garden of Emuna" because it is surely a flowering garden that gratifies the soul, taking it along exquisite paths to the Creator.

We thank the Almighty for the privilege of learning, teaching and spreading emuna. We sincerely thank all those who helped us in the publication of the previous editions of "The Garden of Emuna", and we pray that this edition will illuminate the hearts of people around the world and hasten the day when all of living flesh will call His Name, amen!

Know

that all types of sorrow and tribulations stem from a lack of spiritual awareness. A person with spiritual awareness knows that everything is the result of Divine Providence. He therefore has no tribulations and feels no suffering, for "Hashem has given and Hashem has taken away" (Job 1:21). Even though one must necessarily feel pain, such as the pain of the soul separating from the body and the pain of sickness, since the soul is strongly connected to the body and separation is painful, even though, with spiritual awareness, the pain and suffering are lighter. Suffering is easier to cope with when a person is aware that everything is the product of Divine Providence. If difficult pain and suffering are easy to handle with spiritual awareness, lighter suffering is not felt at all. The reason one suffers is that at the time of tribulations, one's spiritual awareness is taken away, so that he'll feel the tribulations (Likutei Moharan I:250).

Chapter One:
The Foundation of Emuna

The Riddle of Life

This world is full of questions: What's the meaning of life? What's the purpose of a life full of anguish and suffering? What awaits humanity? With so many philosophies on life, who is right? What's the path to happiness? Where am I going? What will be in the end? How should I live my life? Will I ever be happy? Is it possible to find a definite path to happiness? The list is endless...

The drastic and seemingly unfair differences between one person's life and another's frequently perplex us. One person seems to glide on easy street while another person lives a life of excruciating hardships. One person is born with strength and perfect health while another is feeble and crippled. One is rich, yet another is poor. A kind person that never harmed a flea dies young, while a ruthless tyrant reigns until a ripe old age. Why?

Why me?

The ones who ask the most questions are the ones who suffer the most from deficiencies:

The person with a limited income asks, "Why does so-and-so have plenty of money, and even though I work just as hard, I go crazy trying to make ends meet?"

The parent of a sickly child asks, "Why does everyone have strong and healthy children, and I have the hard luck of raising a child that needs round-the-clock medical supervision?"

The handicapped person asks, "Why is everyone so beautifully free and agile while I'm so repulsively limited and impaired?"

The poor look at the rich and ask, "Why do they deserve a silver spoon, when our lives are a never-ending war with poverty and deprivation?"

The lonely individual who is approaching the age of forty and can't seem to find a spouse asks, "Why am I - with all my good qualities - unable to get married, yet others, with all their faults, find perfect spouses at a young age?"

We see that people's questions are endless; you are welcome to add your own to the list...

Changing Times

We have an additional array of questions about the changes in our lives from day to day. Why was yesterday such a splendid day, when everything went according to plan, while today - for no apparent reason - everything's a disaster and I feel nothing but pain and sorrow?

Why did I have plenty of money in my pocket last week, yet this week's unexpected expenses have left me without enough to buy a loaf of bread?

Why did I glean phenomenal joy from my children yesterday, who were the epitome of respect and deportment, yet today they've become miniature terrorists, driving me up a wall?

The questions are endless...

Answer to all the Questions

All of life's questions have one universal answer - **emuna.** Emuna is like a master key to life's locked dilemmas. **Emuna** is the original biblical Hebrew term for a firm belief in a single, supreme, omniscient, benevolent, spiritual, supernatural, and all-powerful Creator of the universe, which we refer to as God (or **Hashem**, which literally means "the name", so that we don't risk using God's name in vain). Emuna teaches that Hashem both created and runs the entire universe, caring for each of us in a unique, tailor-made fashion according to our own individual needs, which we refer to as **Divine Providence**.

As we shall see throughout this book, everything that happens to us in life is the product of Hashem's will and personal intervention in our lives, Divine Providence. Divine Providence dictates every detail in our lives, including the family that we're born into, who are soul-mate will be, how our lives will look, what our talents and aptitudes will be, how much money we'll have and who will be included in our social circles. These and the myriad of additional factors are all Divine Providence's way to help us perform our task in life.

Divine Providence not only determines the overall grand scale of our lives, but how are lives will be on a day-to-day and minute-to-minute scale. Hashem decides when we succeed and when we fail, when times are easy and when they're hard. He alone decides who we'll meet and what we'll do at any given moment. Divine Judgments determine the outcome of every single minute in our lives.

One must know that Hashem's Divine Providence is constant and never-ending, all for the ultimate benefit of each individual. It is designed to direct each person to his or her objective in life, the reason and purpose behind their creation. In His omniscience, Hashem sees that a person won't be able to attain his or her soul correction without the particular circumstances and hardships that they'll encounter in this world. One person's path to success is a road of poverty while another person's is a road to opulence. In like manner, Hashem determines every detail of a person's life, everything according to precision Divine Providence with a zero margin of error. There are no mistakes. Everything is designed to facilitate a person's fulfilling his or her designated mission and function in life.

Divine Will

What is the Divine will, which in essence is your purpose in life? The Creator created you so that you'll get to know Him, as we learn in the holy Zohar, the 2nd-Century C.E. esoteric interpretation of the Torah by Rebbe Shimon Bar Yochai and his disciples. Every single event in our lives is intended to help us get to know Hashem. Hashem knows each of us and knows fully well the exact conditions that facilitate our getting to know Him. Nothing is random and there are no mistakes.

The knowledge of the above concept, namely, that Hashem knows each of us and knows fully well the exact conditions that facilitate our getting to know Him, constitutes "complete emuna" and enables a person to be happy with his lot in life. Despite the fact that he does not and cannot grasp Divine considerations and decisions, by believing in Hashem and accepting his will, one can truly be happy with his lot in life. This is the first step to making the right choice in life. With this in mind, a person is more aware of what is happening to him on a daily basis and uses life's events as a springboard to better knowledge of the Creator.

Every stimulus in life - for better or for worse - comes from the Creator, all designed to help us get to know Him. Consequently, when people ignore Hashem's personal messages, Hashem is compelled to send "louder" messages, in other words, situations of greater difficulty. Those who fail to get to know Hashem in good times risk being placed in predicaments devoid of any natural or logical solution, where the only remaining alternative is to cry out to Hashem. In this manner, Hashem - in His infinite loving-kindness - helps each of us reach Him and thereby achieve our ultimate soul correction and to learn that there is no one to depend on but Him, our Father in Heaven.

The Beginning of Emuna

The holy Zohar states that the beginning of emuna is the thought and recognition that there is not only a physical world of the present but a world to come. Rebbe Nachman of Breslev implores every individual to remember this fact constantly (see Likutei Moharan I:54). Why is this so vital?

Any emotionally healthy individual is not willing to do anything without a purpose. For example, if you tell someone to raise their hand and lower it for an entire hour for no reason, he won't agree - even if you pay him - because he doesn't see the point in such a meaningless task. If humans with their limited intellect understand that they wouldn't do anything without a purpose, then they should realize that the Creator with His Divine wisdom certainly doesn't do a thing without an express purpose.

With the above in mind, it's absurd to think that the Creator created such a world of grandeur with its myriad of details without having a specific purpose in doing so.

There's no way that the Creator would have created man, the most sophisticated of creations with phenomenal intellectual and spiritual abilities, without there being a purpose to each human's life.

Everyone must ask himself: can my purpose on earth be fulfilled in a material world that culminates in death and physical decomposition? Does it make sense that the Creator would give me emotions, creativity, aspirations and feelings just to suffer for eighty or ninety years and then to get buried in the dirt? Does that make sense? Does one's spiritual thirst and aspirations terminate in the grave? That's impossible, for if so, it would mean that there was no purpose to the entire spiritual and emotional aspects of the individual. Therefore, there must be some continuation after the physical life - the body - terminates, where there is an ultimate purpose to the spiritual life - the soul. This makes sense in the context of reward and punishment, where we act in a certain way in the physical world and then receive our reward in the spiritual world.

Even so, there is an aspect of reward and punishment in the physical world. A person enjoys success when he does the Creator's will. Contrastingly, he invokes tribulations upon himself when he transgresses. Yet, these tribulations are not really punishments, but simply prodding agents to lead a person to an upright path. Tribulations are designed to stimulate a person to assess himself and the current path in life that he is pursuing. Maybe it's a mistaken one? Perhaps he should rectify something? As such, tribulations in this world are neither punishments nor Divine revenge. As such, if there were only a physical world, none of this would make any sense.

I Don't Understand a Thing

The Torah in Chapter 21 of Exodus states that a person who accidentally killed someone must exile himself to one of the shelter cities: "But for one who has not lain in ambush, and G-d caused his hand to do so, I shall provide you a place for which he shall flee" (Exodus 21:13).

Rashi explains that the words "one who has not lain in ambush" means that he did not commit premeditated murder. He didn't stalk the victim and he had no intention of doing him any harm. In other words, it was an "accident"...

But, wait a second - look what the Torah says: "and G-d caused his hand to do so." The Torah is revealing that there is no mistake here. Hashem put the guilty individual in a position where he would be the unfortunate one to kill somebody. Hashem orchestrated the "accident". The Midrash adds: "Who are we talking about? One person killed someone unintentionally and somebody else murdered someone in a premeditated manner. In both cases, there were no witnesses." It turns out that neither received his just punishment, for the murderer should have been killed and the accidental killer should have been exiled. So, in this case, Hashem judges them. What does He do? Hashem brings them both an inn. The murderer sits under a ladder. The accidental killer climbs the ladder and falls from it, crushing and killing the murderer. Other witnesses at the inn testify that this was accidental, so now, the accidental killer gets his just due of exile and the murderer gets his just due of a death sentence.

From the above example, we learn the extent of Divine Providence that underlies every occurrence, especially accidents, Heaven forbid. To the innocent onlooker, the man who sat under the ladder was an unfortunate victim. Even so, the person who fell on him and killed him had no intention of doing so. But in truth, everything is a product of precision Divine justice.

The Midrash also relates that Moses asked to understand Divine ways (see Exodus 33:13). Moses wanted to understand the inner mechanisms of Divine Providence. Hashem told him, "Come up to Me on the mountain" (Deuteronomy 10:1).

On his way up to the mountain, Moses saw a strange sight. A person bent down to drink from a spring, and as he did so, a wallet full of money fell out of his pocket without his knowing and he walked away. A second person came to drink from the spring and found the first person's wallet. The second person walked away and a third person came to the spring for a drink of water. While he was still drinking, the first person came back to the spring to search for his wallet but it wasn't there. The first person said to the third person, "Hey, you found my wallet!"

The third person said, "I didn't find a thing."

Enraged, the first person killed the third person.

Moses was amazed by what he saw; he said to Hashem, "Master of the World, explain Your ways to me. That whole incidence at the spring - why did the second person walk away scot-free with the wallet, yet the third person paid the bitter price? He found nothing, yet he got killed!"

Hashem answered, "Everything you saw is truth! The first person stole the wallet from the second person who found it; as such, the wallet returned to its rightful owner. The third person that got killed murdered the first person's father without the first person knowing who committed the crime. As such, the first person became the agent of Divine justice to avenge the death of his father."

The above examples from the Midrash are just a sampling of the exact Divine Providence that governs every event in the world. The Torah's phrase of, "and G-d caused his hand to do so," shows that there is nothing random or happenstance in the world. Divine Providence takes every tiny detail into account in every single happening in the universe, big or small.

In the course of a person's life, one encounters many situations that seem unjust and unfair. The reason is because we mortals can't possibly see the whole picture. This resembles a person who came late to the movies - it's already the second half of the movie and the viewer sees a man mercilessly beating a lady. He blurts out loud, "You villain! Leave the lady alone!"

The other viewers in the theater hush him up. "If you'd have seen the beginning of the movie, you'd have seen the unspeakable things she did to him..."

People are limited in perception - they only see a tiny portion of the entire picture. No one knows the past of every soul, who it was and what it did in previous lives. No one knows what each individual soul must rectify during its current go-around in the physical world. What's more, no one can possibly know the underlying reasons behind each person's personal condition or circumstance.

But, if a person had spiritual eyes that were capable of seeing, he or she would know that Hashem's accounting and individually tailor-made Divine Providence is not only just, but merciful as well; as such, they'd no longer question Hashem.

The Mission

Each individual is here on a mission. His life in this world is temporary; it begins and ends according to the task he must perform. When a person dies, even if the cause of death is seemingly apparent, it is the result of Divine decree - exacting to the tiniest detail. One person comes to earth for a seventy-year tour of duty while another person is on a twenty-year mission. A soul can sometimes fulfill its correction on earth in a mere five years within the body of a child. The considerations and Divine calculations are endless and mindboggling where everything is taken into consideration, past lives, credits, debts and many more.

Some souls come down to earth for a very specific soul correction; as soon as they complete it, there is no longer reason for them to remain here so they hurry back to their rightful place in Gan Eden ("Garden of Eden", the World to Come). Usually, after these souls die, those who knew them say how much those souls were so special and righteous who never did anything wrong. So, don't be surprised when you see young martyrs who were the best imaginable people of the highest caliber. The reason they left this earth when they did was simply because they accomplished the mission that Hashem sent them here to perform.

The very fact that these young, righteous people who didn't seem to have an evil inclination at all died at such a tender age is a giveaway that shows that they came here for a very special purpose. The holy Ariza"l says that the evil inclination puts the most difficult obstacles in the way of the very mission that a person must perform on this earth. When a person has many different evil inclinations, it's an indication that he or she has much to correct in this world. But, those special people, especially the young ones who never did anything wrong, came here for a narrow specific purpose. They complete it and they depart.

Safe Deposit

Rabbi Meir Baal Haness lost two sons on Shabbat. His wife kept this tragic news secret and instead, rejoiced in the Sabbath with her husband. When Shabbat was over, she told him that the time came to return the two jewels that were in their safekeeping to the rightful Owner:

This is the account from the Midrash (Mishli, 31):

One Sabbath, Rebbe Meir sat in the house of study, unaware that both of his sons had died. Bruria, his wife, withheld the bitter news from him, covered the two bodies with a sheet, and moved them up to the attic. That evening, after Sabbath ended, Rebbe Meir returned home and asked, "Where are the two boys?" Bruria changed the subject and served her husband his evening meal.

When Rebbe Meir finished his grace after the meal, his wife said, "Rebbe, I have a question."

"Feel free to ask, my wife."

"If a person gave me a deposit for safekeeping some while ago and now he has come to claim it, what should I do?"

"Simple," replied Rebbe Meir, "you must return the deposit."

Bruria took Rebbe Meir by the hand, led him up to the attic, and showed him his two lifeless sons. Rebbe Meir began to cry, lamenting his grievous loss. "Rebbe," his wife said, "didn't you just tell me that a deposit for safekeeping must be returned when the owner comes to claim it?"

Rebbe Meir stopped crying immediately and quoted (Job 1:21), "Hashem has given, Hashem has taken, blessed be Hashem's name!"

Rebbe Chanina, another holy sage and contemporary of Rebbe Meir, praised Bruria and her poignant consolation that so effectively relieved her husband's grief, and said (Proverbs 31:10), "A woman of valor, who shall find?"

The Talmud (tractate Berachot, 5b) tells of the renowned sage Rebbe Yochanan, who having lost all his ten sons, would walk around with the tooth of his tenth son in his pocket and declare, "This is the bone of my tenth son that died. See how I lost ten sons but am still happy and smiling! I realize that this world is not our principle concern, and those holy souls that were my sons simply finished their tikkun and respective missions in this world, so why should I be sad? They are now in a world of eternal bliss, but we are still suffering on this lowly earth."

Rebbe Nachman of Breslev lost his only two sons, his first wife, and left this world at the young age of 38.

Many Tzaddikim buried loved ones and suffered other grueling tribulations, yet everyone knew that they were pillars of righteousness. Often, there's no connection between longevity and a person's good deeds. We shudder when hearing about the loss of a young person. Actually, the thought of an elderly person's death should jolt us even more, showing us that death is unavoidable. Moses died at 120; if he died, then who is immortal? No one...

When we hear about a young person who died, we all shudder, for it shows how death is right at our doorstep. Indeed, we should shudder even more when we see an elderly person pass away. Why? A young person's death doesn't really prove anything, because it's not an ordinary occurrence. People can say, "That won't happen to me." But, an elderly person's death shows unequivocally that we all share the same destiny. This should awaken us from our spiritual slumber.

Don't Forget the World to Come

Oftentimes a person takes his initial steps as a spiritually-awakened Jew, or Baal Teshuva, and suffers some form of damage - physical, financial, or otherwise. The resulting question usually sounds like this: "Why now, when I've chosen the path of Torah and have started to observe the Sabbath, do I deserve such punishment? Is this the reward of Torah?"

Still other times, a new Baal Teshuva dies a sudden, tragic death. People ask, "How is this possible? What's going on here? A new Baal Teshuva that left a life of glitter and good times to devote his life to Hashem...He should have lived forever! Why did Hashem take him so suddenly?"

The most famous question of the perplexed is: "What about the Holocaust? Why did Hashem allow six million Jews - many of whom were holy and righteous Torah scholars - to die in the gas chambers and concentration camps?"

People forget that this world is a place of temporary significance at best, where a soul assumes a bodily form to perform a mission and achieve a needed tikkun. But, if they'd remember that the World to Come that encompasses the life, destiny and health of the soul is our prime concern - and not the body and the material world - then their questions would fall by the wayside.

Tikkunim: Soul Corrections

Our belief in the World to Come is the foundation of genuine emuna. Life's riddles take on an entirely different meaning when we understand that our lives in the material world are only a small portion of a person's total life, which begins way before birth and ends long after death.

The following story appears in the writings of Rabbi Chaim Vital, osb"m, which he received from his holy mentor, the Ariza'l:

A tragic event jolted an entire Jewish community, leaving many people, old and young, perplexed about Hashem's ways.

A beautiful young lady - daughter of one of the community's most prestigious and respected families - married a righteous merchant, a man of charity and compassion. The early years of their marriage were blessed with happiness, abundance, and children. The modest wife became a wonderful mother, utilizing every free minute from her busy schedule to recite Psalms or to care for the community's poor and underprivileged. The husband, whose successful commerce carried him to surrounding cities and hamlets, never failed to fulfill a strict daily quota of prayer and Torah learning. In addition, he gave enormous amounts to charities all across the country, easing the suffering of thousands of impoverished people.

Suddenly, disaster struck. Their home - a bright beacon of charity, good deeds, and lovingkindness - became the scene of agony. A drunken soldier viciously abused, mutilated, and murdered the couple's three-year-old son!

The entire community was appalled. Thousands joined in the mourning, including the nation's leading sages and spiritual leaders. No one understood. Many vocalized the doubts in their hearts in public: Is this the reward that such a righteous couple deserves? Why did Hashem do something so horrendous like that to them? Why did the poor little toddler have to suffer so severely? Others harbored malice in their hearts against Hashem that weakened their emuna and distanced them from Torah.

The couple reacted with total emuna, capitulation, and loving acceptance of the Divine decree. They continued with their righteous lifestyle as if nothing had changed - the wife with her acts of loving-kindness and the husband with his Torah learning and magnificent charity.

Shortly thereafter, tragedy struck again: Like wildfire, word spread around the town that the righteous merchant had fallen deathly ill. All of the local synagogues mobilized their members in round-the-clock prayer vigils. Everyone loved the merchant. Almost every person in town had benefited from his generosity at one time or another. Understandably, the cries of the community pierced the very thresholds of the Heavens.

The community beadle ran breathlessly into the town's main synagogue, where the head rabbi prayed, and shouted, "The doctors have given up hope! They say the end is near!"

The head rabbi, himself a pillar of righteousness and a learned master of Talmudic law, declared forcefully but calmly, "It shall not happen! No evil shall befall our brother the righteous merchant!"

The pain and bewilderment of the entire town reached new heights when the word of the righteous merchant's death became common knowledge. Such a young man, at the prime of life - didn't he suffer enough? He did nothing but good deeds his entire life, is this what he deserved? The tears of the young, barely thirty-five-year-old widow tore at the community's already perplexed and agonized heart.

A few years passed. One Friday afternoon, the newly-married son of the young widow came to wish his mother "Shabbat Shalom"; she tried to smile but burst into tears.

"Mama," the young man pleaded, "three years have passed already. You've cried enough! Our sages prescribed set times for mourning. If someone cries more than they should, then sorrow never leaves them! We are believers; none of us can know Hashem's considerations. Everything Hashem does is for the very best! Mama, your crying not only saddens us - your children - but it saddens Papa's soul, too. The matchmakers have been chasing after you with several good proposals, and you've been avoiding them. Mama, please, you must continue on with your life."

The young widow took a deep breath. Enough! She made a firm resolve to overcome the sorrow. An encouraging thought flashed across her mind: "Am I more merciful than Hashem? Of course, not! I've always trusted Hashem, so why shouldn't I be happy?!" To the relief of her worried children - that very Shabbat - Mama became a new person.

For the first time in years, the widow slept soundly and peacefully. She realized that a lack of emuna - not her husband's absence - was responsible for the gap in her heart. Now, that gap was filled again.

She had a dream... She saw herself standing in an exotic garden of supernatural beauty, and she understood that this must be the next world. Standing among the aromatic flowering trees, she saw an image of an old man with a long beard, who radiated brilliantly. He approached her and asked if she'd like to see her deceased husband. She nodded in the affirmative. He led her to a magnificent palace where a young man was giving a Torah lecture to thousands of elderly righteous souls. When the lecture was over, the lecturer approached her - it was her husband!

"Dearest husband," she exclaimed, "why did you leave me alone at such an early stage in our lives? How have you become the teacher of so many tzaddikim? You were a merchant and an upright man, but you were never a Torah scholar."

The husband smiled. "In my former life, I was a great scholar, but I never married. When I died, I was told that I can't assume my designated place in the upper palaces of Heaven because I never fulfilled the first commandment of the Torah, namely, that one must be fruitful and multiply. Therefore, I was reincarnated again for the sole purpose of marrying and having children, and to raise them in the path of Torah. That's exactly what I did – I came down to the physical world, I married you and together, we brought children into the world. As soon as I completed my tikkun – my soul correction and my mission on earth – I no longer had to remain down there. That's why I died. Now, as you see, I enjoy the fruits of my labors and live a life of eternal bliss..."

"So many people prayed for you. The rabbi of the city decreed that you shouldn't die. Why did nothing help?"

The husband responded, "None of the prayers were wasted. A portion of them helped me get to where I am today. The rest were used to rescind harsh judgments against the Jewish People and to aid others who needed salvation. But, since my job on earth was finished, there was no chance that I could remain down there. That's why the rabbi's rescinding of the death decree didn't help. But you still have a job to do; remarry and have more children. Take good care of the children you already have – our children. Be strong and valiantly continue on your mission."

"Then why did our little son die?" probed the wife.

The husband answered, "He is the lofty soul of a holy tzaddik, an extremely righteous individual. In his previous life, he was kidnapped at birth and raised on the milk of a gentile surrogate mother. Finally, at age three, he was redeemed by the Jewish community and subsequently became a sage of enormous spiritual proportions. After his death, he was denied his rightful place in Heaven since his early childhood had left a tiny blemish on his soul. His sole tikkun was to return to earth, to be born, nursed, and raised for three years by an upright Jewish woman; you, dear wife, were granted the privilege of being that woman!"

"But why was his death so horrible?"

"Know," continued the husband, "that since our toddler son had completed his tikkun, he was destined to die anyway. At the same time, the Heavenly Court had decreed - in light of the dire sins between man and fellow man in our town - that all its inhabitants be destroyed in a catastrophic pogrom. The righteous soul of our little one volunteered to die a terrible death as atonement for the entire town. He became a holy martyr and sanctified himself as a public sacrifice. No one is allowed to reach his lofty abode except for me, since I was his father. When your time comes, you - as his mother - will also be allowed. You can't imagine the bliss of the Divine light that surrounds our son..."

The husband faded away. Before he departed, his voice reverberated, "Only by virtue of your reinforced emuna was I revealed to you! As long as you were in a cloud of sadness, you almost lost another child. All my requests to be revealed to you were refused... my tikkun is over, but you still have much to do. Go, remarry, and live a life of emuna and joy. Go with my blessing... farewell!" The husband's image disappeared completely.

The widow awakened. She felt like she was born anew into a fresh new world. She realized that her questions - as well as the rest of the town's questions - were needless. If the Torah teaches that Hashem is righteous and just, then there's no need to wonder why Hashem does what He does.

Those of us who don't merit revelations in our sleep should strive to strengthen our emuna. The knowledge that Hashem does everything for our eternal benefit should be engraved on our hearts and minds. The proof of genuine emuna is a person's happiness with his lot in life, for he believes that everything is in Hashem's control and all for the very best. That's the only way that life on this earth makes any sense.

Mortal Man

No one knows **what** he came to this world to correct. We can't possibly know **when** our tikkun has been achieved. No one knows **how** they'll leave this world, either. Yet, we should always remember that we're mortal, and destined to die someday. King Solomon, the wisest of all men, advised (Ecclesiastes 7:2): "It is better to frequent the house of mourning than the house of feasting, for it signifies the end of all men - and the living should take it to heart!"

Apparently, the above advice to attend funerals and visit mourners is simple: By visiting mourners, we remember that someday, our lives will terminate also. Surprisingly though, certain professionals like doctors, nurses, and geriatric attendants see death all the time, yet how many of them are aroused to teshuva? Many of them remained bogged down in the pursuit of material amenities their entire lives. Even the undertakers, who with their own hands bury dozens of people, don't seem to be any more spiritually-aroused than anyone else.

That's why King Solomon stressed, "And the living should **take it to heart!**" All of us must remember that we're mere mortals, here today and gone tomorrow; if we forget, we're liable to fall into spiritual slumber. A person must tell himself, "Hey, the day will come when I die too! People will be sitting shiva (seven-day mourning period) for me also!" If he doesn't do so, he won't wake up from his spiritual slumber, even if he goes to funerals every day. That's why King Solomon implored, "... **take it to heart**!" The contemplation of our final day on earth and subsequent day of reckoning helps us monitor our thoughts, speech, and deeds. We're not talking about scaring ourselves, but simply dealing with reality to view this world in proper perspective.

Since I'm mortal, what should I be doing with my life in this world? Even if I achieve abounding fame and wealth, ultimately, I'll die! No one can avoid this destiny. If so, is there anything of meaning to do in the material world? A person who contemplates life in such a manner will surely arrive at the needed conclusions. He'll realize that there's a Creator to the world, with Whom he should speak to and establish a personal relationship. He should ask the Creator to help him understand why he was created and what his own special mission here on earth is.

Just Passing Through

As soon as a person contemplates his final day on earth, all the lies of the material world crumble. Nothing can fool him! A person who knows that he's going to die someday won't be willing to waste time and effort on inconsequential endeavors. He won't be willing to waste his most valuable asset - time! He has no idea how much time he has here on earth. He doesn't even know if he'll live to see tomorrow. Even if he does merit a long life, one's days transpire like a passing shadow. We look back and we don't know where the time went. Therefore, we must think carefully about how and where to invest our time in such a sorely limited lifespan.

One who is pursuing his purpose in life enjoys every moment. The affairs of the physical world don't interest him. He doesn't care about the type of watch he wears, whether his shirt is a brand name, or if his coffee is sweet enough. All he cares about is utilizing every moment to get to know the Creator, for that's his purpose on earth.

The people whose time and efforts in this world are devoted to material gains and amenities are upset by anything that is not to their liking. They suffer severe tribulations in their quest for worldly success. They have no rest, forever striving for more status, money and amenities. Much of their efforts are in vain. Even the ones who achieve their material dreams must sooner or later leave them behind. All their efforts and material acquisitions no longer help them. They leave here penniless, with no grand titles, no rank and no Swiss bank accounts. It no longer matters whether they drove a Cadillac or a Mercedes. Everything is left behind. They are taken to the next world with nothing of a material nature.

A person who therefore invests his time and efforts into this world is a **double loser**: His life in this world lacks meaning and he forfeits a desirable future in the World to Come. The opposite is also true: a person who devotes his life to his true purpose is a **double winner**. He lives a life of inner peace in this world, with joy and happiness, and he lacks nothing in the next world.

The Lust of Victory

A certain terrible character blemish is liable to lead to a person's downfall. This is what we call, "the lust for victory" when a person wants to win an argument or disagreement no matter what. True or not, he wants his opinion to prevail at all costs. He not only wants to decide how he'll live, but he wants to decide what truth is. He won't listen to anyone or any opinion that disagrees with him. One cannot budge him from his preconceptions. He'll never ever acknowledge a mistake. He'll never change, either. Usually, he ridicules others. All this is the lust for victory.

A person like this, who always wants to win the argument, can never find truth. Why? To find truth, a person must be willing to relinquish everything, including ego. He must be prepared to admit that he erred and be willing to make changes in his life. Even after he thinks he found the truth, he must be prepared to acknowledge that he again made a mistake and once more alter his way of thinking, even if this cycle repeats itself dozens of times. In short, to rectify oneself, one must be willing to acknowledge his or her mistakes.

Rebbe Nachman writes (Likutei Moharan I:122), "The lust for victory - to be right all the time - cannot stand the truth. Even if the lustful person saw truth with his own eyes, he'd deny it because of his lust for victory." As we described above, when a person wants to be right and win the argument no matter what, he'll never acknowledge the truth, for it might cause him to admit his mistake and obligate him to change.

We're Only Human

A person affected by the lust for victory must exert great effort to rid himself of it. When he ponders his limitations, that he's only human, he can do it. As a mortal with sorely limited intellectual and spiritual insight, he knows little about himself, much less about the other creations that are full of Divine secrets, intricacy and wisdom. The fact that "he knows little" is an extreme understatement. If a person looks truthfully at himself in relation to both the macrocosm and microcosm of creation, he truly knows nothing. What's more, he doesn't even know about all the things he knows nothing about. He can't explain what's happening in his own life, let alone explain world events or see into the future. He has no way to protect himself from the perils of the times and of nature.

Most important, he must acknowledge the truth that he can neither help himself nor rescue himself from anything beyond his apparent control. He can't help his own loved ones, let alone his countrymen. As soon as a person is ill in the slightest, and especially if he comes down with a serious illness or disease, the balloon of his pride is completely deflated. Yesterday, he thought that he ran the world and could boss others around. Today, while ill, he is full of anxiety, trepidation and worry about the future. A person can't be haughty when he smells the grass of the cemetery, a place that he is one day closer to.

It's your decision: if you choose, you can cling to your arrogance and feel like you're better than anyone else in the world. You're always right, so you disdain every individual or opinion that disagrees with you. You think you have the truth, but what truth is it? You're full of suffering in this world, you lack joy in life and you are missing the boat of your mission on earth.

On the other hand, you can decide that you have much to learn and that one can learn from every other person, as our sages said, "Who is wise - he that learns from every person" (Avot 4:1). Take into consideration that in order to find and learn truth, one must pass through a series of stages. Each consecutive stage may destroy old notions that you lived by and thought were true. Be ready to change every single day. That way, life is a wonderful, dynamic learning experience full of growth opportunities and joy. This way, you'll find the reason that your soul was created and your purpose on earth.

Proving Emuna

One need not be a genius to prove the truth of emuna. One only needs the sincere desire to see the truth, thereby shedding any lust for victory and winning arguments. Once that has been accomplished, it's possible to prove emuna in one of two ways:

The Negative Way

The first way is the process of elimination, or "proving by the negative way". As in mathematics, sometimes one cannot prove that a given result is the correct answer. But, he can prove that a given answer is definitely not the correct one. So what does one do? He begins a process of elimination, culling out the answers that are definitely incorrect. Result #1 is incorrect; result #2 is incorrect, and so on, until he is left with one possible result that he cannot prove is true or not. Although he cannot prove in a positive way that this result is true, by process of elimination that all other possible answers are not true, he has come to the conclusion that this one answer is true.

We can easily prove that all mundane matters are not the truthful purpose for investing one's entire life. What would you say? That the most important thing in the world is being the best in your profession? Is this your purpose in life? Maybe you think that your mission in life is to accumulate wealth and possessions. Could that be the ultimate purpose of life? So we see that when we use a process of elimination, we can easily see that no mundane endeavor or goal has any purpose for posterity.

But emuna – it's impossible to prove that emuna is not truth! By process of elimination, one can certainly come to the conclusion that emuna is truth.

Here is something that every person should ask him/herself:

Do I want the truth? Have I assessed myself lately, what I'm doing and where I'm going? To what am I devoting my time and attention? Are these things the purpose of creation? Am I fulfilling my mission in the world, the very purpose that the Creator created me for?

If you're honest with yourself, you can easily prove what's a waste of time and what's not truth. Go from amenity to amenity and the things people pursue and you'll find that none of them are worth a garlic peel in helping you accomplish your mission in life. **But, when you get to emuna, you won't be able to prove that it's not true! Please – it's time to try it...**

Open Your Mouth

By process of elimination, we are able to come to the conclusion that emuna is true. But that's not enough. If a person arrives at the conclusion that this whole world is one big mirage of vanity, that might be progress, but he could still be clouded in spiritual darkness. So if the whole world is a mirage of vanity, what's real and what's true? One can understand in his brain that emuna must be true. Yet, emuna must penetrate the heart. If a person doesn't internalize emuna in his heart, no logical proof will help. So now, what?

The Positive Way

We now arrive at the second way of proving emuna, the simpler method: turn to the Creator and speak to Him simply and sincerely and ask Him to show you that He hears you!

Even if someone completely lacks emuna in his heart and thinks that Hashem doesn't hear him - and he looks at himself as a loon who is talking to himself - he should speak anyway, without emuna, as long as he wants to know the truth. Say, "Creator, I'd like to believe in You; I want to get to know You. I know that I can't see You but I can make requests from You. I want You to show me that You hear me. Please, do me a small favor and show me something that I don't expect. Maybe at first, I'll think that it's a coincidence; maybe the second time too. But if You're patient with me and help me believe in You by showing me that You hear me, ultimately I'll be obligated to acknowledge the truth."

In the above simple and candid way, a person can ask Hashem to help him in all kinds of ways. One can ask Hashem to help him solve problems that he hasn't been able to solve until now. By virtue of prayer, salvations come. Speak to the Creator and ask Him to help you believe in Him and to get to know Him.

A person who follows this path will see with his own two eyes - if he only desires - the manifestation of emuna! With your sincere desire to believe in Him and to become acquainted with Him, the Creator will be delighted to oblige, to grant your request, and to help you believe in Him!

Emuna is Prayer

In truth, everyone has emuna but most people don't "live" their emuna. In other words, they don't know how to utilize this prodigious power on a practical, daily basis. The power of emuna is the power to be able to speak to the King of kings whenever you like and to ask for whatever you like. As long as emuna fails to manifest itself in a person's daily life in the form of communication with the Creator, this is incomplete emuna. Therefore, emuna is synonymous with prayer.

The Torah teaches that emuna and prayer are one. When Moses raised his hands in prayer to G-d, the Torah writes, "And his hands were emuna" (Exodus 17:12). Onkeles translates, "his hands were spread in prayer." Our sages teach that prayer overrides nature and is above it (see Rabbenu Bachiya on Genesis 25:21). Nature says one thing, but prayer dictates otherwise (Likutei Moharan I:7).

So why doesn't everyone have emuna? Here are a few of the common obstacles that prevent people from believing:

1. The individual lacks belief in the reality of the Creator and His active intervention in his/her life, in other words, that each tiny detail in the individual's life is the outcome of Divine Providence. Perhaps the person believes in the Creator, that He's somewhere out in space or in the spiritual realm, but He doesn't involve Himself in the individual's life. That's why the individual doesn't speak to Him, especially in matters that worry him.

2. The individual lacks belief that anyone is able or privileged to speak to the Creator in simple language

and to ask for His help or advice in any matter or simply to spill his heart out to the Creator.

3. The individual lacks belief that Hashem hears him, listens to his prayers and to those of every other creation.
4. The individual lacks belief that Hashem loves him and wants to help him, especially those who turn to Him and speak to Him.
5. The individual lacks belief that Hashem's mercy and loving-kindness is infinite; he doesn't believe that there's enough mercy to go around for him and his problems, even for those who don't deserve it.

In light of the above, a person must believe that Hashem loves him/her and eagerly waits to hear their voice. Hashem hears every word and wants to help each of us, His beloved children.

The Creator created all of creation for the purpose of bestowing His loving-kindness on it, for this is His greatest pleasure. The Creator wants us all to have a good life of abundance and success, for this is His honor. His infinite mercy is sufficient to help every single person in any situation, whether they deserve the help or not, if they only turn to Him.

A person who believes that Hashem can help him will certainly seek to speak to Him all the time, telling Him about everything that is happening in his life, especially the difficulties. Such an individual constantly seeks His aid and advice.

The Power of Prayer

Internalize this golden rule: With true emuna, any person – by means of simple personal prayer and dialog with Hashem – can transcend any natural limitation and work wonders! Prayer has the capability of altering nature. Since Hashem is above nature, those who turn to Him raise themselves above the limitations of nature. Jewish tradition is full of stories about how our sages invoked nature-defying miracles with the power of their prayers. For example, the Gemara in Tractate Megilla tells all about the miracles that the Prophet Elisha evoked with his prayers.

You don't have to be a prophet for Hashem to listen to you. Don't ever forget that He listens to, sees, and personally provides for the lowest and simplest creatures in the universe. It therefore goes without saying that Hashem is always ready to help one of His beloved sons or daughters, the highest order of creation, who sincerely turn to Him in emuna. As soon as we activate our emuna and turn to Hashem – in our own words, like speaking to a beloved parent or best friend – we can achieve literally anything, such as a remedy for our ills or the fulfillment of all our needs.

Rabbi Nathan of Breslev, Rebbe Nachman's prime disciple, always used to say, "Wherever I see deficiency, either there was no prayer or insufficient prayer." Consequently, sufficient prayer can invoke a solution to any problem.

A sure-fire spiritual law says that each prayer has its power, and that each request requires a certain amount of prayer – or spiritual power – to bring about its manifestation. Just as an ounce of dynamite is enough to put a hole in a laboratory table, one might need a ton of dynamite to blow a hole in a mountain. By the same token, the greater the request, the more prayer - or spiritual dynamite - is required. Remember, sufficient prayer invokes a solution to any problem. By believing in the power of prayer, we are able to keep praying until our request is fulfilled. The Talmud testifies (tractate Berachot 32b), "Rabbi Chanina says, anyone who prays long enough doesn't go away empty-handed!"

The Midrash explains (Yalkut Shimoni, 31) that when Hashem decreed that Moses wouldn't be allowed to enter the Land of Israel, Moses prayed 515 prayers, until Hashem commanded him to stop praying! Why? With one more prayer, Hashem would have been obligated to rescind the decree.

Why did Hashem allow Moses to pray so long before stopping him? There are two explanations: first, Hashem derived tremendous gratification from Moses' prayers; second, Hashem wanted the merit of those prayers to help the Children of Israel enter the Land of Israel.

We learn from the above Midrash that when we meet the required prayer quota for a given request, the request is filled! As long as Hashem doesn't command us to stop praying, we can - and must - continue to pray until our prayer is answered!

If a person's goal is to fulfill his purpose in life and to get to know Hashem, his prayers will most certainly be effective. But, if a person prays for things that go against Divine will, not only will the prayers be ineffective, but they'll invoke Divine displeasure. This is like a son who asks a father for a $100,000 loan to buy a bulldozer, so that he can destroy his father's house. Maybe he'll use the loan to buy a garbage truck, so he can dump garbage in dad's living room...

The father not only will refuse to grant his son the loan but will be incensed by the son's chutzpa.

That's what the prayers of a lust-seeker sound like. That person wants Hashem to help him succeed in committing more transgressions, thereby destroying and contaminating the world. No wonder such prayers won't be accepted!

One who seeks to fulfill his mission on earth and to get to know Hashem builds and beautifies the world. His prayers will therefore be gratifying to Hashem and readily accepted. Even if they are not accepted right away, it's a sign that Hashem loves those prayers and desires to hear more of them. As we said, everything has a price tag or required prayer.

Hashem Doesn't Want the Horse's Might

We'll clarify emuna in detail in the coming pages, for people lack a basic knowledge of what emuna really is. They don't take advantage of emuna and prayer - the tremendous power that's always at their disposal - simply because they're unaware of their own potential in getting close to Hashem and in improving the quality of their lives.

Some believe in a faraway Creator, or a Creator that has some undefined, removed, and minor influence on their lives. Few fully connect the tiny and mundane details of their daily lives to emuna and to Divine Providence. Emuna shlema, or complete emuna, means that one relates every single happening in life to Divine will and providence. For example, when a wife scolds her husband, the husband - with proper emuna - doesn't lose his temper because he knows that Hashem decreed that she scold him. The same goes for more difficult situations, such as health and financial problems. Emuna means that we accept everything that happens to us as Hashem's will. And, when we need help, a solution to a problem, our daily needs, or whatever we desire, we speak to Hashem.

Dear reader, I know that you believe in Hashem, so why don't you talk to Him? If you don't speak to Him, it's a sign that you don't believe that Hashem can help you; in that case, you must strengthen your emuna.

Hashem wants us to turn to Him for all our needs, big or small. Hashem doesn't care about how much power, money and influence we have. He loves each of us. He simply wants us to turn to Him in prayer on a daily basis, ask Him to help us understand what He wants from us, ask for all of our needs and to seek His help.

Hashem doesn't require us to work double overtime to meet our needs. He doesn't need business acumen, superb intelligence or outstanding ability on our part. King David said (Psalms 147:10-11), "Not in the strength of the horse does He desire, nor in the thigh of man does He favor; Hashem favors those who fear Him, those who long for His lovingkindness." In contemporary jargon, Hashem doesn't need us to show off the "horses" in our fancy stable - military might, technological achievements, or a Swiss bank account. He also isn't impressed by the "thighs" we've developed in our weightlifting, aerobics, or judo workouts. He wants us to pray to Him, to be one of those who "long for His lovingkindness."

Once we become accustomed to praying in every situation, we develop a spiritual sensitivity that is conducive to feeling Hashem's constant presence. When we feel Hashem's presence, we willfully and happily thank Him, speak to Him, and pray to Him all the time. When we're constantly seeking Hashem, He doesn't need to send us wake-up calls of troubles, trials, and tribulations.

The Power of Emuna

Emuna not only helps us to understand the world around us, it is essentially our most powerful asset. Emuna girds us with phenomenal inner strength and enables us to successfully weather any and all of life's difficult tests and challenges, income problems, marital difficulties or whatever they may be. Ups and downs, life's bumpy transitional periods, and times of turbulence all become easier when a person relies on emuna.

If we look closely, emuna is the only real asset a person has in this world, not only accompanying him in the challenges of this world, but even after he enters the threshold of the next world as well. Without this power of emuna, there are situations and tribulations that render a person hopeless and helpless, in utter despair. Life is unbearable when one loses hope. The dead end that a person reaches when he or she can't believe that there's a solution to their tribulations is tantamount to a foot in the grave - a living death.

Despair and emotional breakdowns all stem from a lack of emuna, when a person sees no hope or solution for his predicament and therefore becomes hopeless. He isn't aware of the fact that Hashem can rescue him at any moment. Isaiah the prophet informed King Hezekiah that the latter had been sentenced by Heavenly edict to death. The king answered the prophet, **"Ben Amotz - belay your prophecies and leave! I have a tradition from my great-grandfather King David that even if a sharp sword comes to rest on a person's throat, he should not lose hope in Divine**

mercy" (Berachot, 10a). In other words, a person should not lose hope in his prayers, for they invoke Divine mercy. Even though there's no hope according to nature and logic, by way of prayer - which defies nature and logic - there is certainly hope.

A person who strengthens himself in times of trouble, in other words, he realizes that everything that is happening in his life results from Hashem's Divine Providence and not nature, will turn to Hashem for help and encouragement. By way of his self-strengthening, he weathers challenges with success. Not only that but he saves himself the need to suffer additional tribulations. What's more, the challenges of life make him strong and enrich his spirit. They help him come closer to Hashem and to better get to know Him. He therefore is fulfilling his mission in life. Consequently, his difficulties are all Divine ploys to bring him closer and not to push him away, like so many people mistakenly think.

Rebbe Nachman of Breslev teaches, "One who has emuna is truly alive, and his days are always filled with good. When things go well, it is certainly good. But when one has troubles, it is also good, for one knows that Hashem will eventually have mercy, and make the outcome good. Since everything comes from Hashem, it's definitely for the best. But, Heaven forbid, a man without faith is not really alive. Evil befalls him and he loses all hope. There is nothing to cheer or comfort him, for he has no emuna. He is outside of Hashem's providence, and has no good at all. But with emuna, life is good and pleasant. (Sichos HaRan, 53)."

He Reprimands Those Whom He Loves

The Zohar (Bechukotai, 114) states: "How beloved are the children of Israel before the Holy One, blessed be He! He desires to reprove them and to lead them on the straight path, like a loving father who wields a rod in hand in order to lead the son on the straight path, so that the son shall not stray to the right or to the left, as it is written (Proverbs, 3:12), "Hashem reproves those that He loves, and like a father, mollifies the child." The opposite is also true: if there is someone that Hashem doesn't like - or even despises - He will not chastise that person but will simply leave him.

The root of all tribulations is a person's failure to realize that he is simply a creation, here to do a task, and not lord over his own life. He is certainly not the lord over the rest of the world either.

A believer - who knows that he's a creation - lives an easy and pleasant life. He makes every effort to perform his task on earth and he does his utmost to determine what his Creator wants him to do. He doesn't need difficult tribulations to prod him toward his purpose on earth because the slightest hints from Above stimulate him to assess himself and search for the best path.

A person without emuna entertains the folly that he alone controls his own fate; such people are prime candidates for suffering and emotional ills. Hashem - our loving Father - uses the rod of tribulations as an expression of love, to teach us that we're not "calling the shots", but subservient to a higher authority. Also, to awaken His beloved children from their spiritual slumber, Hashem oftentimes gives us a "jolt" in the form of some difficulty or challenge that forces us to seek His help and to heed His messages. As we said earlier, Hashem doesn't send difficulties to those that He disdains; if He lets a person continue unscathed in his mistaken path, that person is in big trouble. The Zohar says that the Creator hates such an individual.

The Rod and the Staff

Rebbe Nachman of Breslev teaches (Likutei Moharan I: 206) that Hashem immediately calls out to a person that strays from the proper path, beckoning that individual to return. Hashem summons each person in a tailor-made fashion and in accordance with that person's needs. For some, Hashem's call may be a subtle hint; but for others, it could be a vocal reprimand. A "louder" call might assume the form of physical punishment; in the jargon of our sages (Midrash Mishli, 22), "A whisper suffices for the wise, but a fool needs flagellation."

Even extreme handicaps are for a person's own good. Hashem alone knows what a soul's objective is and what it must correct, and thereby places each soul in a circumstance that is conducive for its necessary tikkun, or soul correction. As we are usually unaware of our needed tikkun, we sometimes make wrong choices or entertain useless aspirations; Hashem helps us modify our plans to prevent us from wasting our lives on folly and to direct us on the right path and prevent us from getting lost.

Our task is to develop our spiritual antennae and to discern - by correctly processing Hashem's personal messages to us - what Hashem wants from each of us. Even though these "hints" - or Heavenly messages - are frequently clothed in sorrow, hardship, and deprivation, they are actually the epitome of perfect loving-kindness. How? If a person accepts them with emuna, disadvantages contribute to perfection, as they lead to a life of ultimate good for they enable a person to achieve his correction and perfection of the soul, the greatest achievement on earth. When we accept life's difficulties with emuna - calmly and happily, knowing that Hashem is doing everything to help and thanking Him as well - we literally appreciate our disadvantages for we know that they're all for the best, aiding us to achieve our goal and to find our own personal path.

A person desires to succeed in life. He turns to the right and Hashem blocks his path. He turns to the left, and Hashem blocks that path as well. Without emuna, he'd be disgruntled and disappointed; he'd probably regard himself as a loser and lose his self-confidence. But with emuna, especially emuna in Divine Providence, he doesn't suffer a panic attack. He believes that his current lack of success is entirely for his own good. He tries to understand that direction that Hashem wants him to take. He therefore faithfully and pleasurably accomplishes his mission in life. He readily responds to Hashem's hints, for he is attentive to what Hashem is telling him by way of all the events and catalysts that he encounters. But, a person without emuna is so unreceptive to Hashem's messages that it's virtually impossible to direct him on the right path and to rectify him.

In other words, just as a disciplined child doesn't need to be punished - for a bit of direction and advice suffices - so too a person with emuna doesn't need stern prodding for him to pursue the right path. Yet, the person without emuna is like the unruly child who thinks he knows better that anyone else and therefore refuses to heed his parents and their directives. Such a child is only making his own life difficult.

Lack of Communication

In light of what we've learned until now, a person that ignores Hashem's messages creates a lack of communication with Hashem. Hashem's loving hand tries to direct a stubborn individual on the right path - for his or her own good - but they stubbornly insist on taking a different road, a detrimental one. So time after time, they encounter new obstacles; they get repeatedly kicked and bruised, while their lives are full of suffering. They're bitter all the time, yet they can't understand why their lives are so difficult.

Stubborn people that insist in following the path of their lusts and bodily appetites and against Torah will certainly get hit with painful tribulations. They're not at all in touch with what Hashem wants from them; they repeatedly return to the path of oblivion in pursuing their lusts and fantasies. Only extreme suffering will wake such a person up. When people ignore the delicate signals, Hashem is forced to catch their attention with louder and much more severe signals. In short, when they don't hear the gentle whisper, they risk the ear-splitting wail of a police or ambulance siren.

Even though a person may be following the path of Torah, yet he insists on doing things his way, without heeding the gentle hints from Above, will also fall. For example, he wants to follow a given path, but a Heaven-sent stimulus tries to direct him on a different path. Yet, he obstinately sticks to the path that he chooses. Such an individual demonstrates that he's not interested in knowing what Hashem wants from him; he'll only suffer from his stubbornness. Contrastingly, King David teaches us to seek Hashem's guidance, when he pleads (Psalms 25:5), "Lead me in Your truth," Your truth, and not mine, for only You, Hashem, know what's best for me. He also prays (ibid. 73:24), "May You guide me in Your counsel," Your counsel, Hashem, and not the counsel of my limited human brain. Anyone who doesn't heed King David's advice will struggle in vain and suffer all kinds of needless tribulations.

With Hashem's loving help, this book will help us to understand what Hashem wants from us in every aspect of life, so that each one of us can merit in fulfilling his or her purpose on earth, the very reason that Hashem created him/her. This will not only save us from suffering but will enable us to enjoy the taste of paradise in this world and attain eternal bliss in the world to come.

The Taste of Life

Without emuna, there's no taste for living because in the end, everyone faces the same bleak fate - death. If death is the utter end, then all of life is for nothing. Even if a person achieves his dreams, he won't be able to enjoy them forever. King Solomon says, "As he emerged from his mother's womb, naked, he shall return as he had come, and he can salvage nothing from his labor to take with him" (Ecclesiastes 5:14). All the more so, no one knows when their final day on earth will be. All of a person's grandiose plans are liable to be abruptly terminated at any given moment. He or she will be taken from this world without accomplishing half of what they had hoped to accomplish. Our sages say that no person dies without wishing that he had double of what he had. Indeed, more of life is times of hardship and suffering than it is moments of joy, for King Solomon also said, "For all his days are pain and displeasure" (ibid. 2:23).

One of the great wise men once said, "Everyone says that there is this world and there is the world to come. We believe in the world to come. Perhaps there is a 'this world' too, but I don't know where, because where we are now seems like purgatory, full of suffering and tribulations. In fact, there is no 'this world' at all" (Likutei Moharan II:119).

Look at the people around you - your relatives, your neighbors, your associates at work or school - they all have problems. Some are plagued with health issues. With others, it's an income or emotional challenge. Some have problems with their children and others don't have children at all and wish they did. Even if we look closely at the world-renown success stories, there's a person who hides his or her real suffering behind the mask of glitter. Look at all the bankruptcies, divorces and suicides that accompany the rich and famous. The reality is in our face - no one has true gratification in this world. Without emuna, nothing makes sense and there's virtually no purpose to life.

Emuna gives flavor to life; it's a reason for living. Even a person who suffers his whole life long will find comfort and strength in emuna. He'll also receive the proper guidance how to rectify his life and effectively repent so that he can attain salvation from further suffering. The Almighty doesn't want to make people suffer; the objective of tribulations is to trigger a process of self-rectification that will enable the person to taste a sweet life.

Peace and Tranquility

A person who walks out in the streets sees a tense and angry world. Everyone is stressed and in a hurry. There's dissension everywhere, all the outcome of a lack of emuna. If people had emuna, they'd have inner peace, calm and joy. The world would be tranquil and pleasant. Everyone would know that everything is under Divine control and there's nothing to be anxious or worried about. What a nice place the world would be! Even a lone person with emuna enjoys peace and tranquility. If everyone had emuna, we'd see a world of Redemption that we all dream of.

The war and strife that plagues the entire world would end abruptly once emuna spreads across the globe. Why? Each nation would be satisfied with its share and would lovingly accept Hashem's Divine Providence. They would treat each other charitably and with compassion. Thus, the prophecy for the end of days says, "And the lion will dwell with the ewe, and the tiger with the kid-goat... for the earth shall fill with the knowledge of G-d just as the waters fill the sea" (Isaiah 11:6-9). Emuna is the "knowledge of G-d" that will fill the world and create the wonderful climate of peace.

Rebbe Nachman writes (Likutei Moharan II:5) that as spiritual awareness spreads in the world, there will no longer be cruelty and violence. Together with the spiritual awareness that comes from emuna, both individuals and nations will become merciful, for mercy comes from spiritual awareness.

The Preservation of the World

Without emuna, there's no explanation as to why one must choose good over bad, or why there must be social order, or why one must raise a family. Why should there be responsibility and morality? If life is limited and death is final, then why not let the strongest survive, prevail and have a good time in the meanwhile? If there's no accountability in a next world, no judge and no judgment, why not do everything that you can get away with? But, with emuna, we know there is a supreme Judge and that we all are held accountable for everything we do.

Without emuna, people and nations do as they see fit. The world looks like a lust factory. Without blinking an eyelash, people are unfaithful to their partners in wedlock, even if it's the spouse of a best friend or a relative. People cheat, lie and steal in the name of commercial acumen. Without emuna, they freely covet what's not theirs and invent dozens of justifications in their minds for doing what they want when they want, whether or not it's illegal or immoral. In short, they're not satisfied with their lot in life.

Without emuna, one can create an ideology from any lie, even if it's the exact opposite of truth. To this day, there are societies that glorify murder in the name of their skewed ideology. There are societies that glorify robbery and encourage robbing the rich to give to the poor. If they would only have emuna, they wouldn't arrive at such perverted ideologies. They would know that there is a Master Creator to the world and He alone decides who will be rich or poor, and that no one has the right to take the law into his own hands or to try and overturn Divine Providence.

The whole world is full of these deviated ideologies. Without emuna, everyone decides his own "truth", which is nothing other than a total lie that is liable to lead to the destruction of the world. Look at the revolutionary movements that sprung up in history - Fascism, Communism, military dictatorships and the like. All claimed to be - and still claim to be, wherever they are still practiced - truth. But, with emuna, one connects to absolute truth - the Creator's truth. No deviation of His word would become an accepted school of thought if emuna prevailed in the world, for everyone would know that the only truth in the world is the Creator's word, which never changes. That's why emuna alone can assure the preservation of the world. In fact, it's the foundation that the world stands on.

Truth

Since the Creator has a purpose in creating the world, is it possible that He would demand that a person perform his or her designated task on earth without telling them what that task is? Is it conceivable that the Creator would reward or punish a person without telling him what is permissible and what is forbidden? Do you think that the Creator would leave it up to a person to find out himself what his purpose in life is?

Certainly, the Creator must give a person clear instructions about his purpose on earth. That's why He gave us the Torah and its commandments. The tzaddikim teach us the practical ways of finding and identifying truth that lead us to true emuna.

Only by way of the Divinely-given Torah - which is truth - can one arrive at genuine emuna. Without the Torah, each person decides his own truth depending on his personal appetites and vested interests. As such, as we see clearly in the world, people and governments make tremendous mistakes.

The Golden Path

A person who doesn't live in accordance with Torah is subject to confusion and serious mistakes. One decides to chase money, another decides to chase women, and others chase whatever whim or fantasy their hearts happen to harbor. The result is a world that is difficult to bear - full of hate, jealousy, competition, slander, cruelty, dishonesty, violence and injustice, as well as every additional type of abomination and filth.

But, when people live according to Torah and attain genuine emuna, the world becomes a beautiful place. Everyone is satisfied with his own lot in life and doesn't covet others in any way; he certainly doesn't touch anything that doesn't rightfully belong to him. He respects everyone and desires that they succeed. He is charitable and merciful with everyone. He is honest in business and does good for everyone, never deviating from the truth, all according to the holy principles of Torah and emuna.

Consequently, in a climate of emuna, the world blossoms in all its splendor and sweetness. Only a person who lives a life of emuna can therefore taste life's true sweetness.

Beware - the Torah won't benefit any person who doesn't strive for emuna. Without emuna, a person who learns Torah is liable to make worse mistakes than a person who doesn't learn Torah at all. The core of Torah truth - which is emuna - is only obtainable by way of connecting with the generation's great spiritual leaders, which each generation has ever since Moses. With no connection to these righteous leaders, a person cannot find emuna, even if he intensely learns Torah and fulfills its commandments. As proof, many so-called "religious" people learn Torah and fulfills its commandments, yet lack emuna! They have no personal connection to Hashem and they lack sincere communication with Him. We therefore see that when such people have a difficulty in life, they react just like a person with no emuna; they run to doctors, they're angered by things that upset them, they're worried about income and they become entangled in all types of quarrels.

A Man with Spirit

An unbroken chain of righteous tzaddikim extends from Moses to this very generation. From teacher to pupil, ever since Moses, these tzaddikim received the clear truth of Torah to instruct each respective generation. As we learn in Ethic of the Fathers, Moses received the Torah on Mount Sinai, Joshua received from Moses, the Elders from Joshua and so forth to this very day. The tzaddikim, and their students who follow their path, help us understand the Torah, its commandments, and our individual purpose in life.

Each of us must search for a genuine tzaddik of true spiritual stature that can help us find the way to applying the Torah to our daily lives. A random righteous person that hasn't been the understudy of a righteous spiritual guide before him will not suffice. The expert spiritual guide - whom the Torah calls "A man of spirit" (Numbers 27:18), knows how to apply the laws of Torah for the benefit of each individual's spirit, as the "Kli Yakar" explains in his elaboration of the Torah portion "Vayikra". The "man of spirit" - the righteous spiritual guide - knows how to stimulate and strengthen each individual so that he or she can fulfill the Torah's commandments in the best possible way.

For example, a qualified rabbinical authority who is also "a man of spirit" might permit a certain action under one circumstance, yet completely forbid it under another circumstance. He sees the unique needs of each individual, just as a shepherd knows the needs of each lamb and ewe. Such a rabbi, tzaddik, and spiritual guide knows how to arouse a person from spiritual slumber, strengthen souls, and show them the way to Hashem. This individual must therefore be a person on a lofty spiritual level, full of holiness and devoid of self-and-appetite pursuit. He must have a clear tradition that goes back in an unbroken chain to Moses.

Without a qualified and righteous spiritual guide, a person might learn Torah for a lifetime, yet make tragic errors in spiritual navigation and never attain his or her tikkun. That's why King Solomon writes, "There is a way that seems right to a man, yet it leads to the path of death" (Proverbs 14:12). Two groups of people have difficulty finding their way in the world - those without Torah altogether, and those without a spiritual guide. When we say in our morning prayers every day, "Blessed be He who separates us from the mistaken" (Kedusha D'sidra), we are asking Hashem to save us from both groups.

Rebbe Nachman of Breslev writes (Likutei Moharan I: 123): "The foundation and most important principle - one's connection to the tzaddik of the generation, to accept his teachings about everything, big or small, without straying to the right or left, Heaven forbid, as our sages instructed (Sifri, parshas Shoftim): 'Even if you're told that right is left... ', that one must cast aside his own wisdom, logic, and opinion as if there is no brainpower other than that which he receives from the tzaddik of the generation, and as long as one depends on one's own intellect, he is in a state of imperfection, not fully connected to the tzaddik."

Rebbe Nachman also writes (Likutei Moharan II: 8): "One must search and pray very hard for a true spiritual guide, and insistently request from Hashem that he merit to find a true leader, so he can attain true and complete emuna, for when one connects - Heaven forbid - to a false leader, one is exposed to false beliefs... therefore one must search and pray for a true leader to connect to."

Important Warning!

We must stress here that one can find a true spiritual guide and leader only by way of prayer, for most of us lack the tools to discern between an authentic tzaddik and a good imitation. Furthermore, we may find a tzaddik that may not be the right spiritual guide for us, or an individual of insufficient spiritual stature to guide us on the true path of emuna and tikkun. We must therefore exercise supreme caution in avoiding the pitfalls of criticizing a group or its leader, who doesn't seem to be the right leader for us. Why? Belittling a fellow Jew - let alone an entire group or its leader - is a severe transgression of Torah law. Therefore, to find one's true spiritual guide, he must stick to the path of peace and avoid arguing with anyone.

Those who rely on their own intellectual prowess to search for a proper spiritual guide are prone to mistakes. Therefore, we must pray to find the true tzaddik that can show us the way to genuine emuna and ask the Creator to help us, so that we'll learn true emuna.

Chapter Two:
The Levels of Emuna

Emuna can be divided into three main levels:

A. **First-level (basic) emuna:** This is what Hashem wants - this is the firm belief that everything comes from Hashem by way of perfect Divine Providence, even the tiniest and most seemingly insignificant event.

B. **Second-level (intermediate) emuna:** Everything is for the best! In addition to flawless basic emuna, the intermediate believes that everything Hashem does is for the very best, with no exceptions.

C. **Third-level (upper, or advanced) emuna:** In addition to the above two levels, a person on this level believes that Hashem does everything for a specific purpose and tries to understand the message within whatever transpires in his life.

These three levels are really one, for emuna is essentially one, namely, there is no one or nothing but Hashem. Everything in the world is from Hashem and the outcome of His Divine Providence. Since everything is from Him, it's all for the best. The entire purpose of creation is His desire to bestow good on His creations. Everything in creation has a purpose and is also geared to help the creations get to know the Creator.

Now, we shall explain each level individually:

A. First-level Emuna: This is what Hashem wants

Basic-level emuna teaches that Hashem is the lone sovereign of the universe; His surgically-precise Divine Providence is responsible for every single occurrence in the universe - big or small. We call Him the "Master of all deeds" since the very first of the thirteen tenets of our faith (see Maimonides, The Thirteen Tenets of Faith, appears in most prayer books at the end of Shacharit, the morning prayer service) states: "I believe with complete emuna that the Creator, blessed be His name, is the Creator and Ruler of all the creations, and He **alone** did, does, and will do every single deed." Simply speaking, everything that happens in the world - from the multiplication of a one-celled amoeba to the earth-shaking events that affect entire continents - all come from Hashem.

Let's bring the above principle down to a personal level: **Everything** that happens to us - spiritually or materially, accidental or intended, no matter who or what the catalyst seems to be - comes **exclusively** from Hashem.

Let Emuna precede intellect

Anytime something happens that is not to our liking, we should let emuna precede our intellect and tell ourselves: **this is what Hashem wants.**

This is an important rule of thumb - emuna must be our initial thought! King David tells us in Psalm 111, "The beginning of wisdom is the fear of G-d." Before the brain and intellect begin drawing conclusions and blaming our troubles on "natural" forces and phenomena, on others, or on ourselves, our emuna tells us that our particular predicament or situation is exactly what Hashem wants, otherwise it wouldn't have occurred. Everything is a product of Divine Providence. The things that hurt us are only a stick in Hashem's hands.

Only after we believe that there is no one but Hashem and we don't pin blame on anyone for our troubles, are we allowed to activate our intellect. In fact, we activate intellect for the sole purpose of understanding the intrinsic message within whatever unpleasant experience we are having, for Hashem is calling us to get closer to Him. We must also understand what Hashem is telling us to rectify, according to Torah and common sense. This way, we get to know Hashem much better.

For example, someone that forgets to let emuna precede intellect might blame his or her foot pains on the "natural phenomenon" of a bad pair of shoes. Others might attribute their lack of career success to a tyrannical boss, or torment themselves and blame their stupidity for losing money in a bad investment. Even though the shoes were actually poorly made, or the boss is truly a tyrant, or the investment was surely a silly mistake, Hashem is right there on the scene, hiding behind all the events that He causes to create a certain situation. Life's situations are none other than personal messages for our ultimate benefit.

Letting emuna precede intellect is the proper way to react to any situation. We say to ourselves, "Hashem is making me lose money; Hashem is blocking my career advancement; Hashem gave me the bad shoes!" When we remind ourselves that a given situation comes from Hashem, we're comforted, knowing that everything Hashem does is for the very best. Once emuna precedes intellect, then we're ready to utilize our brainpower in order to understand what Hashem wants from us.

Hints from Above

In the continuation of this book, with Hashem's help, we'll bring several principles that will help us interpret the "hints", or Divine messages within events that occur in our lives. To better understand this chapter, let's take a closer look at the examples we mentioned in the previous paragraphs.

Foot pains: "Foot" alludes to emuna, since the entire Torah stands on emuna. "Feet" refer to arrogance, as King David juxtaposes the two in Psalm 36. "Feet" are also a reference to money, for the Gemara in tractate Pesachim says that a person's money is like the feet he stands on. "Foot" alludes to slander as well, for the Hebrew words for "gossip", leragel, and the word "foot", regel, come from the same root. And finally, a wife is called a foot, since all her husband's success stands on her.

With the above in mind, a person with pains in his feet should now do some soul-searching. Maybe he blemished one of the things that allude to feet, such as he insulted his wife, he breached the principles of emuna, acted in an arrogant manner, made money by dishonest means or spoke gossip and slander. He should make an effort to repent for whatever blemish he finds in himself.

Financial loss: often an indication of dishonest money dealings, insufficient tithing or even an unpaid debt from a former life.

Lack of career success: all the appointments for the year, great and small, are determined on Rosh Chodesh Nissan. The Gemara in tractate Bava Batra 91 says that even the person in charge of irrigating a field receives his appointment from Above. Consequently, if a person is passed over for promotion, it's because he wasn't chosen from Above to get the new job, the greater salary or the promotion. This is his test and he should believe that it's all the product of Divine Providence. His boss or the board of directors do not decide a thing. He should neither hate them nor be angry at them, but continue to love them as before. If he desires career advancement, he should request it from Hashem, and say: "Master of the World, if this promotion or new job is good for me, please give it to me and help me be successful in it, for everything is in Your hands. If it is not Your will that I get the promotion, help me be happy and successful in whatever I am doing right now."

Who Wields the Stick?

The general rule is that Divine Providence is the catalyst behind everything. The old adage tells of a master that uses a stick to punish a slave; the unfortunate slave certainly doesn't blame the stick for his troubles, nor is he angry at the stick, nor does he try to appease the stick...

It's the same way with anything that upsets a person - the "reasons" or "causes" are merely sticks in the hands of the Almighty Himself. Dealing with the "stick" - the cause or the reason - is ridiculous. You would not try to convince a stick.

A person who suffers something that is upsetting or not to his liking must remember: **I am now in a test of emuna.** He must cast aside logic and intellect, both of which destroy emuna and give him all types of reasons to be upset, stressed and angry. Intellect brings him to depression, for he sees himself or others at fault and blames himself or others for his predicament. He is therefore prone to the acid feelings of hate and revenge, all resulting from his logic and intellect. His only hope therefore is to strengthen himself in emuna and remember that **there is nothing or no one but Hashem!** Everything is for the very best! He should devote his main efforts to prayer - to turn to the Creator and appeal to Him for everything.

Free Choice

Most of the things that sadden us fall into one of three categories:

Nature, such as a virus or bacteria;

Fellow human with his or her own free will;

Ourselves, what we often call our own stupid mistakes.

People normally understand that naturally caused tribulations - such as sickness, Heaven forbid - come from Hashem. Sometimes, the same people mistakenly put their trust in doctors and medicines. When the doctors and medicines fail, the sick and their loved ones ultimately turn to Hashem for help. You've never seen or heard anyone asking for mercy from a bacteria or virus.

Since we know that Hashem gives humans free will to do good or evil, many of us think that man's actions are beyond Hashem's control. Our intellect tells us to take issue with the individual that torments us, and attempt to effect a change in his or her behavior. At a superficial glance, the intellect is correct: Why pray to Hashem when here, standing in front of me, is the person that's making me miserable? This person possesses free will, so why not appeal to him or her? Maybe I should just hit them in the face! Who needs prayer?

The truth is that there is no one but Hashem and every single person is an agent in His hands to cause us pain or pleasure as He decides. Sometimes Hashem hardens hearts and sometimes He softens them, all according to His will and according to what the recipient deserves. Therefore, prayer is the only effective answer. Hashem can turn an enemy into a friend if He so desires. With prayer, Hashem can bring the person who hurt you yesterday to become your best friend today.

Your Free Will is All You Have

Know full well that the person facing you has free choice to do good or evil. If he chooses to do evil, Hashem will certainly hold him accountable. Since it has been decreed from Above that you must suffer in some way, Hashem "enables" a guilty person to be the agent of your suffering. Hashem takes advantage of that person's unfortunate choice to do bad things, which of course, he'll pay for. Yet, you have no influence over the other person's choice. The only choice you have is to improve your own ways, to pray and speak to Hashem, to ask for His forgiveness and to request salvation from Him. Once Hashem is pleased with your ways, He'll alter the choice of the person who is causing you grief. That person will not only cease his mean behavior toward you but might even do you a favor in some way.

In Ethics of the Fathers (Mishna, Tractate Avot), Hillel the Elder saw a skull floating on the water. He turned to the skull and said, "Because you drowned others, you got drowned." Certainly, the victims who the "skull" drowned deserved to be drowned; there was no way that they could have avoided this fate unless they would have repented. Yet, the murderer was ultimately murdered as a result of his evil choices.

There's No One to Blame

There's no greater mistake than to blame others for your sorrow. One who blames another - no matter who - not only blemishes emuna, but forfeits the Divine intervention that he or she would have received had they appealed to Hashem. Once a victim forfeits Divine intervention, he or she falls into the hands of the tormentor!

Here's what takes place in the heart and mind of a person who blames others for his suffering rather than appealing to Hashem:

If he feels helpless because he must deal with elements more powerful than him, such as police, judges, tax authorities, bank managers, or employers, he falls into despair. They are prone to frustration, depression, and in extreme cases, suicide, Heaven forbid.

And if he sees his tormentor as an equal, such as his spouse, neighbor, relative or business partner, he entertains thoughts of hate and revenge constantly, day and night. Such people can lose sleep for days, weeks, and even months plotting their retaliation. In other instances, they degrade themselves by flattering or groveling before their tormentor, Heaven forbid. They are liable to become spiteful, angry and cruel for they blame the other person for their suffering, and they become a tormentor instead of a victim. Woe to such a soul! This way, the suffering person kindles Divine wrath and incurs new and additional suffering.

We can conclude that the bitterness and suffering of a person who blames others is unbearable. Such an individual feels hopeless and futile, because he doesn't see any way that he can change or influence the actions of others, especially when they're more powerful than he is. So what can he do?

A person must know that there is something he can do. His life is in his own hands, not in the hands of others. He can appeal to the world's true Authority, the only One Who determines what will happen in his life. From the Almighty, he can receive any assistance or salvation that he needs.

A person must ask the Creator to forgive him for whatever misdeed that invoked the suffering. Once he does, not only will the suffering stop but the person who tormented him will now become a loyal friend. The "Duties of the Heart" writes (see Gate of Trust): "One should remember that both reward and punishment are in the hands of the Creator. If others torment him, he should still think good about them, for his own misdeeds brought about the suffering. He shall plead to G-d and ask Him to forgive him for his sins. Then, his enemies will turn into friends, for it is written, "When Hashem is pleased with a person's ways, even his enemies shall reconcile with him" (Proverbs 16:7).

Can I Help You?

If a person is unwilling to learn emuna, **it's impossible to help him.** Such a person wants the type of help that he understands according to his sorely limited understanding. In other words, he wants you to intervene on his behalf with people, by cajoling them, convincing them or even forcing them to do what he wants. These efforts are worthless and don't solve a thing. Moreover, they only complicate the situation even further. Hashem engineers that such efforts won't work as long as a person thinks that anyone else decides anything other than Him. If so, how can anyone possibly help you in a way that negates Hashem's will? Human intervention or help can't accomplish anything if Hashem decides otherwise.

The only solution for all these problems is to **learn emuna** and to act according to the principles of emuna, as we shall learn them in this book. A person who is willing to heed this book's advice and act accordingly will easily solve any problem. But, it's impossible to help a person who is looking for advice according to his own logic or understanding. He resembles a sick person with limited knowledge of medicine who dictates to the doctor how to treat him. The doctor says, "If you know how to cure yourself, why come to me? But, if you want my help, do as I say, and with the Almighty's help, you'll be healthy."

Half and Half

Some people give lip service to emuna. For example, men come to their rabbi with a marital problem. The rabbi explains that every difficulty their wife causes them is really from Hashem, and that only teshuva will help them. Then they say, "Sure, rabbi - I agree that everything is from Hashem. But... but why is she tormenting me? What did I do wrong to her? Doesn't she understand that she's destroying the kids... ?" In other words, he believes, but. He doesn't seem any more intelligent than a stray dog that gets hit with a stick; he barks at the stick rather than the person who is wielding it. Salvation would be so near if people would only wake up to rectify themselves. As long as they don't, they remain bogged down in the same mistake of blaming others and justifying themselves.

To such people, we say: OK, you want to be right? No problem. Continue to be right, but your life will continue to be purgatory... or, look at the truth, that you are the problem and that you must rectify yourself. Start living with the emuna that there is no one but Hashem and you'll find yourself in paradise instead of purgatory.

You can't escape reality - a person must live with emuna, period. In other words, he must believe that there is no one but Him. All of a person's problems come straight from Hashem. You're dealing with Him only. You're in His hands. Tribulations will end only when He decides.

Your choice is in your hands. You can decide to make teshuva; when you do, your worst enemy will turn into the head of your fan club. Remember, no one suffers for no reason.

Don't Let Me Fall into Human Hands

Suppose that a person is in dire straits: in front of him is a cliff and behind him are murderers that are chasing him. It's better that he jump off the cliff rather than falling into the cruel and ruthless hands of the murderers, for King David said: "I am in a dire strait; let us fall now into the hand of Hashem, for His mercies are great, and let me not fall into the hand of man" (Samuel II, 24:14). When a person with emuna faces a natural calamity, he turns to Hashem only for salvation. He yells out to Hashem with all his might and invokes such Divine compassion and providence that Hashem does a miracle for him. But, when he is faced with a threat from people, he directs his efforts at them. Often, he begs them for mercy and doesn't cast his eyes to Hashem. Maybe he's an expert in Krav Maga or karate and tries to fight them. Either way, he momentarily forgets about Hashem and falls into their hands. That's what happens when he looks at his tormentors instead of looking at Hashem.

People or Snakes

Our sages explain the episode of Joseph's brothers throwing him into a pit in the desert as follows:

Joseph's brothers despised and resented him and decided to kill him (see Genesis 37: 18-24). When Reuven, the eldest brother, saw that the other brothers were firm in their decision, he cleverly saved Joseph by suggesting that the brothers refrain from murder, and cast Joseph into a pit of poisonous snakes and scorpions instead.

Strange, how can this be termed, "saving Joseph"? A pit full of poisonous snakes and scorpions is a certain death! What kind of favor did Reuven do for his brother Joseph? Wouldn't throwing himself at the mercy of his brothers be better than the nightmare of nature's most heinous killing creatures?

The answer to the above dilemma is surprisingly simple: Reuven knew that Joseph was a tzaddik with complete emuna. He knew that the instant that Joseph would be exposed to the poisonous snakes and scorpions, he'd pierce the Heavens with his prayers to Hashem. Reuven knew that Joseph would cry out with every last ounce of his physical, emotional, and spiritual strength; Reuven also knew that Hashem answers such prayers, and would surely rescue Joseph.

Rebbe Nathan of Breslev explains (Likutei Halachos, Birkot HaShachar, 5), that Hashem designed the universe in such a way that prayer can effect a change in nature. When the Children of Israel cried out to Hashem, the Red Sea was required to split its waters (Exodus 14:10). When Joshua was in hot pursuit of his enemies, he commanded the sun to stand still (see Joshua 10:6-16). The prayers of tzaddikim can cool the intense heat of fire (see Daniel

3:10-26) or placate hungry lions (ibid 6: 17-24). In every generation, the true tzaddikim are bestowed with the power to alter the course of nature with their prayers; this power is a condition that The Creator instilled within all of creation."

Yet, Reuven wasn't fully confidant how his brother Joseph, the tzaddik, would perform in a test of emuna against a human of free choice in general, and against his brothers in particular. Reuven knew how difficult such tests of emuna can be. Would Joseph bend under pressure, plead and grovel before his brothers? Would he beg for his life, as if they were responsible for his fate?

Reuven was concerned that if Joseph would depend on logic in the slightest and appeal to the mercy of his brothers, then his complete emuna in Hashem might be compromised. As complete emuna enhances a person's chances to be saved from any peril, a breach in emuna is the gravest danger of all.

Reuven's concerns were well-founded. In the end, Joseph pleaded for mercy, as the brothers later testified (Genesis 42: 21): "Indeed we are guilty about our brother, for we saw his deep anguish when he pleaded to us, and we paid no attention." Reuven's gamble therefore paid off, by throwing Joseph at the complete mercy of Hashem. Joseph cried out for help, and Hashem rescued him.

Know Before Whom You Stand

Let's apply the above lessons in practical terms. From time to time, all of us are faced with a human of free will that's causing us pain or anguish, such as a policeman who pulls us aside, a spouse that's scolding us, or a child that's misbehaving. In any similar situation where another person is causing us grief, we must decide conclusively to focus on Hashem and not on whoever's causing us pain or anguish. This is what our sages teach us, "Know before Whom you stand!"

When we focus on Hashem, we need not flatter or plead to other people. We don't have to crawl on our knees or talk until we're blue in the face to try and convince others to refrain from hurting us, and we certainly don't need to react violently toward them. Emuna means that we focus on "The Master" - Hashem - and not the stick in His hand. We don't resort to all types of ploys or reactions, such as anger, cursing or outright violence, to convince someone or to make a tormentor leave us alone. We turn to Hashem.

Breaches in pure emuna range from the outright to the very subtle, with many levels in between. For example, one who suffers from another person might accept the plight with emuna, speak to Hashem, do some serious soul-searching and teshuva, and yet ultimately appeal to the tormentor and request mercy or consideration. Such an attempt is a flaw in emuna, since the victim attaches importance - even in the slightest - to the flesh-and-blood "stick" rather than to The Almighty's hand that swings it.

Those who place their fate in the hands of humans blemish the very Divine Providence that's designed to guard over them. Conversely, the more we place ourselves in Hashem's loving hands, the more we amplify the Divine Providence that delivers us from any evil.

Don't Let the Setback Depress You

Sometimes people suffer from mistakes or failures that apparently seem to be their own fault. In such a case, we need to remember another important rule: Before making a mistake, a person has apparent free choice not to make a mistake. But, after the fact, one must believe that Hashem willed the mistake! Knowing that Hashem willed the mistake, a person has no reason to be disappointed, depressed, disheartened, and certainly not self-flagellating or guilt-ridden.

With emuna, we attribute our successes to Hashem's Divine assistance.

One who fails to acknowledge Hashem's assistance is - without mincing words - arrogant, for he or she declares, "I succeeded!" To avoid arrogance, we therefore frequently use such terms as "God willing", "with Hashem's help", or "if Hashem so desires". So, if our successes are a result of Hashem's intervention in our lives, then our failures are also the result of Hashem's intervention in our lives. As Hashem knows what's best for us, we should accept our failures lovingly and with emuna, just as we accept our successes.

Those who fail to accept mistakes and setbacks lovingly are angry and disappointed in themselves; the same people pride themselves in their successes. Either way is a clear sign of arrogance, since they attribute their fate to themselves.

Failure is the true test of emuna; by virtue of emuna, we acknowledge that our mistake in judgment, bad decision, or any other setback was Hashem's will. With emuna, we refrain from persecuting ourselves day and night and therefore spare ourselves from untold emotional wear and tear. We can console ourselves that Hashem didn't want us to win the gold medal or the semifinals game. But, we can always take to heart that after any fall, all we have to do is to put a smile on our face, brush ourselves off, pick ourselves up, and start anew with a better effort, as we'll see later in this book.

A person must believe that any sorrow or deficiency in life is the sole product of Hashem's will – **this is what Hashem wants!**

What For?

One who achieves basic-level emuna – the belief in Divine Providence – is well on the way to a life of happiness.

Yet, limited basic-level emuna is deficient; although the basic-level believer attributes everything to Hashem, he or she is still susceptible to questions and complaints about how Hashem runs the world. They're likely to ask, "Why did Hashem do such-and-such to me? I don't deserve this! Why must I suffer?" The grievance list is long.

Any questions and grievances against Hashem are blatant breaches in emuna. The true belief that everything comes from Hashem must go hand-in-hand with the next level of emuna, namely, that Hashem does everything for the very best. King David says (Psalms 145:9), "Hashem is good to all, and merciful on all his handiworks". Since everything that Hashem does is good, one cannot say that he or she believes in Hashem while complaining about their lot in life – such is a contradiction of terms. So, to achieve complete emuna, we must graduate to the next level.

B. Level-two Emuna: Everything is for the Best

The second level of emuna is the belief that everything Hashem does is for the very best, even though it may appear otherwise.

Many are the cases where we see how seemingly bad situations are for the ultimate good. We all have scores of experiences in our own lives. For example, somebody's in a tremendous rush to get to work or to school on time. They sprint to the bus station just as the bus is pulling away from the curb, shouting at the driver to stop and let them board. The driver ignores them.

In the above situation, we might succumb to anger, either humiliated by the driver's lack of regard or frustrated by the impending tardiness to work or to school.

Let's add one missing piece to the above incomplete picture: Suppose that we missed the bus; a minute later, we hear a tremendous crash or explosion and discover that the very same bus has been involved in a fatal accident or terrorist attack, leaving many of its passengers maimed or wounded. Would we still be angry at the driver for leaving us behind? Would we still have complaints against Hashem? The answer is an obvious no. The same bus driver who a minute ago was the brunt of our shouts now becomes the recipient of our blessings. Thank G-d he didn't let us board the bus!

A mortal can't possibly see or understand all the variables that Hashem takes into account, especially when he or she is undergoing a test of faith. Just as a courtroom judge can't try a case - or comes to a mistaken verdict - with incomplete or insufficient facts, none of us are in a position to conclude that a particular situation is bad, without seeing what the future holds in store. In the above example, even if the bus wasn't involved in some sort of calamity, the Creator had good reasons for not letting us board it, reasons that only He knows. We must believe that it's all for the best and not blame the driver, anyone or anything else and certainly not himself.

The above example is oversimplified, for there are many situations in life that every individual must endure where the Creator has a myriad of considerations that cannot possibly be revealed or understood. But, if one successfully passes the test of faith, he or she can frequently see in retrospect how everything actually and truly was for the best, even to their own understanding. Sometimes, this realization comes years later in life. Sometimes, a person never understands how whatever happened was for the best; he or she will only find out when Moshiach comes.

Only Hashem knows the optimum, tailor-made path in life that is perfect for each individual. Sometimes we see the purpose of our suffering, and other times we don't. When we don't understand why we suffer, life's ups and downs can be an insufferable roller coaster; only emuna can put life on an even keel.

"Under fire" - in the midst of a difficult tribulation - we can't see how our current predicament is for our own good. If we could, then it wouldn't be a tribulation at all! But with emuna, we believe that our current predicament is for our own good. Our faith gives us the strength to cope and to function at our best under any situation.

A Basic Requirement

Maybe you think that the level of emuna that everything is for the best is relevant to individuals on lofty levels of piety and spirituality alone. That's not true! This level of emuna is not some spiritual plateau that few can obtain. The Code of Jewish Law (Shulchan Aruch, Orach Chaim 230:5) requires each of us to believe that everything Hashem does is for the very best.

Just as every Jew has the obligation to eat kosher food, to observe the Sabbath, and to comply with any other statute in the Code of Jewish Law, he or she is required to fulfill the above statute (OC 230:5) as well. Not a single rabbinical authority argues against this. So, if the Creator commands that we believe that everything is for the best, then it is certainly within our reach. This chapter will help you attain this level. The Torah is not up in the sky - a person must live with the emuna that everything is for the best.

Everything, not "Almost" Everything

Look at the exact wording of the Code of Jewish Law - "**Everything** Hashem does is all for the best." It says **everything**, with no exceptions to that rule, not "nearly" everything. A person must not say, "I believe that Hashem does everything for the best except for this!" Most people fall down at this point; even when they're willing to concede that everything is for the best, it's only to a certain point. As soon as things go outside their comfort zone, they're unwilling to accept them. As soon as anything negatively affects their pocket, prestige or plans, they're unwilling to accept that it too is for the best. In that respect, they fail to fulfill their obligation to believe that everything is for the best, with no exceptions whatsoever.

The emuna that everything is for the best is inseparable from the emuna in Divine providence; in fact, it is an expression that a person believes that everything is the result of Hashem's precision, tailor-made Divine providence over each individual's life. Since everything is the result of Divine providence, and since Hashem does **only good**, then it's easy to understand that everything is for the best. As soon as a person believes that something in life is not for the very best, it means that he doesn't believe in the Creator. It's impossible to separate between these two levels of belief; if you believe that everything is from Hashem, then believe that it's all for the best.

What is Emuna?

Understanding that a given situation is for the best is not emuna that everything is for the best. From a spiritual standpoint, comprehension is a much lower level than emuna. At the point where the brain no longer understands how Hashem is doing everything for the very best, emuna begins. In other words, emuna kicks in when the brain kicks out. Even when a person's intellect says that a situation is bad, he must cast intellect aside and believe that it's all for the best. He must be happy and thank Hashem wholeheartedly. Only then, can we say that a person has emuna that everything is for the best.

Even if something distasteful happens to us, and we wish that it would be different, we still must subjugate our will to Hashem's will as all our ethics books tell us to. Reconciling oneself with Hashem's will is virtually impossible without emuna, for if a person doesn't believe that Hashem is doing everything for the ultimate best, then why accept Hashem's will? Who wants a life of "bad"? Emuna illuminates our hearts with the confidence that Hashem has a good reason for everything He does, and that the currently rocky roads will eventually lead to smooth and peaceful paths. By letting our emuna override our brains, we can subjugate our will to Divine will and lovingly rise to any challenge that life throws our way.

Everything is Good

When a person strengthens himself in the emuna that everything Hashem does is for the very best - he or she will see the most trying situations in life make complete turnarounds for the better. Rebbe Nathan of Breslev writes (Likutei Halachos, Choshen Mishpat, Hilchos Prika V'taina 4), "If people would truly heed the tzaddikim and always believe in Hashem that everything is for the best, and if they'd give thanks and praise to Hashem always, whether in good times or in bad times, then all their troubles and all the suffering of the Diaspora would completely become null and void, and our people would be redeemed."

Even if a person who is not yet observant accrued verdicts of severe judgments and tribulations, yet he or she believes that Hashem does everything for the best and thanks Hashem under any circumstance, he or she will most likely be spared of most severe judgments. How? Simple and pure emuna neutralizes severe judgments, just like an alkaline neutralizes an acid. That's easy to understand, especially in light of the fact that the main reason for the suffering that comes to the world is the lack of emuna. The Midrash says that as long as there is idolatry in the world, there are severe judgments in the world. Get rid of the idolatry and the severe judgments will disappear (see Sifri, Devorim, 91).

If the emuna of a non-observant person has the power to mitigate or "sweeten" severe judgments, then surely the complete and simple emuna of a person that tries his or her best to fulfill the Torah's laws will lead to a life of gratifying sweetness.

An ostensibly non-observant young man once attended a lecture presented by the author of this book. After the lecture, he approached the author, and recounted the following experience:

"By chance, I happened to obtain a CD of Rabbi Arush's lecture about emuna and giving thanks to Hashem. I wanted to meet the rabbi in person just to say - from my own personal experience - that every single word is true!"

The young man continued, "The day after the lecture, I opened up a Bible to The Book of Job. I read the part where Job's wife tries to incite him against Hashem because of all the troubles in their life, and Job answers (Job 2:10), 'You talk as any impious woman might talk; shall we accept the good from Hashem and not accept the bad?' These words penetrated my heart; I knew that I was hearing pure truth. I decided - no matter what - that I'd thank Hashem for everything in my life, the better and the worse, and bingo! My life has taken a complete turnaround for the better!"

With animation, the young man related a series of miraculous solutions he had received - by Divine Providence and not by his own efforts - to some seemingly-hopeless predicaments that had made his life unbearable. Emuna had triggered a one-hundred-eighty-degree improvement in his faltering marriage and floundering career. He now speaks to Hashem every day and thanks Him. He asks Hashem for advice and asks for whatever he needs in his own words. He sees miracles all the time and he feels Hashem's Divine providence. He has the sweet taste of success in his mouth. In short, he lives a life of emuna and happiness.

You're Unhappy?!?

The same non-observant young man attended another one of the author's lectures, and this time brought his brother, an observant Jew that learns Torah all day long. While the former was pleasantly optimistic, the latter was depressed, complaining about a long list of worries and tribulations. "Nothing goes right in my life," he mumbled. "Were it not for my brother, who lately has been a source of strength and encouragement for me, reminding me that everything is for the best, I don't know what would become of me!" But now, he wanted to ask a question about the way Hashem directs the world:

The observant brother complained about the "illogical" and "unfair" way that Hashem runs the world. "Esteemed Rabbi, I observe all the commandments and learn Torah all day long. Why is my life so bitter? Yet, my brother observes almost nothing, and everything seems to be going his way. What's going on here?"

The author cited a passage from the Talmud (tractate Shabbat 55a) that sin causes tribulations and invokes stern judgments, suggesting that the brother do some soul-searching and teshuva.

"What do I need to do teshuva for?" argued the brother. "I observe the Sabbath, eat kosher food, give charity, send my children to religious schools, and live a life of poverty and deprivation. What's wrong with me? I understand that even the biggest tzaddik can commit a small sin from time to time; but, tell me - how on earth do I deserve such unbearable troubles?"

The author replied, "You obviously think that as long as you don't break any laws, you don't deserve any troubles in life. But, you're missing the main point: Torah and mitzvoth should be bringing you to emuna. You should be thanking Hashem for what you have - such as your wife and your children - and accept the rest of Hashem's Divine Providence happily and with love. Failing to do so invokes severe judgments that manifest themselves in all sorts of suffering and tribulations. Hashem has no joy from the Torah and mitzvoth of a person if they don't uplift him in enhanced emuna and enable him to accept whatever happens to him in life with emuna."

"You yourself prove my point - look at your brother," the author continued. "Despite his non-observant lifestyle, he's all smiles; he thanks Hashem for what he has. His emuna repels severe judgments, so he doesn't suffer from tribulations. Your life is so tough because of your weakness in emuna and your failure to thank Hashem - that's why you suffer!"

"Understand full well that most tribulations come from a person's failure to thank Hashem for everything. One who does spares himself from most suffering. Hashem has special gratification from people with emuna," explained the author.

"What?! Does my brother toil in Torah all day long like I do? He barely opens a book."

The author removed a book from his briefcase, the Ramban's classic commentary on the Torah, and opened it to portion "Bo". He read out loud, "The intent of all the mitzvoth are that we believe in Hashem and thank Him for being our Creator; this is the purpose of all creation. **The sole request of the upper worlds from the nether worlds is that man should thank and get to know his Lord that created him."** Rabbi BenTzion Halevi Bamberger, author of Ginzei Shaarei Tzion, elaborates on the Ramban's principle, namely, that knowing The Creator, accepting His dominion with emuna, and thanking Hashem as a result of getting to know Him is the very purpose of creation, and **without this, all of creation is superfluous.**

A New Light

The observant brother was stunned. He realized that he was further away from truth than his non-observant brother, whom he previously held in disdain. He suddenly realized that Torah learning and mitzvah observance alone are sorely incomplete without attaining the emuna that everything is from Hashem and all for the best.

The author continued, "Now you understand how your brother - who you always thought was so far away from Hashem - is in a certain way closer to Hashem than you are, even though you're the one that's observant! He believes that everything's for the best, and welcomes whatever Hashem does. He thanks Hashem for what he has, and consequently fulfills one of the main purposes of creation, that of recognizing the Creator! What's more, he talks to Hashem all day long and is constantly expressing gratitude. You might be a Torah scholar, but you don't live your emuna the way your brother does. Anytime things don't go your way, you complain, become depressed and persecute yourself. Even though you're accustomed to saying 'thank G-d' and the like, you're never happy with your lot in life. You neither speak to the Creator nor share your thoughts and feelings with

Him. As a result, you are the one that's missing the point of creation - that of recognizing and thanking the Creator - and that's why you have dinim, severe judgments hanging over your head all the time."

As if some bright light suddenly illuminated the darkness, the observant brother began to see a new world revealed before his eyes. He asked, "Rav Arush, please, help me understand: What about desecrating the Sabbath, failing to pray or put on tefillin, and all the other mitzvoth that are the foundation of emuna, which my brother fails to observe? I understand that my brother's thanks to Hashem are important, but what about the rest of the mitzvoth? How can anybody ignore the fact that he doesn't fulfill Hashem's desire by failing to observe most of the mitzvoth?"

"Hashem is patient," replied the author. "Since your brother has awakened to the inner dimension of emuna - that of thanking Hashem and accepting with love all that Hashem does - he'll undoubtedly reach the outer dimension of emuna, that of fulfilling the mitzvoth. Hashem doesn't expect a person to become a Moses in one day; He has patience, and it's worth His while to wait for your brother's return to observant Judaism. You'll soon see how your brother's emuna will lead to his joyous observance of Torah no less than yours. Since his first steps toward Hashem are based on emuna and gratitude - and not on fear of punishment or other self-serving motives - his subsequent steps toward Hashem will lead to his loving fulfillment of the mitzvoth and to his full and complete teshuva. He has already established a pattern of serving Hashem in joy by talking to Him all the time and realizing that everything is from Him and all for the best. His service of Hashem will be in complete love and with great desire."

"But you," added the author, talking straight to the observant brother's heart, "as a person so precise in performing the mitzvoth, could have easily attained a high level of emuna, since the mitzvoth illuminate one's soul with the light of emuna. Why didn't you use the mitzvoth as a means of connecting to emuna and getting closer to Hashem? Why don't you speak with Hashem all the time? It's like a person with a company car that fails to use the car for its designated purpose, and therefore doesn't arrive at his specified destination. On the other hand, your brother is like a person that has reached the specified destination without the benefit of a company car, as if he were driving a donkey cart. Wait and see when he starts to observe all the mitzvoth; this will be the 'company car' that will bring him to more and greater emuna!"

"You therefore get tribulations from Above to wake you up to the mistakes that you currently live by. Start believing that everything is for the best, thank Hashem daily for everything, speak to Him and talk to Him about everything that's transpiring in your life, and you'll begin to be happy," concluded the author.

The above account of the two brothers should stimulate us to readjust priorities and understand that emuna is the objective of our tour of duty on this earth. We also learn that we can't judge a fellow human on the basis of superficial trappings, because no one can know another person's level of emuna, and that is what dictates his spiritual level.

Naturally, simple emuna alone, without observing the mitzvoth, is sorely insufficient. Emuna can't possibly be complete without the fulfillment of the mitzvoth, for there are facets of emuna that one can only obtain by way of fulfilling the mitzvoth. The same Creator Who commanded us to believe in Him also commanded us to observe the Torah and its mitzvoth. We should strive that all the Torah we learn and all the mitzvoth we perform should bring us to enhanced emuna. If not, then we fail to use the Creator's tools properly, just like the misuse of the company car in the previous example.

There is Someone Who Knows Everything

The Creator guides a person along the proper path every single moment of his or her life. Like it or not, there are things along the path that are not to our liking. For example: you might have to encounter people along your path in life who upset you. You'd be delighted if you never met them. But the Creator **does** want you to encounter them, because they are part of your soul correction. There are places where you must frequent. There are tests of faith that you must cope with, without understanding why. They are all part of your mission on earth and the rectification of your soul. In short, they're part of your designated path that Divine Providence dictates for you, whether or not you are pleased with it.

Life's trials and difficulties frequently catch us unprepared and off-guard, often delaying or totally altering our personal plans. Since people are incognizant of their individual tikkun, or soul correction, life's difficulties are liable to confuse and disorient them, imparting the false impression that their lives are ruined. Yet, whenever we rely on the emuna that all the events of our lives are not random, but the result of Hashem's Divine Providence and personal supervision of our lives, we maintain a clear and optimistic outlook no matter how hard we're being tested. With emuna, we're never confused or disoriented. We realize that Hashem is doing everything for our benefit, to enable and facilitate our developing a closer and more meaningful relationship with Him.

Like it or Not

Let's be honest with ourselves: If we must endure the tests of unavoidable tough times, then we might as well accept them with the emuna that everything is for the best. Emuna enables us to be happy and to understand Hashem's individual message for each of us.

Even when a person doesn't succeed in grasping Hashem's message, he or she should accept their current circumstance happily, for such acceptance in itself is lofty service of Hashem. The Code of Jewish Law states (Shulchan Aruch, O.H. 222:3): "A person is obligated to make a blessing on the bad sincerely and willfully, in the same manner that he makes a blessing on the good, since for servants of Hashem, the "bad" is for their benefit and joy, to enable them to accept with love anything that Hashem decrees. Consequently, by accepting the bad, one happily serves Hashem."

We can't hide from life's difficulties; no one asks us whether we're prepared to undergo trials and tribulations - they appear in our lives whether we want them or not. But, we do have the free choice of how we'll cope with difficult situations. Happy is the person that accepts life's trying times with emuna, that they are all for the best; such a positive outlook assures that the tough situation will soon reverse itself. Without emuna, a person is bitter, broken in spirit, disgruntled, and virtually defeated. Bitterness and dark moods are a magnet for additional troubles, Heaven forbid.

There are no Tribulations

The only true tribulations in the world are when a person lacks emuna. Rebbe Nachman of Breslev writes (Likutei Moharan I: 250), "Know that all types of sorrow and tribulations all stem from a lack of spiritual awareness. For a person who has spiritual awareness, and knows that everything in life is the result of Divine providence, he has no tribulations and feels no sorrow." As long as a person clings to the emuna that everything is for the best, and he thanks Hashem for everything, even for that which seems unfavorable, joy overflows within him. Then, everything turns around for the best. Consequently, the only punishment that there is in this world is when a person loses emuna.

Therefore, as soon as a person feels negativity in the slightest, he should ask Hashem to restore him with the emuna that everything is for the best. He should begin thanking Hashem for everything, even if he doesn't yet sincerely feel that it's for the best. The very gratitude that he expresses opens a portal to renewed emuna, and that will bring him to true inner happiness.

Genuine Tranquility

The Torah praises the tribe of Issachar (Genesis 49:14): "He saw tranquility that it was good, and the land that it was pleasant, yet he prepared himself to suffer and became an indentured servant." The holy Rebbe Yitzchak of Varka elaborated on the above verse, and said: "He prepared himself to suffer - the term 'suffer' here has a positive connotation, such as sufferance, when one patiently endures anything that happens in life, the opposite of impatience and intolerance."

We're capable of patiently enduring any difficulty in life when we believe that everything comes from Hashem and that everything is for the best. Patient endurance, the result of emuna, paves the road to genuine tranquility. Genuine tranquility means a worry-free, peaceful, and happy existence. With emuna, we avoid untold emotional wear and tear. Without emuna, this world becomes a purgatory worse than purgatory itself. Our sages teach us that the evil are tried for twelve months in purgatory; but, a person with no emuna dooms himself to decades of living torture worse than purgatory.

A person's most hideous purgatory is the feeling of dissatisfaction and bitterness that he feels in his heart. There is no greater suffering in this world than the feelings of bitterness, despair, and discontent. These negative emotions are a magnet for more types of purgatory such as disputes and arguments, anger, worry, tension, stress, jealousy, sadness, revenge, despair, and depression - all because of a lack of emuna that everything is for the best! But, with emuna, life becomes paradise on earth.

Joy - the Beginning of Free Choice

We're faced with choices every moment of our lives. Most people think that choice begins by weighing the relative advantages of the options at their disposal. In actuality, choice begins with something much more basic; namely, choosing whether we'll be happy with our lot in life or not.

Choice consists of two stages: First, one chooses between being happy and not being happy. The second stage is making the actual choice from the options that a person is faced with. By choosing happiness, one progresses to the second stage, which is weighing the relative advantages of the options at one's disposal, what to do, how to do it, and so forth. What's more, if he chooses to be happy in the first stage, then choosing the best alternative will be much easier in the second stage.

On the other hand, if one fails to make the initial choice of being happy with his lot in life, then he can't possibly weigh his options with clarity of thought and mind. Why? Sadness and depression destroy clarity of thought, and therefore rob us of our free choice. Depressed people are lethargic and ineffective; they perform the simplest tasks arduously. Hashem doesn't bestow His Divine Presence on depressed and despairing people; forfeiting Divine assistance makes good decision-making virtually impossible.

Happiness in our Daily Routine

When we're happy with our lot in life, we can rest assured that at least the first stage of our choices is successful. We see numerous examples of people all around us that are unhappy with their lot in life for no apparent reason. If you were to ask them why they're not happy, they'd probably lack a conclusive answer. In most cases, they're unsure about their path in life and they harbor a constant, nagging feeling that they're missing something. Simply speaking, they're not sure whether they're making the right choices.

In light of what we've said until now, when a person is dissatisfied with life, then he or she is liable to constantly make wrong choices. Proper choices are the result of a clear mind, and a clear mind is a consequence of happiness. Therefore, the prerequisite to living a directed and purposeful life free of unfortunate mistakes is the choice of being happy with our lot in life. Once this initial choice is made, we maximize the chances of success both in the spiritual and material realms of decision making, because when we're happy, Hashem is with us. When Hashem is with a person, then he or she gains clarity, self-composure and confidence in making a good decision. So, if a person doesn't know what to decide or what is really most beneficial for him, then he must strengthen himself from within his current situation. He must know that Hashem is with him so that he can at least make the proper decision in the first stage of his choice and decide to be happy no matter what.

No matter what we're doing - whether at work, in school, or in the home - by deciding to be happy, we subdue the evil inclination's nagging thoughts of dissatisfaction that we're missing something. By being happy with whatever we're doing right now and with our current circumstance, we repel depression and confusion. The evil inclination constantly attempts to inject thoughts of regret and dissatisfaction in our hearts, such as:

"I wish I had a different job..."

"I wish I had married someone else..."

"I wish I lived in a different city..."

The examples are endless, as you well know from your own personal experience. But, by choosing to be happy with our lot in life, we avoid the pitfalls of confusion, disappointment, and depression. We maintain the clarity of mind that enables us to make the good choices that further increase our satisfaction in life. What's more, by believing that everything is for the best, we enable ourselves to function in a happy mode, especially in times of challenges when a person is liable to succumb to all types of despair and negative emotions unless he or she strengthens themselves in emuna.

Aspirations

When we truly desire a change in life, such as a new job or a new home, yet lack the ability to implement such a decision, it's a clear sign that Hashem wants us to continue in our current situation for the meanwhile. In such a scenario, we should accept Hashem's will happily, and know that the current situation is for our ultimate benefit. Nevertheless, we should express any and all of our aspirations in prayer, and devote a special timeslot to telling Hashem about our aspirations, our desires, and the course of our lives. Once we spend an hour a day pouring our hearts out to Hashem, we are able to spend the remainder of the day in happiness. We can then believe that everything has its proper time according to Hashem's master plan.

If you have the option of improving your life, by all means, go forward! But, if you see that you lack options right now, and can't implement what you'd like to, then believe that Hashem wants you to continue for the time being in your current framework; accept Hashem's loving guidance with happiness, with the complete emuna that Hashem is doing the very best for you. On the other hand, continue praying for what you want.

Even with spiritual aspirations, we need to accept our lot happily! So, when we don't make the spiritual gain as fast as we'd like to - we don't succeed in breaking that bad habit yet, praying with intent or immersing ourselves in Torah more - we should ask Hashem for help, tell Him our aspirations, and in the meanwhile learn more about the aspect we'd like to improve on and for the time being, accept our current situation with joy. This will make life easier on us and limit the damages of whatever it is that we must improve.

Falling short of our spiritual goals is a type of tribulation, since our lives are certainly more pleasant when we taste success, understand our Torah learning, overcome our bad habits, and pray with fervor. The tribulation of interim failure in fulfilling our spiritual aspirations is also for the ultimate benefit of our souls, for the following reasons:

1. Lack of spiritual success, despite our best efforts, atones for the period in our lives when we exerted much less effort in serving Hashem or in doing a particular mitzva.
2. Hashem delays granting us spiritual success, in other words, elevating us to a higher spiritual plateau, if our souls are not yet strong enough to receive the enhanced Divine light of the higher plateau. Hashem delays spiritual success until we can properly learn to nullify our egos, so that the success won't lead to arrogance.

Whatever the reason, a person should lovingly accept the delay in his or her spiritual gain, throwing logic aside and activating the emuna that everything is for the best. With continued prayer and teshuva, a person builds the spiritual vessels that enable enhanced success in serving Hashem.

Teller or Talmudist?

A well-known contemporary Talmudic scholar, a pious individual of impeccable character that devoted his life to Talmudic study, suddenly found himself forced to take a job as a teller in a bank. A series of circumstances literally coerced him to trade his seat in the hallowed hall of Torah study for a swivel chair behind a teller's window.

On his first day at work, the Talmudic scholar surveyed the strange and impersonal surroundings of the bank, rubbing his eyes in astonishment: "How did I get here? What am I doing here? Why am I doing such a mundane and unsatisfying task, rather than learning my beloved Torah?" He brushed his mind's questions aside, and decided to think positively at all costs. The teller-Talmudist wouldn't allow himself to sink in despair, despite the fact that he wasn't doing what he wanted to do. He didn't try to avoid or deny his current reality, nor was he angry at Hashem or at himself. He did what he had to do and made the best of his circumstance. During lunch break, rather than eating, he'd find a quiet corner and prayed to Hashem from the depths of his heart that he'd be able somehow to return to his Talmudic study. After outpouring his soul for a few minutes, he would then return to performing his tasks cheerfully for the rest of the day.

Weeks and months passed. The teller-Talmudist was steadfast in his emuna, his joyful acceptance of his current predicament, and in his prayers. Miraculously, the problems and circumstances that had forced him to take a job as a teller reversed themselves for the better, and the teller was soon able to reassume his place in his beloved hall of Torah study.

Veteran Driver

Those who live with emuna that Hashem's Divine Providence is always for the best are happy and confident. They don't suspect Hashem of leading them down the wrong road. Such individuals resemble those who make an intercity bus trip: They're sure that the driver knows both how to drive the bus and how to choose the best route. With nothing else to worry about, they're free to relax in their seats, gaze out the window, and enjoy each minute of the trip.

In stark contrast, those who lack emuna are like nervous passengers on the same intercity bus. As backseat drivers, they think they can drive the bus better than the company driver. They also think they are capable of choosing a shorter and swifter route. Frustrated, they try to drive the bus from their seat in row 12. Each minute passes with bitterness and frustration, for they're sure that the driver doesn't know what he's doing or where he's going. They're worried that the bus is traveling east rather than west. They think the driver's going either too fast or too slow. Those same worried passengers suffer substantial emotional stress because they lack faith in the bus driver.

Without emuna, whenever a person thinks that he or she is "driving the bus" - or in other words, in charge of their own fate. Any time that life doesn't go the way they want it to, such people suffer stress, anxiety, frustration, despair, and even nervous breakdowns. Many of them refuse to reconcile themselves to the fact that we all must undergo tikkunim, those soul corrections that Hashem designs for our individual benefit. They frequently complain about their unbearable suffering;

they're correct, for without emuna, life is surely bitter and unbearable.

No one can escape the fact that life doesn't always proceed along the lines of our personal plans and expectations. The unexpected variables that each of us must deal with lead us down our designated path of tikkun. Why complain, cry, and rant when we can easily strengthen ourselves in emuna and live pleasant lives? All we have to do is to trust the "driver of the bus", our beloved Creator who's capably leading the universe as a whole and doing what's best for each of us. A person must strengthen himself in emuna and realize that this is what Hashem wants, and that it's all for the best. Everyone should make an effort to look for the Divine message in whatever is happening and as Rebbe Nachman says, search for the Divine wisdom embedded in each occurrence.

Patience Pays Off

A person with strong emuna who experiences tremendous difficulties sounds like this: "That's the way Hashem wants things! Everything is for the best!" In the meanwhile, such an individual maintains a positive outlook and copes the best way he or she can with the tools at their disposal, while continuing to pray and express their hopes and aspirations. He or she is all the more delighted and thankful to Hashem when things are going good. Only a person with emuna is happy no matter what, in any situation, for a life of emuna is a life of paradise. The opposite is also true - a life without emuna is a life of purgatory. People who lack emuna are bitter and dissatisfied with life.

It turns out that a lack of emuna is a person's worse punishment.

Rabbi Menachem Rekanati, the famed 14th Century CE Italian kabbalist, was a simple merchant until the age of 80. He dreamed of devoting his life to Torah study, but never had the opportunity. Despite his circumstance, he continued to aspire, to yearn for Torah study, and to pour his heart out to Hashem in daily personal prayer. For decades, he begged Hashem for the privilege of totally immersing himself in the sea of Torah.

After his 80th birthday, a tzaddik came to him in a dream and gave him a golden goblet to drink from. When he woke up, he discovered that the wisdom of Torah had been revealed to him; during the next two years of his life, he wrote some forty texts of intricate Torah and Kabbala commentary!

A Liberated Brain

When a person is happy, he or she is ready to learn the third level of emuna. A happy person's brain is at liberty to search for and understand the messages that Hashem instills within all the stimuli of our environment. Without the chains of negative emotions, we can more readily discern where Hashem is taking us. Even if we don't fully understand what's happening in our lives, with emuna, we can pray and ask Hashem to open our eyes and help us make the right choices.

Understanding Hashem's messages, spiritually awakening ourselves, and learning how to correct what needs correcting are products of upper-level emuna, the third stage in our quest for emuna. But, we can't proceed to the third level until we've solidified our position in the second stage, or intermediate-level emuna.

Remember that we can't make effective choices that result from upper-level emuna until we first internalize our intermediate-level emuna, namely, that everything Hashem does is for the ultimate best. Already at this level, we should be accepting life's challenges with happiness. Once we do, we're ready to understand the message contained within each challenge.

Without a good hold on intermediate-level emuna where a person fully believes that everything is for the best, he or she shouldn't attempt to understand Hashem's messages. Without believing that Hashem does everything for the best, a person can't make proper choices. Truth comes from a free and clear mind; a free and clear mind comes from the happiness in knowing that Hashem does everything for the best. We therefore need intermediate-level emuna in order to avoid erroneous conclusions in discerning Hashem's messages.

Ascending a Rung

With second-level emuna - the faith that Hashem does everything for the best combined with constant thanks to Hashem - we enjoy a pleasant, tranquil existence.

Apparently, if a person has this level of emuna, why go further? He already lives an enjoyable and satisfying life. What's he lacking? Know full well that without using the events of our lives as opportunities for personal and spiritual growth, and without constant introspection, maintaining a hold on the emuna that Hashem does everything for the best will be tricky. Only steadfast second-level emuna can assure happiness, peace of mind, and successful weathering of life's difficult times. The silver lining within any cloud of tribulation is that difficulties stimulate us to seek Hashem and **bring us closer to Him**. That's the very purpose of life – to seek Hashem and to get to know Him and get closer to Him.

Hopefully, learning about third, or upper-level emuna will bring us to complete emuna, thus enabling us to accomplish our mission on this earth and to achieve our soul correction.

C. **Level-three Emuna: What does Hashem want from me?**

The third and upper level of emuna is the belief that Hashem does everything for a specific purpose, and that each of Hashem's actions conveys a special message aimed at helping us perform our task on earth. Moreover, upper-level emuna teaches that Hashem sends us incessant stimuli that call us to strengthen our connection with Him.

Hashem does nothing without a purpose. A person must strengthen his belief in Divine providence and search for the message Hashem is conveying in each occurrence, namely, what He wants from Him. Things happen to us in life to teach us a certain lesson, to stimulate us to take action such as rectifying something or to trigger us to repent for a certain misdeed. Maybe Hashem wants us to strengthen the observance of one of the Torah's commandments or awaken us from spiritual slumber. It's also possible that Hashem is doing what He does to deflate our inflated egos, among a myriad of other possibilities. At any rate, each person on his or her particular spiritual level should try their utmost to comprehend the message that Hashem is conveying and rectify whatever needs rectification.

The overall message that connects between all the events, experiences, and stimuli of our lives is emuna. Hashem's principle desire in His universe is to bring a person to emuna; His actions therefore induce a person to learn emuna. We must consequently search for the message - the "Divine wisdom" - within a given event or experience that's designed to bring us closer to complete emuna. A person who who turns his nose up to emuna is like an Esau, who disdained Divine wisdom, as King Solomon says, "A fool does not desire understanding, but only the wishes of his heart" (Proverbs 18:2).

The matter of searching for the Divine wisdom and message within every creation and occurrence is very broad and deep. In fact, this entire book deals with this search. But, the first concept that a person must internalize in order to merit this level is the notion that "there are no tribulations without prior transgression" (see tractate Shabbat 55b).

Why Do I Have Tribulations?

A person with tribulations should first ask himself if he is pleased with himself and pleased with his lot in life. Everyone should see their own good points, their good deeds, their positive character traits, their compassion for others and their good desires, for everyone is full of worthy aspirations. No one wants to do bad; indeed, everyone would like to be the way Hashem wants them to be. One must therefore simply love him/herself and judge him/herself favorably.

If a person doesn't see his own good, he can't believe in Hashem!

The Creator says to each of His creations: Cherished son and daughter! In the meanwhile, even though you have much to work on, I'm happy with you just the way you are! I take pride in you and I rejoice in you. I just want to bestow more and more good on you.

That's not all! The Creator also says:

I love you, so why don't you love yourself?

I rejoice in you, so why don't you rejoice in yourself?

I take pride in you, so why don't you take pride in yourself?

I am waiting patiently for you. I'm not pushing you, so why are you persecuting yourself? Why don't you believe in yourself, that I love you?

Look, you believe that I can do anything. You believe that I can easily give you what you need. So why are you sad? Why do you despair? Do you think I'm incapable of rescuing you from your current predicament? I want you to be happy about everything I've helped you with until now. First look at everything I've done for you until now, then ask Me for what you need and for My help in the future...

A person is first judged for his emuna. Sadness, depression, self-persecution and bitterness all result from a lack of emuna. If a person would truly believe that Hashem is right there with him, listening not only to his prayers but to every word he says, he wouldn't be sad at all and he'd pray with desire and fervor. He'd surely ask Hashem for everything he needs.

Emuna means to be happy with one's lot in life. Emuna is prayer. A person who is unhappy with his lot in life doesn't pray properly, and that's what he's judged on.

So, if a person sees that he's not content, then it's not the time for self-assessment and teshuva. Why? In his current state, if he tries to rectify himself, he'll only get depressed and will persecute himself; that will make him lose the emuna that Hashem loves him.

A discontented person should strive to be happy. How? He or she should look for his good points and see the good and the beautiful aspects of him/herself. Only after he becomes happy with himself, and he has an aura of positivity, can he believe in Hashem. Then, self-assessment and teshuva become easy. He believes that Hashem loves him and knows that Hashem will therefore help him to improve.

Danger!

Nothing invokes such severe judgments as sadness and bitterness does. The Torah emphatically cites sadness as the root cause of life's curses when it says (Deut. 28:47), "Because you failed to serve Hashem with happiness and goodness of heart when everything was abundant."

The accusation of failure to serve Hashem with happiness becomes even more harsh when it comes to Torah and mitzvoth. The Rambam writes: "The joy that a person has in his observance and implementation of the mitzvoth is a lofty form of Divine service. A person who does not strive for this joy is worthy of punishment, as the Torah says, 'Because you failed to serve Hashem with happiness and goodness of heart when everything was abundant.'" (Laws of Shofar, Succah and Lulav, Ch.8, 15).

Hashem is more than just and He judges us with mercy and lenience. When a person is dissatisfied, he is making a statement that he does not believe that Hashem's Divine providence is just and merciful. This immediately invokes stern judgments that zealously protest any breach to Hashem's honor. The dissatisfied person doesn't think that Hashem is being fair and truthful with him - nothing could be a greater defamation of Hashem's Name.

Since Hashem is rarely, if ever, indebted to anyone, the dissatisfied person's file in the Heavenly archives undergoes immediate examination to determine whether that person's disgruntlement is justified or not. Naturally, the outcome is always that the dissatisfied person has received more than he or she deserves and that the complaints are unjustified. Not only that, but they don't deserve what Divine mercy has already given them. The Heavenly forces of stern judgment now demand justice, with no mercy or compassion. That's when big troubles begin...

If the same dissatisfied person would have been happy with his lot in life instead of feeling entitled to something he doesn't truly deserve, he would have spared himself the troubles and tribulations that he invoked upon himself. He demands justice? The Heavenly Court says fine, we'll give you pure justice, by the letter of the law. King David knew full well to stay out of the Heavenly Court and to rely on Hashem's mercy when he says: "Do not judge Your servant according to the letter of the law, for no living being can be righteous before You" (Psalm 143:2).

There are no Tribulations without Prior Transgression

The principle that there are no tribulations without prior transgression is the foundation of emuna, of Judaism, and of the entire world. The renowned 13th Century

CE Kabbalist and Talmudic sage Nachmanides writes in his commentary on the Torah (Parshat Bo), "A person doesn't earn a share in the Torah until he believes that everything and every event in life is a miracle! Nothing is the product of nature or natural course, whether on an individual or on a collective scale. The reward of one who fulfills the mitzvoth is ultimate success, while the punishment of a transgressor is eventual doom, all by Divine edict." Simply speaking, one must first believe that everything in life is the product of the Creator's tailor-made decree in order to believe that there are no tribulations without transgression. Without such emuna, one lacks a genuine connection to true Judaism.

Those with a general belief in Divine Providence, who fail to attribute their tribulations - even the tiniest - to a transgression, err in one of two ways:

1. They think that Hashem torments His creations for no reason, or that Hashem created the world so that His creations should suffer, Heaven forbid. King David testified (Psalms 145: 17), "Hashem is righteous in all His ways and magnanimous in all His deeds." He also declared (ibid 92: 16), "Hashem is just; my Rock in Whom there is no injustice." One who believes that Hashem torments His creations for nothing consequently has a warped notion of emuna.
2. They really don't believe in Divine Providence like they say but think that their tribulations are the result of fate, chance, or natural course, oftentimes blaming themselves or others for their difficulties in life. Such a notion is contrary to emuna.

We therefore logically conclude that a person who truly believes in Divine Providence - in other words, that everything comes from Hashem - must consequently believe that any sorrow, trouble, difficulty, and deficiency in his or her life come from Hashem as well! Knowing that Hashem does everything for a specific purpose - and that Hashem is loving, just, and compassionate - leads us to the categorical conclusion that our transgressions are the reasons of our suffering.

People ask, "If Hashem is so kind and compassionate, then why does He punish me for my transgressions?" Good question; Hashem knows how terribly transgressions blemish our souls. Blemished souls diminish our ability to receive Hashem's Divine light and prevent us from inheriting an optimal place in the world to come. Therefore, Hashem sends us the tribulations that are capable of cleansing our souls. Life's difficulties are not punishments, but soul corrections from a loving Father in Heaven, designed for our ultimate good and to stimulate spiritual gain.

The belief that there are no tribulations without transgression brings us to happiness, especially when we seize the opportunity of life's difficulties to trigger a process of soul-searching that leads to enhanced spirituality and proximity to Hashem. By viewing our difficulties in life as growth opportunities, we attain true and complete emuna.

The Awe of Heaven (Fear of G-d)

Many regard the term of "Fear of G-d" in a derogatory manner, as if the individual is afraid that a bolt of lightning will strike him in the head if he transgresses. Yet, one must believe in G-d even to attain this low-level fear of Him. On a higher level, Yir'at Shamayim, which literally means the fear of Heaven, better signifies an awe of the Almighty that stems from true emuna. A person without even the basic level of "Fear of G-d", which again is the fear of punishment for transgressing, consequently feels that he is master over himself with no need to heed anyone. Such an individual makes no effort in assessing himself daily, repenting for his misdeeds, asking forgiveness and rectifying himself.

A personal with minimal fear of Heaven is afraid to be punished for his sins. Otherwise, he certainly would assess himself daily, confess his wrongdoings and ask the Almighty's forgiveness. On the next level, he'd beg Hashem to guard him from sinning in the first place.

What's more, the person who fails to engage in daily self-assessment is far away from the most basic measure of personal integrity. Even according to the morals of the world at large, if a person damages or insults another human being, or causes him sorrow in any way, basic decency requires the aggressor to apologize and to ask the injured or affronted party for forgiveness. This should apply all the more so in relation to affronting and transgressing the Creator, Who sustains a person every second of the day. One who commits a transgression should therefore ask forgiveness from Hashem.

A person who fails to assess himself and seek Divine forgiveness doesn't realize the damage that sin does to his soul. This individual if far from any semblance of awe of Heaven. With upper-level awe of Heaven, a person is sorely embarrassed of his blemished behavior that causes such anguish to our holy and exalted King of kings.

We find that the fear of Heaven begins with the belief in the reward and punishment that there is already in this world. This is the outcome of the belief that everything comes from Hashem – one's successes and one's setbacks. Tribulations, like everything else, are also from Hashem,

Who rewards or punishes people according to their deeds. As such, a person who realizes that there are no tribulations without prior transgression will make sure to evaluate himself every day.

Everyone wants to lead a pleasant and successful life. With that in mind, when a person knows that sin is liable to rob his life of success and joy, he'll double-check himself daily to see whether he has anything that needs rectifying. That way, he spares himself the tribulations brought on by uncorrected misdeeds. When a person encounters difficulties in life, he immediately assesses himself, repents for anything he might have done wrong and confesses. If he uproots the cause of the tribulations - the misdeeds he hasn't yet accounted and repented for - then the tribulations disappear. Such a person fears that if he doesn't repent, his tribulations will only become worse. This fear is well-founded, for if a person fails to awaken from his spiritual slumber in light of the tribulations, they only become more severe.

As long as a person blames anything other than his sins for his tribulations, it's a sign that he's far away from the fear of Heaven. He doesn't feel that he needs to account to anyone for his actions. Even worse, he doesn't wake up from the current "wake-up calls", so they only become louder.

We can therefore conclude that without the principle of "no tribulations without prior transgression", there cannot be fear of Heaven. Even the simplest of individuals knows that there are rewards and punishments in the world, the proverbial sticks and carrots. This stimulates his fear of Heaven. Fear begins with the fear of punishment; from there, a person can climb to higher rungs of spiritual awareness until he reaches the upper level awe of Heaven. Rebbe Nachman of Breslev writes (Likutei Moharan, I:15), that the fears that a person has from all types of troubles stems from the stern judgments from Above that manifest themselves within those troubles in order to stimulate a person to fear the punishment and to bring him to pure awe of Heaven.

The Triggers of Tribulations

In effect, this is the proper place to mention what we referred to previously under the heading, "Why Do I Have Tribulations?" The first sin that invokes stern judgments is the sin of sadness. The reason we mentioned it before was because we didn't want to open this chapter with the concept of "no tribulations without prior transgression", for readers might become alarmed and even more depressed unless properly prepared to learn this concept. Once a person is happy with himself, and realizes that Hashem is happy with him, he can move forward constructively.

Therefore, before a person begins to assess himself and to search for what triggered his tribulations. The first thing he needs to know is where he is guilty of whining, complaining and ingratitude. Now, he must work on strengthening his joy and gratitude. Only when a person rejoices in himself and in his good points, can he then be content with his lot in life while praising and thanking Hashem. Once he truly feels that whatever he has in life is a free gift from Above, can he assess himself without persecuting himself and falling into depression.

Transgressions between man and fellow human

Prolonged anguish is often a result of transgressions committed against a fellow human. One who causes pain to another person, even in the slightest, cannot be forgiven for his own sins until he begs forgiveness from the victim of his misdeeds. As long as one's injustices against a fellow human go uncorrected, severe judgments linger. These trigger other inexplicable tribulations that no other penitence can atone for other than apologizing to the affronted individual and seeking his or her forgiveness. Even if the one who harmed his fellow human is righteous and pious in his adherence to the mitzvoth between man and Hashem, it won't help him a bit if he's done damage to another person until he apologizes and seeks forgiveness. Only then will he atone for the transgression and his tribulations will disappear.

Failure to observe mitzvoth

Tribulations are frequently indications that a person is either doing actions that are forbidden by Torah, in other words, the negative mitzvoth, or failing to fulfill the Torah's obligatory actions, the positive mitzvoth.

Arrogance

Tribulations are a direct result of arrogance, for the Torah says, "And your heart became haughty and you forgot the L-rd your G-d..." (Deuteronomy 8:14). Tribulations can also be indications that a person lacks the emuna that "there is none other than Hashem" (ibid, 4:35). Hashem often uses suffering to deflate inflated egos. Oftentimes, a person's downfall is the result or his or her own arrogance. King Solomon, the wisest of all men, said (Proverbs 16:18), "Pride precedes destruction, and arrogance comes before failure." We can usually find a hint of arrogance and complacency before every crisis in life.

Hashem is especially compassionate when He deflates our egos, because an arrogant person can't get close to Him. The sages of the Talmud said (Sota, 5a), "The Holy One, blessed be He, says: The arrogant person and I cannot dwell in the same world." As a result, Hashem removes His Divine Presence from the midst of arrogance and arrogant people. Wherever Hashem removes His Divine Presence, suffering sets in. Who can succeed, or even sustain, without Hashem?

Let's elaborate: since a person's entire purpose is to learn emuna, and arrogance is the total opposite of emuna, Hashem subsequently separates Himself from the arrogant person. Sadness is the greatest form of arrogance, for the arrogant person has a sense of entitlement that is not being fulfilled and feels that Hashem owes him something that he's not receiving. This principle is mentioned in Rebbe Nachman's "Sefer HaMiddot", when it says: "By way of sadness, The Holy One, blessed be He, is not with a person" (Sadness, 14).

Measure for Measure

Hashem frequently employs the policy of "measure for measure" to help a person understand why he or she is suffering. For example, a cab driver that violated the Sabbath suffered two flat tires and a speeding ticket the following Sunday morning, causing him to lose the exact sum that he earned on the Sabbath. Or, a person who was lax in putting on tefillin suddenly gets a splitting headache or a pain in his left arm. We see that Hashem's policy of measure for measure is not a punishment; it's a Divine method of education.

Examples from the Torah

Our sages said (Sota. 8b), "A person is measured in the manner that he measures others. Samson pursued the desire of his **eyes** and therefore lost his **eyes** at the hands of the Philistines[1]; Absalom was haughty about his **hair** and was therefore hung by the **hair**[2]; Miriam **tarried** an hour for Moses, and therefore all of Israel **tarried** for her an entire week.[3]"

Our sages also teach (tractate Shabbat 33a) that diphtheria - a terrible disease that begins with gram-positive bacteria in the intestines and culminates in a fatal growth that blocks the throat - is the result of slander. Just as a person's negative "gut-feelings" against someone lead to slander and an evil tongue, diphtheria begins in the "guts" and progresses to the mouth. The disease progresses in the same way that the sin does.

Elsewhere (tractate Berachot 5b), the Talmud tells the story of Rav Huna, whose four hundred casks of wine soured:

---

1 See Judges, Chapter 16; Samson pursued the desire of his eyes and chose Delila - an idol worshiper, the daughter of an enemy nation, and a person of treacherous character - and ultimately forfeited his eyes at the hands of her people.

2 See Samuel II, Chapter 18; Absalom was vain about his hair, among other things. Absalom also revolted against his father, King David. While riding his mule, his hair became entangled in the branches of an oak tree; the mule kept on going, and Absalom was left hanging by the scalp until death.

3 See Exodus 2:4; Miriam hid by the Nile overseeing her baby brother Moses, who was placed in a wicker basket and cast on the river, until Pharaoh's daughter discovered him. Later, when Miriam contracted leprosy (see Numbers, Chapter 12), all of Israel waited seven days until she healed.

Rav Huna's colleagues told him that he should do some soul searching and contemplate why Hashem made his wine sour into vinegar. Rav Huna reacted, "What, am I suspicious of wrongdoing in your eyes?"

His colleagues answered, "What, is Hashem suspicious of punishing for no reason?"

Rav Huna responded, "If anyone has heard that I've committed a wrongdoing, let him come forward and tell me!"

His colleagues said, "We have heard that you haven't been just with your tenant farmer, and that you failed to give him a just share of the grapevine cuttings."

Rav Huna protested, "My tenant steals me blind! I therefore leave the vine cuttings for myself."

The rabbis remarked, "The folk expression says that he who steals from a thief has the taste of thievery in his mouth..."

Rav Huna conceded, "I take upon myself the obligation to atone and to return the tenant's rightful portion of the grapevine cuttings."

Even though Rav Huna merely committed himself to performing teshuva, but had not yet actually rectified the injustice, Hashem performed a miracle and restored the vinegar to its original state of wine. Another opinion in the Talmud says that the vinegar did not revert to being wine, but the price of wine vinegar skyrocketed and Rav Huna made a handsome profit. Either way, we see how a person's acceptance of Divine justice reverses a situation from stern judgment to miraculous compassion.

Rav Huna transgressed with a grapevine cutting and was subsequently punished by way of his wine. With such "measure for measure" messages, Hashem helps us understand what we need to correct.

Rashi explains (Gen. 37:2) how the episode of Joseph exemplifies the policy of "measure for measure" in Divine justice:

Joseph carried three detrimental tales about his brothers to his father; in each case, he was punished measure for measure, as follows:

1. Joseph said that his brothers ate the meat of a live animal; in turn, the brothers soaked Joseph's cloak in the blood of a slaughtered kid goat.
2. Joseph said that the sons of Leah were calling their half-brothers, the sons of Bilha and Zilpa, slaves; in turn, he was sold into slavery.
3. Joseph said that his brothers were suspicious of illicit sex; in turn, he himself was accused of illicit relations with the wife of the Egyptian minister Potifar.

Jacob was away from home for 22 years; his absence caused anguish to Isaac and Rebecca, his parents. Jacob was punished measure for measure when his own beloved son Joseph was missing and thought dead for exactly 22 years!

Judah fooled his father Jacob by dipping his brother Joseph's cloak in the blood of a kid goat and saying that Joseph was devoured by a wild animal. Judah's daughter-in-law Tamar in turn fooled him with a kid goat (see Genesis, Chapter 38).

Simon advised his brothers to throw Joseph in a pit; subsequently, Simon was thrown in an incarceration pit in Egypt.

Joseph's brothers were caught in a **libelous accusation** of stealing the royal goblet; they understood that they were being punished measure for measure for the **libelous accusations** they made against Joseph.

Thought, Speech and Deed

The Baal Shem Tov teaches that grief from one's children stems from a blemish in neshama, the part of the soul that corresponds to thought, since the seed originates in the brain. Therefore, when a person suffers from his children, it's a measure-for-measure message to help him realize that he must rectify something in his **thoughts**.

Troubles from one's wife indicate a blemish in ruach, the part of the soul that corresponds to speech. Therefore, when a person suffers from his wife, it's a measure-for-measure message to help him realize that he must rectify something in his **speech**.

Financial difficulties indicate a blemish in nefesh, the part of the soul that corresponds to deeds. Therefore, when a person suffers from money problems, it's a measure-for-measure message to help him realize that he must rectify his **deeds**.

Hashem's Children

Since Hashem calls us "His children", problems from our own children are likely to be a "measure for measure" resulting from similar grief we cause Hashem, Heaven forbid. For example, when a person's son is disobedient, then that person has probably been disobedient to Hashem. Insolent children are indications of brazen and insolent parents. In our own soul-searching, we should pay attention to how our children treat us, for that's an indication of how we treat Hashem. Furthermore, we should make a concerted effort to atone for our own sins against our parents. So very often, our own children treat us in the same manner that we treat our parents.

Against or complementary?

The biblical word that describes the wife as a partner in life is kenegdo (see Gen. 2:18); this word has a double meaning, "against" or "complementary".

The nation of Israel is the proverbial wife of Hashem. As such, a wife's treatment of her husband reflects her husband's treatment of Hashem. A disrespectful wife is a sign that a husband is disrespectful to Hashem. A lazy wife is a sign that the husband is lax in his duties toward Hashem, and so forth. Our sages teach that when a husband so merits, his wife is a "complementary" helper to him. But, when he isn't worthy, his wife is "against" him - an enemy! The husband's deeds actually dictate the wife's behavior.

Jewish esoteric thought teaches that a wife is the mirror of her husband - through her, he can see himself, his character traits, his strengths and weaknesses, and the like. For example, if she has a short temper, it's a sign that he has an anger problem. Even if he considers himself even-tempered, if he carefully assesses himself, he'll find quite a bit of latent anger that he perhaps was not aware of until now. She is the microscope that magnifies his faults and exposes his inner dimension. When she is amiss in her performance of a mitzvah, he is most certainly faulty in his observance of the same mitzvah. Even if he outwardly observes that mitzvah, he lacks the inner connection and intent of the mitzvah.

Therefore, he is incapable of shining the light of that mitzvah on his wife, and so on in every other area.

Many marital difficulties are indications of the husband's lack of emuna or his arrogance, or his breach in personal holiness and failure to guard his eyes.

The Blessing Immediately After Washing Hands

Rabbi Chaim Vital once experienced a sharp pain in his shoulder. His teacher, the holy Ariza'l, asked him if he recites the blessing after a meal - Birkat HaMazon - immediately after washing his hands at the termination of the meal, as required according to the law known as mayim achronim, or "final water", to distinguish it from the required hand-washing before a meal. Rabbi Chaim answered that he is not careful about making the blessing immediately. The Ariza'l said that this was the cause of his shoulder pain, since the Hebrew words for immediate - techef - and shoulder - katef - are derived from the same three Hebrew letters- kaf, taph, and peh. The lack in immediacy therefore led to a pain in the shoulder.

The Seemingly Easy Path of the Evil

Hashem uses the policy of tribulations that indicate a needed correction to teach those whom He loves what they need to correct. The Talmud teaches (Berachot 5a) that Hashem sends suffering to those He loves, for He desires to cleanse their souls of blemishes in this world, so that they can earn a lofty place in the world to come.

Some people are so steeped in evil that Hashem doesn't even bother with them. Rather than sending them tribulations that they wouldn't heed or learn from anyway, Hashem gives them their rewards in this world so that they forfeit any reward in the next world. That's why it appears that the evil enjoy money, success and an easy life. But, they pay the full price for their actions in the world to come.

Tribulations of Love

The righteous undergo rigorous soul corrections in this world to enhance their rewards, as our sages teach (Berachot, 5a): "If a person sees that tribulations are coming upon him, let him assess himself, as it is written, 'Let us search and assess our ways, and return to Hashem' (Lamentations 3:40). If he searched yet did not find anything amiss, let him attribute the tribulations to a lax in learning Torah, for it says, 'Happy is the man whom Hashem torments and teaches him His Torah' (Psalm 94:12). And, if he sees that he was not lax in learning Torah, then he should attribute his tribulations as tribulations of love, for it says, 'For he whom Hashem loves, He shall reprove' (Proverbs 3:12)."

From the above we learn that when Hashem wants to add to a righteous person's rewards, He sends him tribulations. The righteous person not only gets rewarded for weathering the tribulations but enhanced rewards for serving Hashem from this level of difficulty. If he wanted to, the righteous person could probably rid himself of the tribulations, praying to Hashem, "I neither want the tribulations nor the rewards."

The Middle Road

Most people don't belong on evil's easy path or on the tribulation trail of the righteous. Our sages said, "We have neither the tranquility of the wicked nor the tribulations of the righteous" (Avot 4:15). The Talmud is therefore telling us that we cannot attribute our tribulations to the tribulations of love that the righteous receive. Therefore, we should assess ourselves, and if we can't find a transgression, attribute the tribulations to a lax in Torah study. Who can testify about himself that he's already on the level of righteousness?

The vast majority of us "middle-of-the-roaders" should remind ourselves that there are no tribulations without transgression. We therefore should train ourselves to look for the turn for a turn in our troubles, so that we'll know what to correct. Once we realize what we've done wrong, we should begin the 4-stage process of teshuva - confess to Hashem, express our remorse, apology for our misdeeds, and commit to improve from this moment on. Once we understand Hashem's message and act on it, Hashem doesn't need to speak to us in the language of tribulations, for He doesn't want to torment us, only to arouse us from our spiritual slumber. Once we wake up and rectify, the tribulations become superfluous and fade away. The prophet says, "Hashem doesn't want the death of a dead person... He wants him to return to Him and live" (Ezekiel 18:32). Tribulations are not a form of Divine vengeance but a loving call to stimulate a person's rectification.

Positive Approach

Nobody wants trials and tribulations. But, once they come, they're a good sign, showing that Hashem cares about us very much. As long as a person harbors sins that are unatoned for, he suffers a blockage of Divine light that causes anguish to the soul. Tribulations are a sign that Hashem is calling us to get closer to Him, so that He can restore the full measure of Divine light that this person is capable of receiving, and his life becomes sweet and beautiful.

In the midst of suffering tribulations, a person frequently has no idea what Hashem wants from him. In that case, he should first of all strengthen himself in emuna and remind himself that there is no mistake in Divine Providence - Hashem didn't hit the wrong target. What's more, there are no tribulations without prior transgression. He should therefore turn to Hashem and say, "Master of the World, this is surely no mistake and no random occurrence. I believe wholeheartedly that my tribulations are due to my misdeeds. But unfortunately, I don't know what I did wrong to trigger this particular suffering. Please illuminate my eyes in understanding, so that I'll know what I did wrong and how to rectify it. In the meanwhile, please forgive me for whatever I did wrong that caused these tribulations. Help me do Your will always..."

If he still suffers tribulations after these prayers, let him cast intellect aside and simply believe that it's all for the best, accepting everything with love and humility. He should tell himself, "It's not enough that I upset Hashem to the extent that He was forced to send me tribulations, I haven't repented either. What right do I have to complain? Maybe these tribulations are coming to me because of previous incarnations or something else that I'm incapable of understanding. The least I can do is to accept them lovingly and humbly, and that way, they will atone for my sins."

When a person fulfills all three levels of emuna - knowing that everything is from Hashem, all for the best, and asking himself what Hashem wants from him - this is called complete emuna!

Obstacles

Two main obstacles prevent us from successfully weathering tribulations with emuna, as follows:

First, when we say, "I'm not strong enough to hold on! This is going to break me!" Such a feeling reflects a lack of belief in our own inner strength and capability to withstand stress. In order to overcome this obstacle, we must internalize the vital spiritual law that **Hashem doesn't give us trials and tribulations that we're incapable of withstanding.**

Second, when we say, "Let me live in peace!" or "I don't feel like dealing with this." This is a request to go through life with no teshuva, no soul corrections, no ups and downs, and no stormy weather. In other words, he's disconnected from his purpose in life and has no interest in true success. He doesn't care about what Hashem wants from him or about the world to come. He just wants one thing, an easy, tribulation-free life.

Hashem desires that we strengthen our souls; we can't strengthen our souls without being tested from time to time. Only by way of the trials and tribulations that build our emuna, do we achieve true tranquility of the soul. Trying to run away from life's difficulties rather than coping with them makes them even more unbearable. Hashem won't give in: He knows what we have to correct. The fact that we might not "feel like" correcting doesn't mean that Hashem will forget about effecting the needed tikkun, whether in this life or in a subsequent reincarnation. Our sages warned that any difficulties in this life are preferable to an additional reincarnation.

We can't live in a stupor of imaginary calm and achieve our needed soul corrections at the same time. Our entire purpose on this earth is to attain our tikkun, or soul correction. Therefore, ups and downs, difficulties, trials, and tribulations come with the turf. Our sages teach us that we come to this world whether we want to or not (see Avot 4:22). That means we must endure everything that comes our way. But even more, we'll be judged as to whether we did everything in our power to rectify ourselves. That means using life's stimuli as a mode to get closer to the truth.

A person can't decide to sit on the sidelines in this world. Once we're born, we're on the playing field; that means we have to pick up the ball of life's challenges and begin running with it toward our goal. But, we can't say that we don't want to play. We can't run away from the championship game called "life" where the winner - he or she who performs their mission in life - gets unfathomable rewards in the next world and in the meanwhile, enjoys a meaningful life in this world. You can't refuse to play, and you certainly shouldn't resist or complain.

By withstanding tests of emuna, a person rises to great spiritual heights, attaining a measure of spiritual growth that no other mitzvah could accord him. What's more, he'll have a gratifying life. For those who are unwilling to invest effort in correcting their soul, life will ultimately yield a worse collection of trials and tribulations. Therefore, whenever we strengthen ourselves in emuna, prayer, and the fear of Hashem, we make life so much easier.

With Hashem's help, the coming chapters will show how to apply emuna to our daily lives.

Chapter Three:
Sudden Tests of Emuna

This world is a classroom of emuna. Since the entire purpose of our life on earth is to learn emuna, then literally everything that happens to us in the course of the day is a test of emuna.

This chapter illustrates several of the typical and seemingly "natural" occurrences that are none other than Divinely-initiated and individually-tailored tests of emuna. With Hashem's help, we'll learn how to evaluate our performance and how to pass these tests with maximum success. Our final score in each test reflects our level of emuna proficiency. The higher our score, the better our lives will be in this world and in the next world.

Pull Over to the Side!

We're startled by the whine of a siren. We look in our rear-view mirror and see the flashing blue and red lights of a state trooper's car. A patrolman with an iron jaw motions for us to pull over to the side of the road. Whether or not we broke the law is now immaterial; this is a sudden test of our emuna. Now is the time to activate the lessons of emuna that we learned in the previous chapter, as follows:

1. **We should believe that our current predicament is from Hashem and exactly what Hashem wants.** Consequently, there's no need to blame ourselves (why wasn't I more careful?), the other driver (he was creeping - I had

to pass him!), or our spouse (honey, can't you go any faster? We're gonna be late...). Certainly, there's no need to harbor malice toward the policeman, even if we think we were unjustly pulled aside. According to state traffic laws, we might be innocent of wrongdoing. But, according to the guidelines of emuna, we deserve to be pulled aside; the policeman in this case is an enforcing officer of Hashem's absolutely just legal system.

2. **We should believe that what's happening to us now is for our own ultimate good.** Therefore, we should cast aside the nagging thoughts in our brains that what's happening to us is not good. Furthermore, we should happily thank Hashem for sending us the state trooper, as this situation is certainly for our ultimate benefit.

3. **We should believe that everything in life has a reason and a purpose, and that there are no tribulations without transgression.** The state trooper is none other than Hashem's catalyst to initiate a process of soul-searching and teshuva for something we may have inadvertently done wrong. Although we were pulled aside because of an apparent traffic violation, the "natural" circumstance is only a vehicle of Divine justice designed to arouse us.

Speak with Hashem

Before we say a word to the state trooper, we should perform some quick soul-searching, think about making teshuva, and speak to Hashem in the following manner: "Hashem, You know why You sent me this tribulation. Please forgive me for my wrongdoings; help me rectify whatever I did wrong. Help me identify and correct the reason that I deserve to be punished; help me to know fully what You want from me. I hereby commit to give (name an amount) dollars to (name your charity); in the meanwhile, please don't punish me by way of this policeman. Have mercy on me and help me correct the core sin that caused me to be punished."

Of course, one should neither complain nor protest to the policeman. Anger is also completely uncalled for, and flattering is just as bad. Don't argue or curse, and don't do or say anything disrespectful to the policeman.

If we've succeeded in remembering the three lessons of emuna while focusing on Hashem, and we've avoided the pitfalls of anger, blame, and negative emotions, then we score an A-plus in emuna. With emuna, we see any outcome for the best: if the state trooper lets us off with a warning, then we're certainly delighted. And, even if he does give us a ticket, we activate our emuna to remember that Hashem is doing this for our very best; we accept the outcome lovingly. Either way, with emuna, we're always living a good life.

On the other hand, people that lack emuna think that their fate is in the hands of the state trooper. They regard their current predicament as random or natural, and not the product of Divine Providence. Such folks sometimes try to sweet-talk the law-enforcement officer, and subsequently get in worse trouble. A concrete law of spirituality teaches that whenever people trust in anyone other than Hashem, they fall into the hands of the object of their trust; that's bad news, since no human has Hashem's capacity for mercy and compassion (see "Duties of the Heart", Chapter 4, "The Gate of Trust," introduction).

Usually, whenever a person tries to flatter a policeman, the policeman becomes even more stringent. Frustrated, the flatterer often reverts to anger and epithets, and unjustly accuses the policeman (you're just trying to fill your quota at my expense; hey, loads of people are going a lot faster than I was; why are you picking on me, etc. - the list is long), further complicating an already sticky situation. Rather than rectifying the wrongdoing that led to this predicament, the person that lacks emuna accrues even more transgressions by insulting or falsely accusing the policeman. The transgressor adds insult to injury, for now he is committing a heinous sin between man and fellow man by insulting the policeman with no justification at all. This is a transgression that is difficult to atone for. As long as the sins between man and fellow man go uncorrected, then severe judgment hovers like an ax over the neck of the transgressor, making life even more unbearable. Hashem refuses to forgive a person for affronts to one's fellow man; the transgressor must apologize to and beg the forgiveness of the person he harmed.

From here, a person should be stimulated to realize how serious the matter of man and fellow man is. As long as there are harmed and insulted people walking around in the world, there are troubles and stern judgments. Hashem is so merciful and forgiving when it comes to an affront against Him; Hashem often forgives a person at opportune times like a family celebration or when a person has the slightest contemplation of teshuva. But when it comes to transgressions between a person and his or her fellow human, there is no Divine mercy; Hashem will not forgive until the harmed individual wholeheartedly forgives.

A person who desires to rectify the wrongs he did to others must remember all those whom he harmed, find them and ask their forgiveness. Since this is virtually impossible, a person should exercise extreme caution in saying or doing anything that is hurtful to others.

Unsightly conduct between man and fellow man is the result of a lack of emuna. In our case at hand, of being stopped by a policeman, if a person has a non-emuna, "might of my right hand" mentality, he thinks he can talk his way out of the traffic ticket or appease the policeman in some way. When he fails, he tries to force the issue and then gets himself into worse trouble. A person likes this doesn't pass this sudden test of emuna. He'll see the results of his failing the test in this world as well as in the next world, for already, his life will be filled with sorrow, turmoil and more tribulations. Such people miss the entire point of Hashem's message to them when they bitterly blame their ills on the policeman. That's a gross lack of emuna, since they see the policeman as the one who determines their fate rather than seeing that Hashem is standing behind the policemen. Ein od milvado, there is no one but Hashem - everything is Him.

Charity Saves Fines

Many financial penalties and fines stem from a person's insufficient giving to charity.

The Talmud teaches (tractate Bava Basra 10a) that a person's income is preordained from Rosh Hashanah, just as his losses are preordained from Rosh Hashanah. If one so merits, money given to charity takes the place of financial loss. When one lacks the merit of charity, financial loss manifests itself in taxes, penalties (such as traffic and parking tickets), doctor bills, broken appliances, and so forth. Consequently, charity prevents penalties.

Rebbe Yochanan Ben Zakai had a dream on the night after Yom Kippur (ibid), that his nephew was destined to lose seven-hundred dinars that year. Rebbe Yochanan therefore hounded his nephew all year long for donations to a number of charitable endeavors. By the year's end, Rebbe Yochanan had extracted 683 dinars in charitable donations from his nephew.

On the eve of Yom Kippur, a Roman tax collector appeared on the nephew's doorstep and demanded the sum of seventeen dinars in back taxes. The nephew and his family trembled even after the tax collector left, worried that they were now under the close inspection of Caesar's cruel occupation government. When they expressed their fears to their saintly uncle Rebbe Yochanan, he said, "Don't worry! The seventeen dinars is all that you are liable - you won't have to pay an agora (cent) more!"

"How do you know?" questioned the skeptical nephew. "Do you have connections with the tax authorities, or maybe you're a prophet?"

"I have no connections to the authorities, nor am I a prophet or the son of a prophet. Yet, I do have connections with the supreme ruler - Hashem! At the beginning of this year, He showed me how much you stood to lose - 700 dinars. I almost succeeded in extracting the entire sum from you for charity. But, since you still owed seventeen dinars, the tax collector served as a messenger to complete your predestined loss! If you hadn't previously donated the 683 dinars to charity, then you'd have lost the entire 700 dinars to tax collectors and other cruel messengers, receiving only grief in return. But, since you now have the merit of charity, you'll see blessings and success in everything you do!"

"Dear Uncle," cried the nephew and his family, embarrassed by all the time and effort their saintly uncle exerted in their behalf all year long, "why didn't you explain that to us in the beginning of the year? If we knew that the financial loss was preordained, and that charity is a substitute for penalty, we'd have gladly given the entire sum to charity!"

"I wanted you to give charity with no ulterior motive," replied Rebbe Yochanan ben Zakkai, "and not just to save yourselves from a Heavenly edict." The nephew and family thanked him and committed themselves to give as much charity as they could possibly afford, having learned the power of this lofty mitzvah.

Frequently, the financial loss that people suffer is simply the completing payment of a preordained penalty for the current year. Heavenly accounting is exacting to the penny; but, whenever we take the initiative and willfully give to charitable causes, we prevent the anguish of losing money in all kinds of negative circumstances.

Atonement for sins

The preordained annual financial losses aren't the only root causes of losing money. Transgressions can also invoke additional financial loss, for one's dearest possessions - health, money, and so forth - are atonements for sin. Preemptive charity prevents penalties in this area as well. A person who willfully gives charity not only cleanses sin but reaps the wonderful benefits of this important mitzvah. Without charity, a person becomes a triple loser: First, he or she will have to involuntarily part with their money; second, they'll have to suffer the pain, anguish, and accompanying aggravation that are related to a specific financial loss; and third, they forfeit the benefits that they would have earned had they given charity. The Gemara teaches, "Rabbi Elazar says: 'In the time of the Holy Temple, one's participation in the purchase of ritual sacrifices atones for him; when there is no Temple, his charity atones for him. When he fails to give charity, the authorities take his money forcefully'" (Bava Batra 9a).

To avoid becoming a three-time loser, one should become accustomed to giving charity on a regular basis. The satisfaction of donating to the worthy poor, to the sick, to those in need (both material and spiritual), and to the advancement of Torah study in the world is infinitely preferable than losing money on medical bills, broken appliances, car breakdowns, taxes and fines. Whereas the latter brings only grief, the former serves as a first-class ticket to success in this world and eternal happiness in the next world, since it has the power to atone for one's sins.

Let's go back to the state trooper that pulled us aside: Our quick self-evaluation should be whether or not we gave enough charity. Without thinking twice, we should pledge an additional amount to charity, and say outright, "I hereby pledge (such-and-such amount) to (your favorite charity)!"

Charity is a tremendously worthy endeavor. If the lack of charity was the reason that we were stopped by the policeman, then the pledge of charity can almost instantaneously tip the scales of harsh judgments in the opposite direction. Even if the lack of charity was not the reason that the person was pulled over to the side of the road, the act of charity can still tip the scales of harsh judgments and invoke a favorable outcome in the Heavenly Court. This favorable outcome manifests itself in the state trooper's change of heart, where a five-hundred dollar, four-point fine or even potential license suspension becomes a mere vocal warning. With charity, the entire predicament can turn itself around for the best.

The Prosecutor Becomes the Defense Counsel

A trial or court case is a classic test of emuna. Like in any other challenging situation, remembering the three basic laws of emuna is the key to success. Whether or not a person is guilty of wrongdoing in this world, by contractual, federal, or state law is immaterial; the fact that he or she is faced with a court case is an indication from Heaven of outstanding spiritual debits that need rectification.

One should know that the outcome of a trial or hearing is actually determined in Heaven. A person that appears in the flesh before a judge and/or jury is simultaneously being judged in the Heavenly Court, which scrutinizes the individual's credits and debits. Once the Heavenly decision is reached, Hashem subsequently instills the "upstairs" verdict in the hearts of the judge and/or jury members in the "downstairs" courtroom.

Even though a person tries his or her best to succeed in court by hiring the best legal counsel, seeking the best witnesses and evidence, and carefully preparing arguments, a true believer knows that one can't fool the Heavenly Court. No fast-talking attorney can alter the truth of one's deeds or misdeeds as recorded in the Heavenly Court register. The verdict upstairs will dictate the verdict downstairs. Therefore, to win a court case, one's plea bargaining should be first and foremost with Hashem.

Sometimes, a person feels that he or she has an open and shut case, with complete success assured. Other times, a person may feel that there are no chances of success. Both feelings are false; he doesn't know whether he is innocent or guilty in the Heavenly Court, and that is what dictates the verdict down here on earth. Even if the defendant is innocent according to the local law, if there's a stern judgment Above, he'll be found guilty below. Therefore, the best way to prepare for any day in court is to carefully examine oneself, confess any and all wrongdoing to Hashem, express remorse for one's sins, ask for Hashem's forgiveness, rectify one's actions, and make a firm commitment to improve from this point onward. Effective teshuva mitigates and even neutralizes stern judgments, and the individual will be found innocent of charges.

Even when a person makes a sincere effort of teshuva - something that will undoubtedly help one's case or ease a severe verdict - he or she should be emotionally prepared to accept an unfavorable outcome. Who knows if his or her teshuva was sufficient enough to completely nullify the harsh judgment? So whatever the outcome, one must accept it with emuna.

Even a favorable verdict is a test of emuna. A person shouldn't attribute it to luck, to the legal system or to the attorney's cleverness.

On the other hand, one's emuna undergoes a special test in the face of a negative outcome or judgment, when found guilty or liable; this is the time to summon the power of emuna. The unfavorable decision is not the result of the other side's superior lawyer, our lawyer's mistakes, insufficient preparation, or untrue testimony. The judge and jury aren't to blame either. Negative judgments in a flesh-and-blood litigation are the sole results of insufficient teshuva. The task at hand is to accept the court's (Heavenly and earthly) decision lovingly and with emuna and to increase one's efforts of teshuva and prayer until the trouble is over.

When we make genuine heartfelt teshuva, we witness how Hashem turns a prosecutor into a counsel for the defense.

By making teshuva in preparation for our day in court, we receive a perfect score in emuna. We'll enjoy the fruits of our efforts even in this world, as follows:

1. We are spared from harsh judgments.
2. By strengthening our emuna, we merit enhanced proximity to Hashem.
3. We avoid slander, anger, frustration, bitterness, and blaspheme, and we earn the rewards of happiness and emuna.

The above fruits are immediate rewards in this world. Even more, the tremendous dividends of teshuva and emuna assure our eternal bliss in the next world. Nothing brings a person closer to Hashem than passing difficult tests of faith in this lowly and oftentimes confusing material world.

On the other hand...

People that lack emuna think that flesh-and-blood judges, juries, attorneys, and witnesses dictate the outcome of a case. Such folks harbor hundreds of trepidations and limitless complaints about the judges, their own legal counsel, and the other side. They'll readily depart from the truth to advance their case. When they put their trust in their lawyers, their lawyers frequently become the reason of their failure in court.

A concrete law of spirituality states that whenever people trust anything or anyone other than Hashem, then Hashem lets them fall into the hands of the source of their trust, which usually turns out to be miserably helpless and pitiful. Trusting in anything or anyone other than Hashem is a complete failure in the test of emuna.

Don't think that winning a day in court by way of teshuva and emuna is a fantasy. Dozens of people that implemented the author's advice discovered that even hostile judges came to their aid. Many have reported the amazing results that preparations of teshuva and prayer bring about in the courtroom.

Positions of Authority

People with positions of authority such as judges, law-enforcement officers, military commanders, government and municipal officials or public servants who wield power over other people should know that their test of emuna is tremendous. If they pass their test, they merit huge rewards. Not only that, but they faithfully perform their mission on earth and make the world a better place. If not, they are liable to cause indescribable ruination that is most difficult to atone for.

This is for several reasons:

A. A public servant comes in contact with many more people than a private person does. Whereas the latter's life centers around family, close friends and a few colleagues or coworkers, the public servant encounters a vast number of people who are directly affected by his decisions and conduct. So, if the public servant or the person in a position of authority performs his task in good faith, he benefits many people. He'll see blessings in everything he does and his merit will accompany him to the world to come. On the other hand, if he fails to use his authority in good faith and is cruel to people and unjust to his subordinates, he will accumulate a mountain of stern judgments very quickly. Since he so freely and frequently transgresses the commandments between man and fellow man, he won't be able to make amends to all those whom he harmed. This will manifest into all types of troubles in his own life. He shouldn't be surprised when he sees that life slaps him in the face so often. His life will become a nightmare.

B. Such an individual has great responsibility on his shoulders, since the success of his subordinates depends in a great measure on his conduct of affairs. For example, a teacher's manner affects a student – for better or for worse – the student's entire life. A bank officer or public servant's snap of the fingers can influence the future of entire families. A judge can decide between life and death, Heaven forbid. A policeman can save a life or unjustly take a life, and so forth.

C. A person of authority or a public servant must be much more cautious about character refinement that an ordinary person. He undergoes many test situations that he won't be able to pass without good character. Every moment of the day, he can choose between being benevolent or cruel, compassionate and caring or cold and aloof. He often has the authority to grant amenities or deny them, to punish or to forgive. He can act respectfully to those who need his services or trample and disparage them. He, more than anyone else, must have a fear of Heaven and the awareness that he is accountable to the Creator for everything he does.

In general, a person with authority should be aware that he is an emissary, a conduit of Divine will. Therefore, he should be benevolent and perform his mission faithfully. If he is a haughty tyrant, thinking that he is the overlord of other people's lives, he'll crash, and will be punished as well.

Remember, you are only an extension of Hashem's long arm. You can choose to be a hand that slaps or caresses; you can be either Hashem's punishing rod or a walking cane for people to lean on. From Above, good people merit bringing good to others, while wicked people become the agents of pain and suffering. From the way you treat others, you can understand which function you are performing. Don't forget though, the emissaries of good are rewarded, whereas the agents of sorrow and suffering are fully accountable and punished for the grief they cause others.

This behooves the person of authority and the public servant to devote at least an hour of daily to personal prayer and self-assessment making sure that he is only an agent of good. That way, Hashem will enable him always to bring good to the world.

An individual of authority should do his best to do his task the best way possible. He should be considerate of other people's feelings and never be cruel or degrading. Indeed, he should preserve the dignity of all those with whom he comes in contact and not take advantage of his power of authority to torment other people. If he must exercise stern discipline, then he should do so in a fair and merciful manner. If he must punish someone, he should exercise restraint and explain his considerations, where his objective is to educate rather than torment.

Know full well, that if you have authority over others, this is not a sanction that allows you to transgress the commandments between man and fellow man. If you cause sorrow to others for no reason, even if you do teshuva, you'll have to ask Hashem's forgiveness a thousand times. And, as long as you don't placate the injured party, stern judgments will hover over you.

On the other hand, if you do good to others, and help them improve their deeds, your tremendous rewards will stand to your credit for posterity. Don't ever forget - there is an eye that sees, an ear that hears, and all your deeds are inscribed in a book (Avot 2:1).

Compassion vs. Cruelty

Cruelty is a severe test of a person who wields authority, for every person has a cruel streak that he or she enjoys using. As long as a person is not in a position of authority, this tendency of cruelty is latent. But, as soon as he gets a position of power, he gets a delusion of grandeur that he can now act in any manner he likes. He is liable to enjoy meting his cruelty out. This is his test of emuna - will he be compassionate or cruel? There are many cruel people in positions of authority, but there are those who are very compassionate and earn prodigious rewards.

The Midrash tells us that in the future, Hashem will settle accounts with equestrians who were mean to their horses. If that's the case, imagine how Hashem will demand justice from those who were cruel to their fellow humans. Therefore, we should all pray to break our tendency to be cruel and substitute it with compassion.

Honor

Another difficult test of emuna for a person of authority is his lust for honor. Since people need him, they often flatter and kowtow. He should therefore break this fantasy lust of honor for it is nothing more than a fantasy. Would people honor him if he didn't sign their paychecks? Probably not. Our sages tell us that true honor is the respect of one's fellow human. So, if a person with authority respects others, he becomes truly honorable, and not when others dance around him because they need him. A person should therefore never use his authority to demand honor or any other favors or services that he is not rightfully entitled to.

A person who feels an inflated ego and false sense of importance will certainly fall, for King Solomon says that "pride comes before a fall" (Proverbs 16:18). At first, he delights in the homage that people pay to him and he thinks that this is reality. This causes him to get slapped; at home, his wife and children give him grief and fail to respect him. At work, both his superiors and subordinates rise up against him. That's not all the disparagement he gets, all because of his arrogance.

Disparagement

Another test of faith is when a person suffers insult, embarrassment and disparagement in the course of his job. Even when according to the laws of this world, the insults appear to be unwarranted, according to Divine jurisprudence, it's all precise justice. Hashem makes no mistakes and if a person must endure the pain of humiliation in some way, he'll get it. The suffering is paying off a spiritual debt and the person who insulted or humiliated us is only an agent in Hashem's just hands; if not this agent, then another agent...

Once, the holy Ariza'l turned to his students and asked, "How would you like to atone for your sins? Would you choose poverty?" His students answered no. "Sickness?" Again, no. "Strife with your neighbors?" Still no. "Exile?" Emphatically no.

"If that's the case," he told them, "accept insult, embarrassment and disparagement with love, and that shall atone for your sins."

That's why we must accept everything with love and to repent as well. Don't think that you're entitled to return insult for insult or to wield your power by belittling or cursing someone. One will be completely accountable for such an act. It's as if a voice from Heaven says, "It's not enough that you ignored these tribulations that came your way and failed to repent; you made things even worse by transgressing the Torah commandment that forbids verbally abusing another person. You should have realized that Hashem was sending you the insult, not the person who insulted you; you had no right to insult him in return."

Avshalom revolted against his father, King David. King David was forced to flee Jerusalem; as he did, Shimi ben Gera cursed him and hurled a string of the worst insults and epithets at him. Not only that but he threw stones at King David and at his attendants (see Samuel II, 16:5-8).

Avishai the son of Zeruiah, a valiant army officer who remained loyal to King David, upon hearing Shimi's unprecedented insolence said, "Your Majesty, why should this scoundrel curse my lord the King? I'll go forward and behead him!" (ibid, 9). This was no empty threat; at that moment, Shimi's life expectancy was about to expire.

King David would not allow Avishai to avenge his honor. He knew that the disparagement was from Hashem, so he said, "So let him curse, because Hashem said to him, 'Curse David'; who then shall dispute Hashem?" (ibid, 10). At that point, a voice called forth from Heaven and declared that King David would be the fourth wheel of the Divine chariot.

Within the framework of a person's job, he might have to suffer insult and humiliation, even embarrassment in public. He should accept this lot with love and not try to take revenge against those who disparaged him. Indeed, he should overcome and convert his anger to mercy. A sin against you is no license to sin in return.

Position of Authority = Position of Emuna

There's a marked difference between the way a person of emuna fulfills his position of authority and the way a person devoid of emuna does his job. The person of emuna knows that the Creator sees his every action, so he tries to conduct all his dealings in an upright manner.

Conversely, the person who lacks emuna thinks that he can throw his weight around and do as he pleases, taking advantage of his position for his own personal enjoyment and aggrandizement.

Let's view a few specific examples of the different challenges specific people of authority must cope with, and how to successfully deal with them.

The Public Service Clerk

Any clerk who must serve the public, whether he works for the government, a bank or a utility has an important task and a challenging test of emuna. He must believe that he was chosen from Above for this job, for his soul rectification is to help people. Therefore, he is given the opportunity to meet many people and to help them. If he treats them with respect, kindness and consideration, he'll be performing his mission on earth in the best possible manner.

Therefore, he should take advantage of his position to help everyone he can, acting with patience and with courtesy. He should avoid insulting anyone and rid himself of any trace of cruelty. Even if he receives grief from the public, he should believe that this is from Above and accept it lovingly. This is his test of emuna.

Just imagine how many people a public-service clerk deals with in a day. If he takes advantage of his position to do good for people, he accumulates a wealth of merit that will guarantee him blessings in both worlds. People will love him, which is also a sign that the Creator is pleased with him. Anyone that does good for people emulates the Creator and therefore invokes enhanced Divine love and compassion for himself.

But, if he doesn't perform his job faithfully, is arrogant toward people and not helpful, he'll be digging a hole for himself. Before he knows it, he'll have accumulated a long list of demerits for the negative, uncaring and haughty way he treats those who seek his assistance. Ultimately, he'll find himself in an abyss of personal troubles and tribulations, for many people will have malice in their hearts for the way he treated them.

The Policeman

The Creator wants law, order and justice to prevail in His world, so the policeman fulfills a vital role in society. As an officer of law and order, he is in a unique position to prevent suffering, for without his enforcement of the law, there would be chaos. But just as his task is so important, so is his responsibility.

The main test of a policeman is to avoid being cruel and to avoid being iron-handed. He must know that he is an emissary of the Creator, and therefore resist and correct his natural inclinations of being cruel and ruling over others. He must use his authority in an upright manner, knowing that he has a wonderful opportunity to do the Creator's will, to maintain the law and educate people rather than being tyrannical toward them.

For example, if a highway patrolman stops a person for a traffic violation, he shouldn't yell at him. Aggressive behavior will bring out the worst from the other side. Rather, he should approach him respectfully and say, "Good day, sir. I have nothing personal against you, but you have violated the law; you were driving twenty miles an hour more than the clearly-posted speed limit. It's my job to protect you as well as the other drivers on the road, and you should know that driving in such a manner endangers you, your passengers and everyone else on the road, including the pedestrians. Be honest with yourself, acknowledge the truth and accept your verdict willfully."

Even if the patrolman has the authority to give the person a stiff penalty, he should be merciful and considerate wherever he can. Clearly, a first offender deserves more consideration than a serial offender. Yet, he should never give a bigger penalty than what is stipulated by law. Policemen who receive incentive percentages of the fines they give out are frequently over-zealous. Their personal gain should not affect their decision-making. They should realize that the Almighty determines their income and they will never lose by giving a person a more lenient fine than what they could have given. The Creator has endless ways to augment the incomes of the upright.

The Judge

Judges play a critical role in society, for without the judicial system, there would be chaos in the world. Understandably, their influence on and responsibility to society are tremendous; this puts them in a dangerous situation.

A judge should know that the Creator alone is Judge of the universe. Mortals can easily be swayed; therefore, they must pray profusely that they don't make mistakes of judgment. The lives of people hinge on their verdicts. Judges should steer clear of hastiness and cruelty. They should take advantage of their power to educate and help the people to better their ways. Therefore, even when they mete out punishments, they should make sure that an educational message is in each punishment they give a person, in a way that will help that person mend his ways.

The Bible tells of the wisest of men, King Solomon, who could have asked the Creator for anything, but sought wisdom, for he realized the heavy responsibility he bore on his shoulders as King of Israel. He therefore pleaded to the Creator for the necessary wisdom and insight that would enable him to judge in the fairest and most accurate manner possible.

Parking Inspector

A person must do everything to avoid causing pain and bitterness to someone else. Parking inspectors, or as the British nickname them, "meter maids", have an important task in maintaining order in our cities' streets. They prevent hindrances to traffic and help enable the smooth flow of city life. They keep entrances to buildings and driveways from being blocked, and their work can actually prevent loss of life. Nonetheless, they must do their job with fairness and consideration. Even when they issue tickets justly, they are still liable to cause damage by causing sorrow to people. All the more so if they issue an unjust ticket. Imagine a situation like this: a person double parks for a moment in a no parking zone to pick up a heavy appliance he purchased. He is obstructing no one, and he plans to move on as soon as he places the appliance in his car. The parking inspector, who was waiting in ambush, slaps a ticket on the man's windshield and is unwilling to listen to any explanations, and so forth in similar situations.

To summarize, a person who lives with emuna knows that there's a Chief Justice in the world, who sees everything and punishes those who act unjustly. Yet, the rewards He gives for those who act righteously are of much greater proportion than the punishments. With this in mind, the parking inspector or any other public supervisor should act with fairness and decency, and never with anger, cruelty, hatred or spite. If he or she keeps the Creator in mind and acts in emuna and in compassion, then they'll certainly benefit in this world and in the world to come.

He Who Frees the Imprisoned

Incarceration is an extreme test of faith. A person in jail can't blame anyone for his or her predicament - not the judge, not the prosecutor, and not the witnesses. He can't even blame an informer who turned him in to the authorities. Why? It's a Divine decree that puts people behind bars to atone for their sins.

Sometimes innocent people are found guilty and convicted. Usually they suffer from extreme feelings of anger, frustration, and bitterness because of the injustice that has been done to them. But, if they would earnestly search their own souls and objectively evaluate their deeds in light of the Bible's commandments, they'd find themselves guilty of serious wrongdoing. Why? The Heavenly Court doesn't decree incarceration for no reason. So, even if a person is innocent of the charges against him, he might be guilty of some other wrongdoing that led to the Heavenly verdict of imprisonment. Therefore, one should accept the predicament lovingly and use it as an opportunity for penitence and personal growth.

Even though a person is behind bars as the apparent result of a worldly-court verdict, he should know that penitence, prayer, and charitable deeds mitigate stern judgments. The Almighty is not interested in tormenting people; He desires to bring them closer to Him. Therefore, the more a person earnestly tries to get closer to the Creator, the less he needs the prodding of stern judgments. Therefore, the incarcerated individual should talk to the Creator as much as possible in personal prayer, asking Him for strength, guidance, a shortened sentence, and a quick release from jail.

Confessing to the Creator is vital for an inmate's spiritual and emotional welfare, as are the other principle acts of penitence, namely, expressing remorse for one's transgressions and deciding to improve from this point on. To merit true and complete atonement, a person must also pray constantly for Divine assistance and guidance, as well as asking the Creator to have compassion on him and to lead him on the right path, and especially to help him overcome his evil inclination. He must also pray that the Creator protect him from negative friends and influences, and send him good messengers that will help him correct his life. The more prayer - in one's own language - the better!

Note: The subject of profuse prayer and supplications is also applicable to most of the cases mentioned in coming chapters, in dealing with any of life's challenges and difficulties. Profuse prayer and penitence invoke Divine compassion. If a person tries to depend on other ploys instead of prayer, he'll likely trigger worse difficulties that will serve as stronger stimulants for prayer. Therefore, one shouldn't wait; he should begin to pray as much as possible starting right now.

Dancing and Rejoicing in Jail

A person in the test of incarceration - a certainly difficult test - should strengthen himself to accept his lot with love. If he does, everything turns around for the very best. The Bible teaches us this principle by the example of Joseph.

Joseph was incarcerated on trumped-up charges (Genesis, 39). Even so, he accepted his plight with happiness. Tradition tells us that Joseph was accustomed to singing and dancing all day long as an inmate. How could he act like that, as a lone Hebrew prisoner in a cruel Egyptian jail? He simply trusted in the Almighty, and believed that everything was for the very best.

By virtue of Joseph's amenable, cheery disposition, the warden took a liking to him and placed him in charge of the other prisoners. Joseph literally did whatever he pleased whenever he pleased. The minute his Heavenly-decreed sentence was up, he was virtually rushed out of prison to become the second most powerful man in all of Egypt - the world's greatest superpower at that time - overnight!

Suppose Joseph would have lacked emuna, and would have moped around his prison cell with a long and sour face, complaining about his lot in life. The Divine presence departs from the midst of depression and complaint. Without Divine intervention, Joseph certainly wouldn't have become the warden's favorite inmate. As a lone, dejected Hebrew prisoner, he might have suffered all kinds of torments from the other prisoners - murderers, thieves, and rapists of the meanest and lowest order. He could have rotted in jail for years, not even daring to dream of freedom, much less of meteoric success as the vice-premier of Egypt! In short, without emuna, he would have suffered a living death.

Let's not forget that Joseph was prodigiously righteous and innocent as well. Even so, he accepted his lot with joy, devoid of even a trace of bitterness. All the more so, a person who is not completely righteous and not completely innocent of wrongdoing should lovingly accept the Divine decree that has led to his imprisonment.

A long list of innocent and righteous men spent time in prison as a result of false accusations. They had every right to be bitter. Yet, they took advantage of their predicaments to devote their entire time and energies to prayer and spiritual gain, using their challenging tribulations as springboards to greatness. Many even authored classic works of spiritual thought behind bars.

No matter how unbearable a situation may seem, a person can take solace in knowing that his or her life is in the Creator's hands and under His personal care. In retrospect, we always see how He does everything for the very best. For that reason, even if a person is innocent according to the law down here, he should accept everything that is decreed from Above with love.

God Reproves those He Loves

A prisoner should never forget that the Almighty loves him, listens to his prayers anywhere and anytime, and wants him to make amends. If he's smart enough to utilize his time for prayer, penitence, and whatever good deeds he can do behind bars, then the Creator will surely help him find favor in the eyes of the jailers, the warden, and the parole board. A person should maintain the faith that the Creator has an infinite number of ways to free him from jail.

It's important to emphasize that the Heavenly Court has a serious complaint with a person who doesn't take advantage of imprisonment for spiritual growth, prayer, and penitence. In jail, one need not worry about making a living, paying bills, or going to PTA meetings. Most inmates have plenty of time at their disposal; the Creator gives them conditions that are conducive for introspection and penitence.

Logically, and in accordance with emuna, an inmate should be well-disciplined and respectful to the guards and prison authorities, and kind to his fellow inmates. A person with emuna who is striving to repent will also be careful about fulfilling the commandments between man and fellow man. Noble deportment behind bars invokes everyone's admiration, as well as enhanced Divine compassion. The inmate must respect everyone from his fellow inmates to the guards and the prison authorities, never deviating from the bounds of decency.

All of a person's good deeds and upright conduct add up. Ultimately, he receives a reversal of the Heavenly judgment that manifests itself as a speedier release from prison. Also, righteousness makes a person's term in jail all the more bearable, even pleasant, to the extent that he doesn't feel that he's imprisoned at all. As such, a person with emuna can attain complete inner freedom even within the confines of incarceration. Many former inmates told me that their self-strengthening in emuna made their lives behind bars so much easier. What's more, emuna helped them to rehabilitate themselves and to achieve the personal growth that stayed with them all their lives.

There are many people outside of prison who are nonetheless shackled in a jail of lust and monetary pursuit. They suffer untold difficulties and disorientation. On the other hand, there are those behind bars who enjoy true personal freedom, for they have learned to get to know the Creator. Such people gladly serve the Creator wherever they are. To them, it makes no difference if they are in prison, in the study hall or at home.

"And I Shall Cure You of Your Ills"

Illness is a severe test of emuna. Therefore, a sick person must recognize the three principles of emuna, as follows:

1. The Creator makes a person sick; one should avoid attributing sicknesses to natural causes or to human error.
2. One must know that sickness is for a person's ultimate benefit; as such, he should thank Hashem.
3. Hashem does everything to draw a person closer to Him; consequently, the sick person should initiate a process of self-evaluation, attempting to identify any possible wrongdoing that might have led to the sickness, and then make amends accordingly. Only afterwards, should he pray to be healed from his sickness.

A Divine License to Heal

Apparently, medicine is an applied science just like all the other applied sciences. Researchers delve into the cause of disease, experiment with various disease-inhibiting agents, and then convert successful laboratory findings into commercial medicines and modes of treatment.

Medical research appears to be straightforward and logical. The Almighty instilled us with the intelligence to observe, investigate, and solve problems for the betterment of mankind. Not only that, but it's our duty to devote our mental resources to worthwhile endeavors, particularly for the benefit of society. Electricity, computer technology, and labor-saving appliances are a few examples. Man should therefore invest his God-given power of intelligence to cure illness and relieve human suffering.

The above outlook is furthermore reinforced in the Torah, for we are told that a physician has a Divine license to heal, as part of man's tasks in this world. As such, even (and especially) people of Israel's spiritual leaders were famous healers, such as the Rambam, the Baal Shem Tov and many others.

In conclusion, logic tells us that medicine is an applied science just like all the other applied sciences, and apparently, the more we devote to medical research, the more we'll overcome illness and suffering, gaining the ability to maintain our health. Is that really the case?

The Influence of Divine Providence on Humanity

Medicine would be a simple, straightforward applied science if its sole challenge were healing a physical body, such as an animal. But, that's not the case. The body is lifeless without its spiritual life-spark, the soul. Physical treatments and medication can't cure an ailing soul. Since body and soul are connected, then their mutual health and wellbeing depends on more than nature and natural law. Human health depends on Divine providence, the Creator's personal intervention in our lives.

The simple conclusion we arrive at is that since all of creation was designed as an agent to facilitate man's free choice on earth, we can understand how man benefits from the Almighty's personal attention to the tiniest detail of his life in general and his health in particular.

Nature operates according to Divine will, even though it's not always apparent. The further away a creation is from man and the less it directly affects his life, then the less apparent the Divine providence. Therefore, it seems that the stars and the great galaxies go their merry way in their clear and predefined celestial lanes, according to the dictates of nature and seemingly devoid of Divine intervention. This is only an illusion, since the galaxies don't appear to have anything to do with our daily lives. In truth, their orbits in space are the product of Divine decree, as King David says that Hashem, "Has placed them forever; He issued a decree that shall not be violated" (Psalm 148:6). The stars, planets and galaxies simply have a static task that doesn't change.

As opposed to the stars and other faraway creations, dynamic daily change in our lives is an indication of Divine providence. Look how things change so drastically from day to day: One day, we're challenged with income problems. The next day, our children act up. Then, a health crisis pops up. Such matters as income, health, marriage and child-rearing are ways that the Creator sends each individual the messages that he or she needs to stimulate character improvement and personal growth.

One's Body is Dear to Him/Her

Divine Providence plays a greater role in a person's health than in any other area of a person's life. Pains and afflictions of the body and soul are the Creator's prime tools in arousing people to correct what they need to correct, for several reasons:

First of all, a person might remain apathetic about a variety of other trials and tribulations. He or she won't necessarily undertake serious introspection after losing a hundred dollars. Yet, few are able to ignore something that directly affects their own bodies, such as sickness or severe negative emotions.

This is what happened to Job. At first, the Creator gave the Satan license to test and torment Job, but not to strike him down with illness. And, that's exactly what the Satan did.

Even though Job lost his money and buried his own children, he didn't crack at the emotional seams. The Satan said to the Creator (Job, 2), "A person will give anything for his own skin. Afflict his flesh, and we'll see if he continues to bless you!" The Satan claimed that no test of faith is as difficult as a sickness or injury. Job's steadfast faith was shaken once his entire body was afflicted with infectious boils, and he began to harbor disgruntlement in heart about the Creator's way of doing things.

We therefore learn from the Book of Job that body and soul afflictions are the most difficult type of tribulations for a person. This is a phenomenon that needs no explanation. The moment a person becomes ill, he loses all joy in life. Even wealth and other material amenities are no consolation. On the contrary, they heighten the person's feeling of misery for he can't enjoy them. What good is a big bank account, diamonds and jewels to a person with an ulcer, diabetes, and a cardiac condition whose diet is sorely limited and can't even enjoy a meal? And what good is a healthy body if a person suffers from a tormented soul? Since one cares so much about one's health, the Creator frequently arouses a person by way of his or her health, for health issues catch a person's attention more than anything else.

There's an additional reason: the human body comprises 613 parts that correspond to the 613 commandments of Torah. The 248 limbs correspond to the 248 positive commandments while the 365 tendons correspond to the 365 negative commandments. When a person violates one of the Torah's commandments, he or she is therefore damaging that commandment's corresponding part of the body. The type of ailment a person suffers from is therefore an indication of what he or she must rectify.

The holy "Baal Shem Tov" of blessed and saintly memory once visited a sick man on the verge of death. At the man's bedside, the Baal Shem Tov discussed his condition with the attending physician. The doctor said that there was no hope for the man to live more than a few hours, because his disease had caused massive internal damage.

The Baal Shem Tov asked the physician to wait for a moment while he approached the sick person, who lay unconscious in bed. A minute or two later, the patient opened his eyes and asked for a sip of broth. Gradually, the color returned to his face. The physician couldn't believe his own eyes. He said to the Baal Shem Tov, "I can't believe what I'm seeing! This is impossible, for I know for certain that this patient's entire body was destroyed - there was no way he could live. What did you do?"

The Baal Shem Tov replied, "You are correct. Not only that, you are truly an expert physician. You made no mistake - the patient did suffer massive internal damage. This person repeatedly transgressed the Creator's commandments, which caused extreme damage to his internal organs. Only now, I spoke to his soul, and he agreed to atone for his sins. Once he committed himself to repenting, his organs regained their vitality."

Divine Considerations

The Creator runs the world in accordance with our actions. He created the world in order to show us His glory and greatness. By way of His world, we learn how

Hashem directs things. Sometimes, He runs the world mercifully and at other times with exacting stringency, all according to our actions. When people behave in an upright manner, then the world is a place of harmony and loving-kindness. On the other hand, injustice, immorality, and cruelty invoke stern judgments and calamity. This is the Creator's "measure for measure" mode of running the world. Even more so, people are treated from Above in the same way they treat others.

Sickness is directly rooted in a person's misdeeds. Consequently, medicine and medical professionals - as advanced and as skillful as they might be - cannot possibly take into consideration such Divine considerations as the patient's spiritual debits and merits, his efforts to atone and improve, and so forth. No professional - as talented as he or she may be - can override a Divine decree. If the Almighty decrees that a person should be sick for a week, then no treatment in the world will help him get well any faster. The opposite holds true as well - if Hashem decrees that a person shall recuperate - despite all medical logic - then that person will get well immediately.

Imagine two identical twins who grew up together in the same home with the same parents, ate the same food, and so on. Maybe when they were small, they appeared to be equally healthy. But, as they grew older, each had his own separate health problems. This is proof that one's health is not determined by nature, but by one's actions. If nature were the determining factor, then both twins who were born and raised in identical circumstances should have identical health profiles.

Miracles and Wonders

The principle that nature plays no role in human healing becomes even more apparent when we see that as soon as a person corrects the spiritual cause of his or her ailment, the ailment disappears without any natural intervention at all. If nature governed healing, then the sick person should have continued to suffer despite whatever efforts at repenting that he or she made. And, in the cases where seemingly irreversible damage had been caused, nothing should have helped!

Since nature does not dictate health, and we see with our own eyes that people who have earnestly repented have miraculously recovered even from terminal ailments, we can conclude that health and healing defy natural laws.

Frequently, as I've seen with my own eyes while accompanying patients and guiding them, that as soon as they repented, they were cured, often in a manner that defied both nature and the doctors' estimations. I've seen such phenomena on my own body, how once I realized what I must rectify, my afflictions desisted immediately and totally.

On one instance that I can talk about, I was suffering from a massive toothache on Shabbat. My entire jaw was swollen and infected - the pain was excruciating. I understood that I needed a root canal treatment, and that's what I told my family.

"What?!" they reacted, startled. "You're going to the dentist on Shabbat? Since when is it allowed to do a root canal on Shabbat?"

"Yes," I said. "I must have a root treatment - I'm suffering terribly. Since when is it permissible to suffer on Shabbat? But I'm not going to the dentist you're thinking of - I'm going to the chief dental surgeon - Hashem, blessed be His Name."

I went to a nearby field and asked the Creator to enlighten me as to the spiritual root of my ailments, in other words, to show me what I did wrong to deserve the toothache, the infection, and the resulting swelling. I did some serious soul-searching until I laid a finger on something I shouldn't have done. I asked forgiveness for this misdeed and made complete atonement the best I could. Within a few minutes, the swelling went down and the pain disappeared, with no antibiotics or any other natural explanation. I realized that the toothache was only a wake-up call, and as soon as I rectified my actions, the wake-up call became totally superfluous.

There is No Nature!

Our encouragement to the sick is, "Don't despair - there is no nature!" Whoever chooses the option of teshuva and prayer will see major miracles. When the Creator decides to cure someone, He doesn't need any help.

Rebbe Nachman of Breslev teaches (Likutei Moharan I: 62) that the principle misconception of those who are far away from emuna in Hashem is that they visibly see a world governed by various natural forces that intercede between a person and the Creator. Each person has his own misconception: Some think the world is governed by nature, and that the world behaves according to natural law; yet, natural law and nature are only a means, a tool Hashem uses to run the world. Others believe that there is a Creator, but that they must worship the means, or an artificial intermediary, such as the Israelites did in the sin of the golden calf (see Exodus, Chapter 32).

Many get caught in the trap of the "means" - the way Hashem implements His decisions - and make the means into an intermediary. This is just another form of the golden calf! In other words, they believe in Hashem but they also believe that the intermediary determines their fate, such as their business or livelihood. They then invest their hopes and main efforts to their business dealings, since they believe that their business dealings determine their livelihood, and without their business dealings, which are nothing more than a means, Hashem won't be able to provide for them, Heaven forbid. The same goes for medical matters, when they put their faith in the intermediary rather than in the Creator, it's as if, Heaven forbid, Hashem won't be able to cure them without doctors and medicine.

This is not so! The Creator is the cause of all causes and the reason of all reasons. One must believe in Him only, and not make any intermediary, means, conduit or other cause the object of their belief.

Revealed Miracles

To further reinforce our principle at hand, here are two stories that many people witnessed, which show that there literally is no nature at all.

Story 1 - Mentioned in Sichot HaRan, Discourse 187:

Once, a person came to Rebbe Nachman with a terrible pain in his hand, so bad that he couldn't move it. His arm was hanging in a sling, the way people often do in such a case. The man's pain was unbearable. People were talking within Rebbe Nachman's earshot that the sick person needed to soak his hand in Epsom salts and other such treatments.

The ailing man was very poor and he couldn't afford any type of medicine or medical care. On Shabbat in the morning, as Rebbe Nachman sat down for his Shabbat morning meal, he commented to those in attendance, "The man with the ailing hand certainly has emuna." Those present agreed. Rebbe Nachman made the same comment a second time and a third time. Those present at his table agreed again. Rebbe Nachman then told the sick man, who was one of those in attendance, "Take your hand out of the sling." The sick man was dumbstruck; so were the others in attendance. What a strange thing for the Rebbe to say! The man had been sick for a long time and it was clear that he couldn't move his hand, much less remove it from the sling...

How could the sick man do such a thing? Without waiting for the man to react, Rebbe Nachman's disciples present at the table snapped into action and took away the sling, which was made out of a strip of an old bedsheet. The man not only lowered his arm but flexed his hand, which had returned to a state of complete health, to this day...

This episode that many people witnessed proves that there is no nature. The same body cells and tissues were so sick that no cure on earth could have returned them instantly to health. Conventional healing takes time, even if one is so fortunate to overcome an ailment. But on the spot recuperation? Who can make that happen? Only the Master Physician Himself can do that, Hashem, blessed be His Name. Therefore, only the sick person's power of emuna merited him an instant recovery.

The second story is about the "Baba Sali", the holy Rabbi Yisrael AbuChatzera of saintly and blessed memory who came to Israel from Morocco. In front of many witnesses, he ordered a crippled person to stand up from his wheelchair. That person had been paralyzed for years; how could he suddenly stand up? How could the degenerated muscles, tendons and cells return to life? This was the Divine power of reviving the dead, invoked by the prodigious emuna and prayers of a holy righteous man. That's what's capable of lifting a person out of a wheelchair.

The Professor of Annipoli

Hashem is the physician of all flesh and only He can cure. Once, a person sought the advice from Rebbe Mordechai of Neshchiz, complaining of a severe illness. The Rebbe asked, "Have you visited the famed professor from Annipoli?" The sick person replied that he never heard of such an individual. "In that case," added the wise man, "go see him - he can surely help to cure you!"

The sick person heeded the wise man's advice, and made a difficult, backbreaking wagon trip to the remote village of Annipoli. When he arrived at the township, he asked the first person he encountered where the famed professor lives. The local shrugged his shoulders and said that there's no such thing as a doctor or medic in all of Annipoli, much less a famous professor. The sick person's heart broke - had he made this entire excruciating journey for nothing?

"What do you people do when you get sick, with no doctor or medic in town?" asked the sick person.

The local answered, "Whenever people here are ill, they repent, pray to the Creator, ask Him to cure them, and then they get better."

The sick person, brokenhearted, turned his horse and wagon in the opposite direction, and made the long, hard, bumpy trip back to the wise man, complaining bitterly: "You know how sick and weak I am! Why did you send me all the way to Annipoli for nothing? There's not even a country doctor in that one-horse town!"

Rebbe Mordechai of Neshchiz smiled patiently. "Didn't anyone there explain to you what they do in case of sickness if they don't have a doctor?"

The sick person replied, "Yes, they did; somebody gave me a perfunctory answer that they pray and repent, then they get better."

"That's the professor of Annipoli," answered the wise man. "It's the Creator! Whenever people turn to Him, He cures them. He's the professor that the people of Annipoli turn to. He's available 24 hours a day and doesn't charge for house calls. He can even turn bread and water into miraculous medicine, for it is written (Exodus 23: 25), 'He shall bless your bread and your water, and remove sickness from your midst.'"

The son of Rabbi Yisroel Meir Kagan, the famed "Chofetz Chaim" of saintly and blessed memory, related that his mother seldom sought the services of a physician during the years that she raised her children. Whenever someone in the family became sick, his father instructed her to bake and distribute forty pounds of bread to the poor, and he himself would pray for several hours in the attic. Shortly thereafter, the sick child would recover.

Only Hashem Knows

The Gemara says, "At the time tribulations are sent upon a person, they are sworn that they shall depart on a certain day at a certain hour, and by way of a certain person and a certain substance" (Avoda Zara, 55a). Rebbe Nachman of Breslev adds that since all these conditions must be met for a sick person to get better, how can a physician be presumptuous enough to think that he can cure a person by way of all types of ploys? The physician doesn't know if the appointed day and hour have arrived or if his prescription is the particular substance that will cure the person. He doesn't even know if he is the designated emissary to effect the cure (see Likutei Moharan II:3). If so, and if the person's recovery all depends on a decree from Above, why do people place themselves in the hands of doctors?

From the above, we learn that relying on doctors is a gamble - maybe the conditions for healing will be fulfilled, and maybe not.

Pidyon Nefesh: "Redemption of the Soul"

There's another way, however, to nullify such a decree, enabling to person to get well any time by way of any doctor and through any medicine. The way is by doing teshuva, going to a tzaddik, having him pray for the sick person, and make a pidyon nefesh or soul redemption.

As Rebbe Nachman explains, "However, when one makes a pidyon and sweetens the judgment, the Heavenly decree is canceled and the doctor is able to heal the person through medicines, as there is no longer any decree. For in this case, the doctor no longer needs to specifically use the certain medicine that had been decreed, as now there is no longer any decree! So in actuality, it's impossible for any doctor to heal a patient without making a pidyon nefesh. But the pidyon nefesh needs to be done first, to sweeten the judgment, for only after doing so is the doctor given permission to heal."

If a person gives money to a tzaddik and does the pidyon nefesh, then his efforts will yield results, bringing health and life. One must always be careful, though, to connect with tzaddikim who know how to do a pidyon, meaning sages and scholars from the Breslever community who are familiar with the correct text. One must also be careful not to be stingy or miserly, as Rebbe Natan brings down in Likutei Tefillot (123), "Be merciful when bringing a pidyon, and **don't be stingy**. Give what you need to give in order to remove the decree."

The Pidyon Nefesh is especially effective. We've seen and heard first-hand how people have been cured from serious ailments and other severe decrees as well by way of Pidyon Nefesh.

A certain man who wasn't feeling well asked his rabbi if the rabbi thought that he should go to see his doctor. The rabbi answered, "Why are you in such a hurry to go to see your doctor? Did he make you sick? Hashem made you sick! Instead, go to Him and ask Him to show you what you have done that has resulted in you becoming sick. Then, do teshuva the best way you can and give a Pidyon Nefesh."

"Only after you've done everything you can to cancel the harsh decree," the Rabbi added, "and you've asked Hashem to cure you, then you can do the basic hishtadlut (effort) of going to the doctor. But, going to the doctor without first doing what you must in turning to the Physician of All Flesh, is a lack of emuna."

Physicians cannot add to our Heavenly allotment of longevity, but they can shorten it, Heaven forbid. But

Hashem - the Master Physician - can certainly extend a person's longevity if He so decides. That's why our main efforts in seeking relief from sickness should be devoted to turning to He Who grants life.

Give Thanks and Be Healed

The most conducive thing in the world for healing is emuna. Therefore, a sick person must thank the Creator that he is sick, for the Creator surely caused him to be sick for his ultimate benefit. A person who sincerely expresses gratitude for his sickness can be easily healed, for gratitude is the greatest expression of emuna, where a person believes that everything in his life is the product of Divine providence and all for the best.

One of my students, a "basic trainee" on the start of his path in emuna, was sick for many years, suffering immensely. Nothing he tried helped, not even penitence and prayer. Then, he heard my lesson on gratitude, which clarified the point that since everything is for the best, one must profusely thank the Creator for his tribulations and deficiencies with a whole heart.

This student decided to devote his entire daily hour to gratitude. Daily, he thanked the Creator for his years of being sick and for all of his suffering, for surely the merciful Creator has done all this for his best interests, as a soul correction, an atonement and as a catalyst to bring him to repentance.

Daily, he would stand before Hashem for an entire hour and thank Him, not even asking for a cure to his ailments. Within two weeks, his sickness disappeared with no medicine, no treatments and no ploys. He had suffered for years and nothing had helped, until he started to say, "Thank You!" Gratitude is the height of emuna. Since lack of emuna is one of the main causes of serious illness, the opposite - strong emuna - is strongly conducive to good health.

Intrinsically, the only suffering a person has in this world is when his emuna is taken away from him. As long as a person believes that everything is from the Creator and is all for the best, he doesn't feel any suffering. Therefore, by strengthening oneself in emuna, the harsh Heavenly decrees are nullified and a person has no tribulations. Therefore, a sick person must ask the Creator to give him the emuna that everything is for the best, thus enabling him to wholeheartedly thank the Creator. The suffering that a person feels is from his lack of emuna. If he seeks emuna and merits to wholeheartedly thank the Creator for everything, his situation will surely turn around for the very best!

The Main Thing is Emuna

There are serious ailments, Heaven forbid, that are triggered by a lack of emuna. Rebbe Nachman of Breslev writes, "The main thing is emuna. Each person must assess himself and strengthen himself in the area of emuna. For there are serious ailments, **indescribable afflictions**, that a person is liable to suffer because of a lack of emuna, as the Torah says: 'And Hashem will cause... great plagues, and of long continuance, and sore sicknesses, and of long continuance' (Deuteronomy 28:59). If a sickness is rooted in a lack of emuna, no medical care, no prayer and no merit of ancestors will help" (Likutei Moharan II:5).

We see from the above that a lack of emuna is the worst transgression there is - more so than any other sin, transgression or misdeed! The punishment is terrible, Heaven forbid, with terrible ailments that only the greatest efforts in teshuva and strengthening emuna will help. **The main penitence for lack of emuna is to learn emuna and pray for it.**

People of Compassion

Anyone in the medical field must know that he or she performs a lofty task in the world. Usually, those who choose a career in medicine are people of compassion. The characteristics of mercy and compassion combined with the desire to aid humanity are wonderful incentives to learn medicine.

Nevertheless, physicians must avoid the pitfall of arrogance and remember that they are only messengers of healing, for Hashem alone decides who will live and who will die. He also decides how much a person will suffer and whether he or she will be cured or not.

A physician must pray daily before he begins his day's work that the Creator will help him be a worthy emissary. His prayers should also include a special request that he merit being an agent of healing, and not an agent of death, Heaven forbid, for a doctor's slightest mistake or misjudgment can have tragic or even fatal results. Therefore, medical professionals should always plead to the Creator for Divine assistance in everything they do. They should also ask for patience, understanding, and sensitivity with their patients, helping to instill hope and strength in anyone who seeks their assistance.

There is No Despair!

"And he shall be entitled to heal" (Exodus 21:19). From this passage, our sages teach that physicians are granted a Divine license to heal (Berachot 60a). That doesn't give them license to discourage or dishearten patients. In many cases, doctors give patients and the family members of patients a pessimistic outlook and a feeling of hopelessness. Telling a patient that he only has so much time to live is a terrible mistake.

Medical research shows that optimism and a happy attitude play an important role in healing, recovery, and resistance to disease. Such nuances as laughter therapy have reportedly helped cure a number of ailments. Today in Israel, many hospitals employ "medical clowns" whose job is to make the patients laugh and divert their focus from pain and suffering. No wonder Rebbe Nachman of Breslev stresses the importance of maintaining happiness and avoiding sadness and depression at all times and at all costs, writing that sickness and disease are the result of a breakdown in happiness (Likutei Moharan II:24). Since emuna leads to happiness, emuna facilitates recovery from sickness and ailments.

Therefore, a doctor must avoid saddening or discouraging a patient. Indeed, one of his most important tasks is encouraging a patient. A doctor's word of encouragement carries far more weight than a layman's word. A doctor should also use his good influence to help reinforce his patient's emuna. Such spiritual and emotional support is inestimably beneficial to every patient.

The Prognosis

The claim that a doctor must give patients truthful assessments of their situation is a fallacy. A patient shouldn't be robbed of his hopes to recover. And, even if the sick person is destined to die, he should still be surrounded with optimism and encouragement.

Those doctors who frighten and discourage patients, especially those doctors who forecast how long an apparent terminally-ill patient has to live, are actually robbing them of any chance for recovery.

Hashem doesn't reveal the day of one's death, for such knowledge could have a detrimental effect on a person. If He hides the day of death, then how can a mortal be presumptuous enough to think he knows it? Negative prognoses are sometimes completely inaccurate.

Even in apparently terminal cases, a gloomy prognosis robs the patient of his right to die with a feeling of optimism and faith in his heart. The doom prognosis leads to a bitter death accompanied by feelings of despair, bewilderment, and even anger at the Creator, Heaven forbid. When doctors say that the end is near, they deny patients their lone lifeline - emuna - by sealing their fate.

Stop and think for a moment: Who says that the patient's condition won't make a sudden or dramatic change for the better? We've all heard of clinically-dead people that have come back to life! Are the doctors G-d, that they know what has been decreed on each patient? Only Hashem can change anything in the world from one moment to the next. Therefore, a sick person can recover despite all the doctors' negative predictions.

A patient's tiniest commitment to penitence, self-improvement, or a commandment such as giving money to charity can lead to recovery where natural methods have failed. His entire condition can make a dramatic turnaround. By improving his spiritual status, he improves his physical status as well. Whereas before penitence, his medical tests results were alarming, after strengthening emuna and penitence, the recent tests no longer reflect the patient's improved situation.

In all fairness to the doctors, sometimes the patient's family members put tremendous pressure on them, demanding to be told the "truth." In such situations, a doctor should be cautious and say that according to natural circumstances, the situation seems critical, but experience has proven that Divine intervention can alter the picture from one moment to the next and override any natural laws.

The Best Advice

A physician with emuna knows that a patient's condition can improve from one moment to the next, depending on his efforts in prayer, penitence, and strengthening emuna, or his friends' and family's efforts on his behalf. The opposite is also true: A patient can feel better and then renege on a commitment or fall from emuna and then suddenly relapse.

Either way, a physician should avoid giving gloomy forecasts: If the Creator decides to revive the patient, then the physician will lose face. On the other hand, if the physician is accurate, what does anyone gain? By scaring the patient - even truthfully - the physician is guilty of causing anguish to another human being, the opposite of healing. The "truth" could have made the patient suffer even more by losing hope and falling into despair. This is exactly that idea that Job expressed when he said, "For the thing which I feared has come upon me, and that which I was afraid of has overtaken me" (Job 3:25).

The best advice for physicians is therefore to avoid saying anything of a committal nature, even if the patient's family applies tons of pressure. There are plenty of verbal escape routes, such as "it's too early to tell" or "we don't have enough information to make an accurate prognosis."

There are situations when a doctor wants to force his opinion on the patient with regards to a certain treatment, medicine, or operation. This is also a mistake. Even if the doctor is convinced that his recommendations are accurate, the patient must not be deprived of his free choice. Even though the doctor undoubtedly wants to help the patient, he shouldn't dramatize his own opinions by pressuring the patient and forcing advice on him.

Do you want to be a doctor? Do you want to help people? Do what you can, but don't rob a patient of his emuna. If a patient doesn't listen to your advice, that's his problem. Don't paint your opinions with doomsday scenarios and dark colors.

The underlying principle in healing is that only Hashem decides the fate and outcome of each patient. The doctor's task is to be a worthy emissary of Divine will and providence and pray that he'll be fortunate enough to be an agent of healing and not of death.

A physician should therefore tell a patient, "I'll do my best, but you should know that your health doesn't depend on me; that's why you should do your part –

strengthen your emuna and trust in the Creator! No matter what the outcomes of tests are, there are many surprises in medicine and the Creator can override any natural circumstance, as difficult as it may seem. I pray that He will give me the best advice in regards to your case, but you can contribute so much to your own recovery with prayer, charity, penitence, and emuna. If we work together, hopefully the Creator will grant you a full and speedy recovery."

The Main Thing - Don't be Afraid at All

The message to physicians is to know your place and don't try to be G-d.

The message to patients is not to be afraid of doctors or their forecasts, because everything depends on the Creator anyway, so take courage and be strong.

Blindly trusting in doctors and medicine is itself a form of heresy. Belief in doctors and in medicines are a source of lack of belief in the Creator. Many people are afraid to sever their dependence on doctors and medicine, as if their lives were dependent on the man with the stethoscope around his neck rather than in the hands of the Creator. As such, patients whose doctors try to scare into taking certain treatments or medicines shouldn't be daunted at all. One should fear the Creator only and not the doctors or their admonitions. Those fear tactics are the opposite of emuna and weaken a person into thinking that he or she is at the mercy of the elements, as if nothing can be done.

Psalms

Psalms have enormous power, tantamount to an intravenous infusion of trust in the Creator. Trusting in Him is very conducive to a person's full and speedy recovery. There are dozens of stories about people who merited miraculous recoveries from reciting Psalms.

There's a story about a little boy whose best friend became very sick. The doctors appeared to have given up hope. He picked up his book of Psalms, and with poignant innocence said Psalms for an entire hour on his friend's behalf. He closed the book, ran to his friend's house, and asked if there was any improvement. His friend's mother tearfully shook her head in the negative. The little boy ran home and said Psalms for another hour. Once again, he ran to his friend's house and asked if there was any change in the situation. Once again, the answer was no. The little boy ran back and forth for most of the night, when his friend's parents finally informed him that their son's fever had broken and that he was sleeping peacefully now...

The Names of the Tzaddikim

Rebbe Nachman teaches in Sefer HaMiddot (The Aleph-Bet Book), "By mentioning the names of tzaddikim, we are able to bring about a change in the Creation of the world, meaning to change the course of nature."

A woman came to see me with an X-ray in her hand showing a uterine tumor. The doctors told her that she had to undergo surgery and would never be able to have children. I told her to read the names of the tzaddikim every day. After a period of time, she went in for additional tests and X-rays, and the new films showed that the growth had completely disappeared – without a trace, as if it had never been there – and she merited to have many healthy children!

(Today, you can obtain "The Names of the Tzaddikim" online at www.breslev.co.il or by calling 972-52-2240696).

Likutei Tefillot – **The Anthology of Prayers**

A person suffered from severe chronic back pain that was so bad that he was unable to lift even the lightest weight. He went to one of the generation's tzaddikim to ask him what he should do. The tzaddik told him that he should say all of the prayers for healing found in the book, Likutei Tefillot. He followed the guidance of the tzaddik and began to say all the prayers in the order listed. After a short period of time, the pain that the doctors had given up hope of relieving was gone.

Everything Will Turn Around for the Best

Never forget that the Creator can do anything He wants, whenever He wants - Hashem is G-d! Any Divine decree can be overturned with prayer, penitence, and charity. Our sages teach that even if a sharp sword rests on a person's neck, the person shouldn't give up hoping for Divine mercy. Our sages say that "mercy" means prayer, and the most cogent prayer is the sick person's own prayers, as we learn from the passage in Parshat Vayera, "And the Lord heard the lad's voice..." (Genesis 21:17). Rashi elaborates that a sick person's prayer for himself is readily accepted. Even though Hagar Ishmael's mother cried, Hashem heeded the cries of Ishmael himself, according to the Siftei Chachamim.

Even though Pidyon Nefesh and the Names of the Tzaddikim as well as other ploys we learned are important, nothing so invokes Divine compassion for a sick person as his own personal prayer - speaking to the Creator in his own words. A person should ask for all his needs from the Creator, and especially for healing and good health. These prayers should not be limited - the more the better. One should devote as many hours as he or she is able, asking for all their material and spiritual needs. King David said (**Psalms, 30:3**), "I cried out to You, O Lord, my God, and You healed me."

One of my students was in a near-fatal automobile accident that left a gaping hole in his back that exposed his spine. The gap almost reached his kidneys. The wound became infected and the doctors had given up hope. My student was conscious and well aware of his critical situation. There was no rational procedure or cure.

Up until the accident, my student would devote a few casual minutes to personal prayer, but nothing more. Now, I asked him to commit to speaking to the Creator for two hours a day - he agreed.

Every night when most everyone else was sleeping, he'd wheel himself out in a wheelchair to the hospital terrace. For hours on end, he'd beg God to stimulate new tissue growth around his kidneys and spine. Little by little, to the amazement of all the doctors, new tissue began to grow until the gap was completely healed.

Rebbe Noach of Lachovitch says, "When the doctors tell a patient that there's no cure, and the patient reinforces himself with complete trust in the Creator, then all the gates of salvation and healing are opened...

Why? As long as the physicians tell a patient that there is a cure, it's difficult for the patient to put all his trust in Hashem, for he puts his hopes in doctors, treatments and medicines. A patient shouldn't wait until the doctors say that there's no hope, but from the start, he or she should put all their hope and trust in Hashem.

Don't Waste a Moment

A sick person should utilize any and all available time for self-evaluation and soul-searching. Many patients lie idle in hospital beds for hours; freed from the demands of a normally busy routine, the bedridden should take advantage of the time at their disposal. This is directed from Above so that they'll have an ample opportunity for self-evaluation. Oftentimes, a sick person's bodily urges diminish dramatically, enabling him or her to look at the world objectively. At such times, the soul's delicate voice gets a fair hearing. How terrible it is to stick a television in front of a patient's face, for it drowns out the soul's voice and distracts a person from what he should really be doing, praying and assessing himself.

Much Success!

A person who became sick, yet acts according to the principles of emuna, earns a high score in this world and in the next. He succeeds in rectifying many misdeeds, for he became aware of the relationship between his sins and his sickness. He gets to know the Creator, he becomes spiritually strengthened and his recovery is hastened. He lives a good life in this world and in the next.

In stark contrast, a person without emuna suffers from fear, anxiety, worry, depression and negative thoughts about Hashem. He thinks, why do I deserve this? What did I do wrong? Such a person fails to profit from his experience with illness and just suffers all the more. He puts his trust in doctors and medicines, and he's simply a candidate for more disappointment, Heaven forbid.

A person must know that when he passes the test of emuna, he brings gratification to the Creator. Hashem created the world so that people would learn emuna. As such, the sick person or anyone else who strengthens emuna is fulfilling his mission on earth, and thereby merits a high score in the test of emuna as well as full and complete healing.

Emotional and Mental Health

Rebbe Nachman of Breslev writes that the soul and emuna are one aspect (Likutei Moharan I:173). Consequently, one's emotional health is directly related to the level of one's emuna. We therefore conclude that emotional disturbances result from a breakdown of emuna. Emotional confusion results from confused emuna. Emotional weakness is the outcome of weak emuna. This is a rule of thumb for all mental illnesses. When we see that a person is born healthy, but at a later age succumbs to fear, anxiety, depression, and even schizophrenia, or any other mental or emotional difficulties, the root of the problem is a breakdown in or insufficiency of emuna. But here's the good news: If an emotionally-disturbed individual learns all about emuna and prays for emuna, he or she will recover from the ailment. The more a person corrects and strengthens emuna, the more he or she will enjoy mental and emotional health, for as we learned, emuna and the soul are one aspect.

Every person - even the so-called "normal" person - suffers from emotional problems to a certain degree.

In addition to fear, anxiety, and depression, people are plagued with boredom, lack of satisfaction, anger, worries, nervousness, and extreme mood fluctuations, just to name a few. If he or she strengthens emuna, they will overcome all these emotional ills.

Why Be Afraid?

Many people suffer from varying degrees of anxiety: They fear other people, their bosses, the IRS, terrorists, other motorists - the list is long. Any time they get a muscle spasm, they envision some imminent crippling or terminal disease. All these fears are expressions of a lack of emuna, particularly the lack of emuna that the Creator does everything for our very best. A person with emuna doesn't fear anything, for he knows that he is in Hashem's care and that everything He does is for the very best. This saves tons of emotional wear-and-tear; since the Creator does everything for the best, then there's nothing to worry about. Did you ever see a person who knows that a wonderful gift is waiting for him worry about it?

According to emuna, everything that happens in our lives is the product of precise Divine providence and not nature, luck or fate; even more so, it's all for the best. As such, a person who devotes an hour a day to self-evaluation, penitence, and personal prayer in particular has nothing to worry about. If a person is making his best effort at self-improvement, then why should the Creator punish him? Such a person doesn't need wake-up calls, because he's daily arousing himself to penitence and to self-improvement. The result of an hour a day in personal prayer is increased happiness and decreased stress and worry.

Be Happy

Know also that stringencies and nitpicking in the fulfillment of mitzvoth is craziness. A person should not be too exacting with himself. He shouldn't tremble in fear as to whether he is fulfilling his obligations or not; indeed, he should perform the mitzvoth with simple innocence the best way he can. Hashem gave the Torah to flesh-and-blood mortals, not to arch-angels. Those who are too exacting with themselves, adapting all kinds of stringencies, bitterness and extremes do so because of arrogance, thinking that they are capable of perfection. If they had the slightest spark of Hashem's truth, they'd be happy with what they are reasonably able to do without the extraneous stringencies.

Belief in the Wise

In "Rebbe Nachman's Discourses" (67), we learn that whoever doesn't heed our truly wise spiritual leaders is liable to go insane. A person goes "insane" when he or she ignores the voice of "sanity". If the insane individual would have heeded the voice of sanity, then he would not have become insane in the first place. In his spirit of folly, he thinks that he must walk around in rags and roll around in a garbage heap, and all types of insane things like that. If he would only nullify himself to the person who is wiser than him, his insanity would be nullified. But, since he will not heed the voice of sanity, he remains insane; understand this critical point.

Everyone must heed the wise spiritual leader, the voice of sanity, who completely knows the wisdom of emuna, and to heed his teachings. Anyone who does will enjoy emotional health. Most important, he must believe that Hashem dictates and supervises every detail of his life, loves him and does everything for the best - there is no bad in the world! Hashem doesn't harbor petty complaints at anyone and doesn't expect anything that's beyond a person's ability. Hashem knows that no one can make teshuva in a day. On the contrary, Hashem wants us to make slow and steady progress at a pace we are capable of. In fact, this entire book is a manual of emuna wisdom, the best possible cure for the soul.

Learning the Holy Torah

Learning Torah has the power to save a person from craziness, as we learn in the abridged (Kitzur) Likutei Moharan (145:1): "The evil inclination wants to drive a person literally insane, G-d forbid, because a person who sins is mad, as our rabbis have taught, 'A person does not do a transgression unless a spirit of folly enters him.'"

How can he (the evil inclination) come to a person and make him crazy suddenly? The method used by the evil inclination is to pretend that something is a mitzva and mislead a person by inciting him further until he does full transgressions intentionally, G-d forbid. This is very much like the way an insane person behaves, as he is so confused that he thinks bad is good. Nevertheless, he still has some sparks of rationality and common sense so as to realize that he shouldn't do certain things. Yet he compulsively can't control himself and continues to do them. For such insane people two strategies are required: first, they must be beaten to subdue their wickedness, so that they won't feel comfortable with their insanity and at least won't so readily do things that they themselves realize are insane and foolish.

Second, he should wear amulets containing Hashem's holy names to expel the evil spirits that confuse him and drive him insane, to the point where he says that evil is good.

The same two strategies also need to be employed when healing a person from the madness of the evil inclination. First, his evil and malice must be subdued so that he will not compulsively do what he himself understands and knows is bad. In addition, he must expel the evil spirit that disguises itself as mitzvot, and misleads him by pretending to encourage him to do a mitzva. This can only be completely accomplished by occupying oneself in Torah, which is the only thing able to integrate both strategies.

Contemplations

Rebbe Nachman teaches in Likutei Moharan (I:60:3) that lewd contemplations and thoughts focused on bodily lust, Heaven forbid, lead a person to insanity.

"The proper function of the intellect, so that it can observe cogently, requires the oils in the body. The intellect is like a lit candle that continues to burn as a result of the oils that are drawn to it, as oil is drawn to a burning wick. But when there are no oils in the body to serve as fuel, the intellect cannot be lit in cogent observation, and this causes people to go insane, by way of the body fluids drying out. For it's this lack of oil to burn that damages the brain."

As is known, the main way that body fluids dry up is by blemishing personal holiness, particularly wasting one's seed. In addition, immoral thoughts and lustful desires, which women can also be guilty of, destroy the brain even more than the actual act itself, as our Sages have taught us: "Contemplating sin is worse than the actual act" (Yoma 29a).

Insanity begins with the two provocateurs of sin: the eyes. Many young boys go out of their minds, having fallen into the sickness of looking at women, lewd magazines and filthy movies that drive them crazy with burning lust. They can't find a way to dissipate their burning passion, until eventually their brain burns up and their mind becomes totally disoriented. Sometimes they look for relief by turning to various hallucinogenic drugs. Even though, on the surface, there are people who use these drugs and appear to be sane, internally they are completely mixed up and bewildered. They lack any semblance of inner peace, are forgetful, angry and depressed, even if they might appear to be more or less functioning normally.

The best advice to anyone who has harmed his body fluids is to start guarding his eyes and thoughts. He shouldn't allow his mind to roam into lustful thoughts which make him crazy. If he is unable to do this, at least he should focus his mind on physical things, such as a job or some kind of craft. It's known that one of the ways of treating insane people is by giving them employment that occupies their mind and prevents their thoughts from uncontrolled wandering.

As we mentioned earlier, immersing oneself in Torah learning is the best ploy for purifying lewd thoughts and contemplations. There's an advantage of focusing on Torah over focusing on a job or a handicraft: the Torah diffuses the spirit of folly and instills a fear of sin as well as a sense of right and wrong in a person. This encourages normal behavior.

The insane individual is usually in self-denial - he does not acknowledge his problem. Therefore, he must first shed his arrogance and acknowledge the truth, that he is currently in a state of mental disorder. He must nullify his brain to the wisdom of the wise spiritual leaders, the tzaddikim who teach us the true wisdom of Torah. He must beg Hashem to grant him mental and emotional health. He must apologize to Hashem for contaminating his brain, which houses the soul. He must ask for complete emuna in Hashem as well as emuna in the true tzaddikim, the spiritual guides of our generation. He must heed them without veering to the right or to the left. He must ask for joy, which comes from the good spirit of holiness that chases away all the bad spirits of arrogance and promiscuity. He must strive to be truly happy and sing melodies of happiness.

Happiness and song are cogent cures for all disease and particularly for mental illness. Since mental illness is on the rise in our generation, we must ask Hashem constantly for emuna, happiness and trust. Surely, anyone who prays profusely for happiness will merit emuna and a good spirit.

Income

The quality of a person's livelihood depends on his or her trust in the Creator. By way of emuna, one attains trust in the Creator. Consequently, concentrated efforts to reinforce emuna and trust in Him are capable of improving one's livelihood.

Emuna teaches us that the Creator sustains all His creations, from the one-celled amoeba to magnificent galaxies, from the whale and the elephant to human beings, who are the crown of creation. Our sages say that

He who gives life also gives livelihood. In other words, if one believes that the Creator is the life-giving Creator, one should also believe that He sustains His creations.

Complete trust in the Creator includes the trust that livelihood is part of His Divine Providence over all creation. It is Hashem's task to worry about one's livelihood and not the individual's; therefore, one who trusts in Him is relieved of worry about livelihood and free to concentrate on his or her specific task on earth with a clear mind. Such people know that the Creator will certainly fulfill His task faithfully.

The distinct sign of trust in the Creator is when a person's thoughts don't focus on money. Those who trust the Creator don't worry about where their next meal is coming from. Even if money is tight, they know that their financial problems come from Him. Therefore, they don't blame themselves or anyone else for their difficulties.

When experiencing a financial loss, whether in the form of a theft, a lost possession, or a breakdown, one should revert to the three principles of emuna, as follows:

1. Everything comes from God, as does this particular loss. Not only does everything come from Him, but this is exactly what He wants.
2. This particular loss is for the best, as everything else God does.
3. The loss is a message from Heaven to stimulate self-evaluation and soul-searching for something that needs to be corrected, because there are no tribulations without transgression. In addition, there are certain transgressions that cause financial loss, as

explained in the book "The Garden of Riches" by the author.

Examples from Sefer HaMidot, **"The Aleph-Bet Book"**

"Losing a possession indicates a loss of faith".

"He who sells liquor diluted with water, thieves pounce on him." In other words, just as he dilutes a product, thieves dilute his assets. This saying includes all types of swindling, counterfeiting and short-changing that are basically acts of thievery, which therefore invoke thievery in a measure-for-measure fashion.

"Inconsequential endeavors (such as watching television or reading newspapers) invoke the coming of thieves."

"Listening to nonsense (such as television, social media, etc.) invokes the coming of thieves."

"Lying invokes thieves", for lying is also tantamount to stealing.

People with emuna know that the Creator is the Provider; therefore, when they encounter financial difficulties, they react by putting their emuna to work, as in the three-stage thought process above based on the principles of emuna. They compensate for deficiency by penitence, namely, rectifying the misdeeds that caused the deficiency in the first place. They pray and appeal to Divine mercy, that He should provide for them and fulfill their every need, as we explain at length in this book. They certainly don't try to attain money in a dishonest fashion. Only by power of emuna can a person glide through financial difficulties. With emuna, he attains the attribute of trust in the Creator, an attribute that accompanies him for life.

The Sweat of Your Brow...

Those who lack emuna attribute their financial difficulties to a long list of "villains": Either they blame themselves or others, curse their bad fortune or bad luck, or go on witch-hunts after bad omens, evil eyes, and other nonsense. Sometimes, they lament that God doesn't love them or care about them, and harbor resentment towards Him. They think of a hundred different ploys to make money or otherwise obtain what they want, including illegal means such as cheating on taxes or outright stealing. They do everything instead of what they should be doing - turning to the Creator and praying. They wrack their brains deciding whether to beg, borrow, or steal; they work overtime or travel abroad for lengthy durations at the expense of health and family. Rabbi Yisroel Salanter says that without emuna, a person amplifies the curse of living by the sweat of his own brow (Genesis, 3:19). They lack inner peace both in this world and in the next.

Thou Shalt not Steal

The more a person lacks emuna, the more he or she is liable to contemplate illegal means of making money. Dishonesty and lack of emuna are notorious partners. But, with emuna, one understands that God provides a livelihood within the framework of Biblical principles. Any money destined to reach a person does so permissibly and by honest means. Remember this important spiritual rule: Money that one obtains by transgressing biblical laws (lying, cheating, withholding a worker's salary, fraud, and stealing, just to name a few) is not only cursed, but it also damages one's legitimately-earned money, just like a rotten apple damages the good apples in the same basket. Dishonest money invokes a torrent of troubles and tribulations, Heaven forbid.

Trust

Those who desire to solve their financial problems once and for all should learn to trust the Creator, knowing that He is the One who provides for us. Everyone should learn "The Gate of Trust" in Rabbenu Bachiya's classic book, "Duties of the Heart". The first day, one should learn fifteen lines, no more, and review that segment four times. The second day, learn a second segment of fifteen lines and review that four times as well. Repeat the same every day for additional segments, until finishing the entire chapter. Now, keep reviewing the entire chapter until you feel a tangible strengthening of your trust in Hashem, for that is the main conduit for income.

Afterwards, a person should pray for his every need. The Talmud says that when a person turns to the Creator at the time of suffering, his livelihood is enhanced.

Know full well that those who desire to perform a spiritual "root treatment" for their financial problems should not ask for money at all in their prayers; instead, they should ask the Creator for emuna and trust. Why? When we pray for money, the prayer serves as a temporary solution, like a patch on a torn pair of jeans. Prayers for money won't solve core financial difficulties. Unless we reinforce our trust in the Creator, one financial crisis will lead to another. But, by strengthening emuna and trust in Him, our income problems will be over! The Creator wants us to learn to trust Him; once we do, He doesn't need to prod us with financial tribulations. With emuna and trust, we merit a pleasant and sufficient livelihood for life.

Those who are buried in debt should spend at least an hour a day in personal prayer, seek the Creator's help, make penitence, and try to correct the misdeeds that generated the debt. They should pray to Him for emuna and trust, thus creating a strong spiritual vessel of trust that's a worthy recipient for Divine blessings of abundance. As such, they merit that their prayers alone generate an abundant income.

Emuna and Worry are Mutually Exclusive

A young man complained to me about financial difficulties. I told him to pray to the Creator and request emuna. The young man protested, claiming that there's nothing faulty with his emuna. "I have emuna!" he exclaimed, "but I'm worried about my old debts, my new bills, feeding and educating the children..."

I told him, "Your ears should listen to what your mouth is saying! In the same breath, you say that you have emuna but you have worries too. That's a contradiction, for if you have emuna, then you don't have worries. A person who believes that the Creator gives him his livelihood simply does not worry! Have you ever seen a worried three-year old? No! A toddler doesn't have to worry - daddy is responsible for making a living! He trusts his father completely. By the same token, you should trust your Father in Heaven while concentrating on your own task in life, without worrying either, for it's his job to provide for you and He will surely do so!"

"Your task in life," I continued, "is to serve the Creator and to repent. Let Him take care of your financial situation and income worries. Speak to Him in this manner: 'Master of the World, there's no one else I can turn to but You, for the universe and all its contents are Yours, and You sustain all Your creations as You see fit. My livelihood is in Your hands alone and not up to me. You are the One who gives income and no one else. It's not my job to worry about where my livelihood will come from - I don't even care at all. Please, beloved Father in Heaven, send me my livelihood as You deem befitting, and teach me how to strengthen my faith, to serve You in happiness, and to have absolute trust in You and in whatever way You do things. Help me cling to You always."

Once we believe with complete faith that the Creator is the only address to turn to for income, our hearts fill with joy and trust, knowing deep down that He will never leave us. Just as the Creator always sent a means of sustenance until now, He shall continue to do so in the future.

He who Trusts in Hashem is Encompassed in Loving-kindness

A person must believe that the Creator gives a person a livelihood with no connection to that person's efforts or righteousness. Think about the example of a small child: When the child misbehaves, does the parent withhold food, clothing, shelter, or medical attention? Of course, not! If such is the case with humans - and the Creator is infinitely more merciful and compassionate than a human - it's surely the case with Him! He provides for His creations regardless of their righteousness, simply as a result of His abounding mercy and compassion for everyone, even to those who do not deserve. He who gives life also gives sustenance, unconditionally.

Even so, financial difficulties are frequently a message from the Creator for a person to start soul-searching. Maybe that individual has committed certain transgressions that are directly detrimental to making a living, such as fraud, theft, dishonesty, infidelity, anger, sadness, spilling one's seed in vain, birth control (without the sanction of a qualified clergyman) and worry. These transgressions are serious breaches of emuna; if a person suffers from financial troubles and is guilty of one or more of these transgressions, then confessing to the Creator, atoning and praying for enhanced emuna will most certainly be conducive to a better livelihood.

If a person assesses himself and doesn't find that he committed any of the abovementioned transgressions, then the financial difficulties are likely to be an indication of an overall lack of emuna and trust. He should therefore concentrate on reinforcing all aspects of emuna by learning about emuna and praying to the Creator and seeking His help in attaining and strengthening emuna. He should also do daily self-assessment, especially in the area of emuna, atoning for any lack of emuna.

Livelihood is the prime testing ground for emuna. Here, one can't "fake it," because the results of emuna are reflected in one's inner peace, or lack of it. Either you believe that the Creator provides for you, or you run around in a frenzy thinking that you provide for yourself; if you're worried or over-exerting yourself about income, you're still far away from emuna.

A well-known Breslever chassid and Holocaust martyr from Poland, Rebbe Yitzchak Breiter, may Hashem avenge his blood, worked for years as an accountant at an important firm in Warsaw. Before the war, he made a fine living and had ample free time to serve Hashem peacefully while enjoying financial security.

Prior to World War II, hard times befell Poland and Rebbe Yitzchak was forced out of his job. His family was in shock, but he did not lose his calm demeanor. When he saw that he had no way to make a living, he sat himself down in the study hall and learned Torah and prayed with great diligence.

As his financial situation worsened, he intensified his Torah study and prayers. He knew what his job was. When Rebbe Yitzchak experienced hard times, he understood that he must make an effort to do his own job much better. And when the situation got even worse, he understood that perhaps he had more work to do - more learning, more praying, more emuna and more trust.

As the economic situation became progressively worse, Rebbe Yitzchak continued to forge ahead with his studies and Divine service, all the while relying on Hashem - completely trusting Him to sustain him and his family. During the entire financial crisis, while everyone else was suffering, Rebbe Yitzchak and his family received their sustenance through Divine Providence and literally supernatural miracles.

One day, when he was sitting alone in the study hall, a Jewish acquaintance came in and gave him a sizeable donation to support his family. Rebbe Yitzchak did not show any excitement, thanked the man and returned to his studies. The Jew, who had begun to leave, turned around, stood before Rebbe Yitzchak and said to him, "One question is bothering me. King David said in Psalm 37:25, 'I was a lad and I have also aged and I have not seen a righteous person abandoned or his offspring requesting bread.' If so, how can it be that a righteous person like yourself, who serves Hashem day and night, is forced to ask others for his sustenance?"

Rebbe Yitzchak said to him: "Go to the marketplace and find the shop of the wealthy Mr. X. Look at his son, standing at the entrance to the shop, shouting his wares and convincing passers-by to enter the store and buy their merchandise. The boy has to put in a lot of effort until he can entice somebody to buy from his father - isn't this a perfect example of 'his offspring requesting bread?'"

"I, on the other hand, sit here in the study hall and serve Hashem. Did I ask you to come here? Have I ever asked you to support me? You came here of your own free will and gave me my sustenance..."

Our Sages say that when a person believes that Hashem sustains him, he merits the World to Come. The Talmud (Brachot, 4b) explains that whoever recites Chapter 145 of Psalms three times a day merits the World to Come. Why? Because this chapter is imbued with emuna and trust in Hashem, Who feeds and sustains all: "You open Your hand and satisfy every living thing with favor." (Psalms, 145:16). Accordingly, the main tool for livelihood is emuna. Conversely, worry is the main thing that causes a lack of sustenance.

Our Sages provide us with more information about the connection between emuna and livelihood: (from Sefer HaMiddot)

- A person who has knowledge (emuna) will ultimately become wealthy.
- Emuna increases a person's livelihood.
- Constant joy (joy means emuna) is a conduit for success.

- He who shares his sorrow with Heaven (pouring his heart out to Hashem in personal prayer) has his livelihood doubled. His livelihood flies to him like a bird, as well.
- Emuna is good for livelihood. See Rashi on the verse in Psalms 37, "And graze emuna:" Rashi explains: Eat and make a livelihood in the merit of emuna.
- A person who does not have livelihood should study Torah and then pray for his livelihood. Surely his prayers will be accepted.
- Poverty stems from blasphemy.
- Sadness (lack of emuna) creates a lack of livelihood.

We have seen that a person's main focus must be on emuna, through which he'll merit his every need.

The Debtor

Debt is a test of emuna. Does the debtor blame himself, others or his bad fortune, or does he look at his predicament through eyes of emuna? If he opts for emuna, he should tell himself, "Emuna says that this is the way that the Creator wants it and that it's all for the best. The Creator obviously wants me to rectify something so that I can get closer to Him." Our sages tell us that there are no tribulations without prior transgression. Debt is certainly a tribulation! Consequently, he knows that teshuva must be the only advice in overcoming his debt problems.

Rebbe Nachman of Breslev writes (Sichot Haran, 112): "there is a certain transgression, which invokes the punishment that the transgressor is in perpetual debt. Even if he does all the tricks in the world, it won't help, and he'll remain in debt. This transgression sometimes brings others down in debt."

He continues and writes, "There is a moment when a number of people fall in debt in the world, because of the aforementioned transgression becoming rampant in the world, Heaven forbid. The advice for this is to engage in complete repentance, and to beg Hashem to rescue him from this transgression. One must believe that he is capable, with the spiritual confidence that is known as expansion of the mind, show remorse to the Creator and do teshuva for what he did. For the opposite, contraction of the mind where he doesn't believe that he is capable of teshuva is an aspect of being a debtor. Our sages say (Kiddushin 49b): "Ten measures of slumber came into the world; the slaves took nine of them." Slumber is also an aspect of contraction of the mind, and a slave is an aspect of debt, as it is written, 'The borrower is a slave to the lender' (Proverbs, 22:7). So, when a person has an expansion of the mind and does teshuva, then the punishment of debt is nullified."

As such, a person with debts must first strive to be happy. Once his mind is free, he can atone for the blemishes that are the spiritual roots of his money problems. He should therefore devote time and effort to self-assessment, asking the Creator to help him realize what he must rectify, especially those misdeeds that led to his owing money.

Business

A businessperson without emuna is miserable. A depressed and harried merchant once came to me, seeking my advice. I told him, "Your business and money problems result from the fact that you think you're the boss, and therefore all the worries are on your shoulders. You depend on your brains, your business acumen, and your talent, and therefore suffer bitter disappointments when things don't go the way you want them to. Even worse, you put your trust in people - customers, suppliers, banks, and the like - and they let you down, lie to you, and cheat you."

I continued: "If you only realized that the Creator runs your business, and you're only a mere clerk, then your job would become much simpler; you wouldn't need to worry, you wouldn't need to suffer, and you wouldn't need to lose your temper. As a clerk, you could concentrate on doing your job and let the Big Boss - the Creator - worry about the rest. Tons of pressure would fall off your shoulders. You have no way of knowing if the individual you're about to do business with - whether a supplier or a customer - is honest or not."

"You therefore must pray to the Creator," I continued, "asking for His assistance and guidance in every transaction you make. He who puts his trust in the Creator will be surrounded with Divine compassion. Ask Him to let the deal go through if it is His desire, and to fall through if it is not His desire."

A businessperson who prays for enhanced emuna learns to manage affairs without stress and anxiety. When he puts his trust in the Creator, nothing upsets or frightens him. He doesn't fall into the heretic mindset that the "might of his right hand" - his prowess or his ability - is the source of success. He turns to the Creator for everything and constantly seeks His advice. He trusts in the Creator exclusively, so no one can scare him.

Basically, we can choose one of two paths in commercial life (or any other phase of life): Either we appoint the

Creator as the Chief Executive Officer of our all our affairs, business and otherwise - consequently enjoying a smooth, enjoyable and worry-free life - or we shoulder the problems on our own, with the accompanying stress, worries, nerves, and health problems.

Juggling Money

"Financing" is a disease. The banks are happy to loan money at killer interest rates. They are a treacherous entity to trust in. One who borrows money from them doesn't make the proper calculations, namely, that the cost of financing often exceeds the profits. The ready cash in his hands blinds him and obscures his better judgment. In the end, the burden of heavy debts break his back.

This of course is the result of faulty emuna. A person forgets that the Creator alone decides how much money we have. He also gives each of us the necessary funds for whatever He deems that we need. A person with emuna knows that if the Creator wants him to invest a large sum, He will provide him with the funds. Does the Creator lack the necessary capital? Does the Creator need banks or loan sharks? If the Creator provides us with a small sum, it's a sign that in the meanwhile, He wants us to run our business on a small scale. When we do, we see a blessing in what we do. But without emuna, people entertain delusions of grandeur; they think that they can only succeed by doing business on a grandiose scale. Who knows if they'll succeed? Who knows if they'll be able to pay back the tremendous loans they took?

The biggest mistake people make is thinking that they're making more money by juggling big sums. If they'd check carefully, they'd see that the cost of financing eats up all their profits. Moreover, "jugglers" are dependent on the mercy of cruel institutions like banks and finance companies. As soon as a bank or finance company closes the loan faucet for a juggler, he or she falls on his or her face. Ultimately, a person can't earn a cent more than the Creator destines on Rosh Hashanah for him to earn during the course of the year. When the smoke clears, the jugglers see that they didn't earn any more than a simple salary.

The only way to increase our financial portion is to increase our prayers and our donations to charity, especially giving tithe properly and faithfully. Then, it is possible to attain an increase in our Rosh Hashanah allotment from Above.

If the financial juggler simply failed to make as much money as he dreamed of, then that wouldn't be so much of a problem. The real problem is that when the jugglers entertain delusions of grandeur and invest sums they don't have, they end up taking more loans, wasting money by hiring more workers that they don't need, spending needless funds on advertising, or by disproportionate spending trying to increase their business. Not only do they squander their annual allotment, but they sink into debt as well.

A person's income is the result of Heavenly decree - he can't make any more than his allotment from Above. But, he can lose more, for there is no limit to the losses he can incur. He should therefore do business in accordance with his ability and with the resources at his disposal instead of needlessly inflating his business, trying to earn more than what's allotted to him. One should therefore avoid the ensnarement of doing business on a larger scale than what he can manage, financially and otherwise. People who disregard this rule end up owing millions in debt, Heaven forbid.

Your Accountant

A person with emuna fulfills the passage (Proverbs, 28:20), "A man of faith will increase blessings, but the impatient to be rich will not be exonerated." In other words, the people of faith are satisfied with the Creator's blessing and happy with their lot in life. They don't chase after money and wealth. Even though they seek advice from experts such as investment brokers, accountants, or other financial advisors, people with emuna ask the Creator for success before finalizing any transaction, praying in this manner: "Master of the Universe, thank You for providing my daily needs until today. Guide my current and future investments and/or transactions in such a way that I make a profit, so that I'll be able to give substantial amounts to charity and to perform good deeds. Please help me accept any outcome - whether profit or loss - with complete faith."

The prophet describes people like this and says (Jeremiah, 17:7), "Blessed is the man who trusts in Hashem, and Hashem will be his security." King David promised that those who trust in the Creator will always be encompassed by Divine compassion (Psalm 32:10). On the other hand, those who lack emuna and put blind trust in financial advisors or other flesh-and-blood, as if the mortal they depend on gives them their sustenance, are almost always disappointed. The prophet also said (Jeremiah, 17:5), "Cursed is the man who trusts in people and makes flesh-and-blood his strength." Trusting in anyone or anything other than the Creator is a formula for failure.

Rebbe Menachem Mendel of Kotzk explains the Midrash (Mechilta, Beshalach 17), "The Torah wasn't given to anyone other than to those who eat manna." He writes that the Torah was only given to those satisfied with what they have every day, are happy with their lot, and are not worried about the future. In the desert, the manna that fell from the heaven was a daily portion. This continued for forty years - as long as the Jews were in the desert! And so it continues in future generations, until today. Only a person with emuna and trust in Hashem merits the Torah, because with no trust, he wastes his life chasing after income, and won't be free to learn Torah.

A Good Merchant

A foundational principle of emuna that is the root of all commerce, financial and income affairs is that the Creator provides each individual with his or her allotted income.

The practical manifestation of emuna is trust in the Creator, including the awareness that the Creator sustains all His creations, and that He does His job dependably. As such, a person will receive whatever is predestined for him, without a doubt. He knows that his livelihood doesn't depend on his efforts, cleverness or righteousness. He also knows that no one can touch what is destined for him, to prevent or obstruct his heavenly-allotted income. Our sages say (Yoma 38b), "No one can touch that which is destined for someone else," in other words, that which doesn't belong to him.

Trust in the Creator - internalizing the fundamental principle of emuna that our livelihood is predetermined and exclusively from Him - enables us to conduct our business affairs with confidence, a clear mind, and a healthy outlook, while steering clear of any stress, anxiety, worry and forbidden business practices.

With trust in the Creator, a person doesn't think about money all day long. Peace of mind is only two words away - God provides. Period.

Your Allotment will Reach You

Business is one continuous test of faith. Businesspeople are tested every single second: If they believe that their livelihood comes from the Creator, then they're calm and composed, conducting their affairs on an honest basis. If they believe otherwise - that their income depends on their own efforts and aptitude - then they're most likely working much too hard and wasting energy looking for all types of ploys to make money.

One's entire life depends on the emuna that the Creator provides for every creation. Emuna creates a clear, clean, and shining spiritual pipe that abundance flows through, directly from Heaven to a person's bank account or dinner table. Drinking from the pipe of emuna is like drinking from a silver goblet. He can choose to receive his income by way of such a sterling silver pipe - in other words, with honesty, integrity, joy and inner peace - or to receive income by dishonest means and with the negative emotions, bad health, and damage to the soul that accompany a lack of emuna. That's like drinking from a sewer.

Simple emuna is the basis of income. Believe that the Creator predetermines your income, and that every last cent designated for you will reach you at an exact time and in its entirety, if not from one source, then from a different source, if not today, then tomorrow. It's your choice between drinking from the silver cup of honesty and self-composure or drinking from the sewer of illegal and dishonest business procedures, court cases, audits, hypertension, ulcers, and cardiac arrests.

Remember! A person receives his or her Heavenly stipend to the last penny. By cheating, lying, or dealing dishonestly, a person won't earn a cent more. Indeed, whereas the honest person enjoys every cent he earns, the dishonest person will only suffer from the money he makes.

There's no middle ground - either you believe that you'll receive what's destined for you at the exact time you need it, and if not from one source, then from another, and if not today, then tomorrow. The result is that you live a tranquil life that's free of headaches, dishonesty and shady business, Heaven forbid. Or, you don't believe, and the result is that you're stressed out of your mind, entangled in all types of complications and problems and even a defendant in court or an inmate serving time for tax evasion, laundering money and all sorts of crimes committed because of a lack of emuna and trust in Hashem. The latter is a life of purgatory.

Remember, every person's allotment is exact, and he or she won't make a cent more than what's destined. If a person earns his money honestly and with emuna, he'll enjoy every cent for it will be money with a blessing. If he earns his money dishonestly, he'll still get his allotment, but the money will carry a curse and he won't enjoy it; indeed, he'll suffer from it.

The Thief Steals His Own

The following eye-opening story exemplifies the above principle:

The Baal Shem Tov had a disciple named Yossele. Yossele's evil inclination tempted him to steal. Unable to overcome his urge, Yossele decided to try and steal at night, when the entire township was fast asleep. He set his first sights on Lady Sara's mansion, the vast three-story residence on the outskirts of the township where the rich spinster lived.

Sara was the only daughter of a wealthy merchant who died and left her all his wealth.

Yossele sneaked up to the mansion, and to his delight, found the gatekeeper snoring away in a deep slumber. Two overfed dogs sat by the gatekeeper wagging their tails. Yossele couldn't believe his good fortune - even the front door to the mansion was unlocked! Not a single servant was in sight.

Quietly, as if walking on eggs, Yossele entered the mansion. He never saw so much abundance in his life - rich carpets from Persia, crystal chandeliers from Vienna, paintings from the leading galleries of Paris and Amsterdam. He tiptoed through the parlor to the drawing room; once, Yossele had come here to receive a donation from Sara's father, who made no effort to conceal the whereabouts of the safe.

He moved aside the painting of the waterfall in the drawing room, and lo and behold, there was the safe. Yossele barely turned its dial, and the unlocked door simply popped open! Diamonds, gold, and stacks of paper currency stared him in the face.

Yossele was astonished at how everything proceeded so smoothly: The guard slept, the dogs didn't bark, the front door was open, all the servants had disappeared, and even the safe was unlocked. As strange as it seemed, Yossele felt like he was receiving Divine corroboration!

"Why's Hashem making this so easy for me?" Yossele asked himself. "Strange, it looks like all these riches are just waiting for me to take them." The more he stared at the wealth before his eyes, the more his heart pounded with guilt. He remembered his Gemara that said a person's livelihood is predetermined. "If so," he argued with himself, "why should I be touching anything that doesn't belong to me?"

Yet, the diamonds and the stacks of money seemed to be calling his name - "Yossele, take us... "

Yossele's Torah background, his conscience, and his good inclination were gaining the upper hand in his inner struggle; a spark of emuna kindled a fire of faith in his heart. "If all these riches are really mine, then they'll come to me by honest means; certainly - there's no need for me to transgress Hashem's commandments and steal!"

Suddenly, Yossele felt an awesome fear of Hashem, as he stood on the verge of a terrible felony. "Hashem, save me!" he yelled, turning abruptly and running out of the house without taking a thing.

The following day - in the evening hours - after having spilled a river of tears and a flood of remorse while begging for Hashem's forgiveness, Yossele received a summons from the Baal Shem Tov. Obediently, he proceeded to his master with no delay, but he was scared out of his wits. The holy tzaddik would surely know what his sinister intentions were.

"Sit down, Yossele," said the Baal Shem Tov cordially, offering him a chair. "How are you feeling?"

"F-fine, b-baruch Hashem," stuttered Yossele, expecting the worst chastisement imaginable.

"Yossele," said the Baal Shem Tov, "I received a message from Lady Sara - do you know who I'm referring to?"

A tremendous lump parked itself in Yossele's throat; he could barely breathe, let alone speak. He cleared his throat several times, while his face alternately changed colors from a bright crimson to a pale yellow to an ash white. He was sure that Lady Sara reported the attempted theft to the Baal Shem Tov. Even if she didn't, nothing escaped the limitless spiritual vision of the tzaddik. Yossele wanted to jump in a hole and then have the ground devour him. He was so ashamed...

"Yossele," the Baal Shem Tov continued, "Lady Sara, as an orphan and as an only child, has asked me to be her guardian and to advise and assist her in conducting her affairs... ". The Baal Shem Tov paused, and his probing, Heavenly, ice-blue eyes seemed to penetrate the fibers of Yossele's soul.

"... Lady Sara asked me to find her a suitable chattan; she wants to get married. She desires a pious husband, who'll spend every waking hour in the study of Torah and in the service of Hashem. She doesn't want a businessman who'll manage her commercial affairs, for she can do that herself; her father trained her well, and she's most adept in the business world. She wants a husband that will be isolated from the outside world, whose entire energies and aspirations will be channeled toward Torah."

Yossele nearly fell off his chair; he was expecting to be consumed by a bolt of lightning at any second, but instead...

The Baal Shem Tov smiled warmly. "You know, Yossele, when Lady Sara first approached me several weeks ago, I couldn't think of a suitable candidate. Later, Hashem gave me the idea that the time has come for you to take a wife, and that you and Sara would make a splendid match. I want you to prepare yourself for the wedding; the High Holidays are drawing near, so I think that you and Sara should be married with no further delay."

Any bombshell - even a sweet one - requires time to digest. Yossele stepped out of the tzaddik's house, his head spinning, into the warm midsummer Ukrainian sunshine. He sat down by the river and contemplated the vastness of Hashem's Divine Providence to the tiniest detail, His mercy, and His phenomenal lovingkindness. "What if I hadn't withstood the test?" he asked himself, and almost fainted when he contemplated the hypothetical consequences. If he'd have stolen, he'd have stolen money that would ultimately have come to him by permissible means! Instead of being Lady Sara's bridegroom and a pious Torah scholar with all his needs taken care of, he would've been a lonely, common thief out on the street with nothing - no money, no Torah and no Judaism...

Yossele thanked Hashem for giving him the strength to withstand temptation and to pass the test of faith. He also realized that good fortune and abundance readily come to a person without forcing the issue. Hashem has His timetable. A person can either force the issue and suffer or depend on Hashem that he'll receive what's destined to him at the exact opportune moment. This is the wonderful story of Yossele.

Understandably, not everyone receives such a clear preview of the abundance that's in store for him like Yossele did. Also, few realize that their future needs are already taken care of. Our efforts in making money are merely tests as to how we'll make our money - in honest, straightforward means, or by shady deals, bickering, fraud, swindling, and the like. Even if he doesn't resort to financial transgressions, but he forces the hour by pressuring, borrowing and lacking patience, he'll suffer. In essence, we are all like Yossele - with emuna and patience, we'll receive all our needs.

Maybe you're thinking about Yossele's good fortune in marrying a rich woman. Know full well that even if Yossele didn't marry Lady Sara, if her money was earmarked for him, he would have received it anyway, by any number of means. Hashem is not limited in the number of ways He sends people their livelihood.

Everything Has its Hour

A merchant with emuna needs to know that every article in his or her inventory is under the influence of absolute Divine Providence. Hashem decides when a certain object - whether a twenty-room mansion or tube of toothpaste - is sold, to whom, and at what price. According to Kabbalistic thought, each object has spiritual sparks of holiness that belong or gravitate to a certain soul; that soul will ultimately acquire the object, as a soul correction both for the object and for itself. Elaborating on this concept, Rebbe Nachman of Breslev writes (Likutei Moharan I:54) that everything in the world has its sparks of holiness... and its hour, when it ultimately returns to its spiritual root."

Consequently, if a business transaction occurs, it's only because Hashem so decreed. When the appointed time comes for certain goods to change hands, then the Creator in His magnificent Divine providence creates the catalysts that make it happen. All of a sudden, someone wants to sell something and someone else wants to buy it. Why? The sparks of holiness of that particular object are destined to change hands, for the seller no longer needs them but the buyer needs them for the completion of his or her soul.

Here's another example: suppose that the sparks of holiness in a particular carrot are rooted in the soul of a tzaddik, the tzaddik's wife will eventually go to a certain vegetable stand on a certain day and pay a certain price for a certain pound of carrots. She'll then come home and feed her husband the certain carrot whose spiritual sparks are rooted in his soul. Once the tzaddik makes a blessing over the carrot and eats it, the carrot attains a lofty spiritual correction. In the case of a carrot or other foodstuff, it physically becomes a part of the tzaddik!

In light of the above example (which is none other than a drop of water from a vast sea, for the subject of soul corrections necessitates an entire volume in itself), any business deal - barter, trade, purchase, or sale - occurs **only** when and where Hashem decides. When the time is ripe for a certain commodity or piece of merchandise to reach the domain of a particular soul, the transaction is completed - not before and not after.

If a purchaser and an object don't have a spiritual common denominator, they won't come together at any price or under any circumstance. Therefore, it's senseless for a pushy salesman or overpowering merchant to try and force something on a customer that he or she doesn't want.

Many businesspeople have related stories about seemingly useless merchandise that they sold at a tremendous profit, or about products that they thought would be best sellers that ended up collecting dust on the shelves. Realtors have all experienced prospective buyers that turn their noses up at a certain house or piece of property, and three months later end up purchasing the very same piece of real estate. Every field has its own examples of Divine Providence. Everything has its hour.

Negotiating in Faith

A businessman with emuna is satisfied with his lot in life, for he conducts all his business affairs faithfully. The Creator desires a healthy and just society; He therefore wants people to be fair and honest in commerce. A businessman with emuna therefore conducts his business with emuna. Emuna in business means that a person is fair, honest, and sticks to his or her word. With the emuna that livelihood comes from the Creator, a person doesn't resort to criminal or immoral means in acquiring money. He also doesn't try to pressure people to complete a deal, for pressure in business is liable to lead to undesirable things such as customer resentment and ill feelings that invoke anything but blessings. That's the first thing a person is asked when he or she leaves this world: Did you negotiate fairly, with no dishonesty or swindling?

Businesspeople with emuna don't try to make high-pressure sales or misrepresent their goods. Nothing frightens a businessperson with emuna. He or she isn't disappointed when a prospective customer walks away. With emuna, one knows that if profit doesn't materialize from transaction A, then it'll materialize from transaction B. Such a businessperson earns a high score in emuna and lives a calm and good life in this world. In the next world, he will merit a favorable judgment by virtue of his honesty, decency and upright character, for he never caused sorrow to others.

On the other hand, businesspeople who lack emuna think their livelihoods depend on customers. Such folks believe that money and success depend on their own acumen, and therefore will readily stretch the truth or compromise their principles in their exaggerated efforts to make a living. They often make promises they can't keep or slander their competitors, violating the biblical ordinance of wholesome speech. Inadvertently, they accumulate a long list of spiritual debits that leads to further suffering.

Businesspeople or other professionals who lack emuna are almost always plagued by arrogance and an inflated ego. When the Creator grants them success, they pat themselves on their backs telling themselves how clever, wonderful, and talented they are. When they attain more money than they deserve by deviating from the realm of integrity and fairness, they pride themselves in their ability to "make" money. But, money made in such a manner will ultimately sour. Dishonest money is poison, both spiritually and materially. One must therefore pray, "Merciful Creator, help me make an honest living." No matter what the merchant does, he won't make a cent more than what has been allotted to him from Above.

Have you ever seen an arrogant person fail to complete the transaction that he or she wanted to complete?

Some vent their frustrations in temper tantrums, curses and complaints; others eat themselves up inside. Such an individual earns a low score on his test of emuna.

The Choice

Apparently, there's room for confusion; we frequently see successful businesspeople who couldn't care less about emuna. Furthermore, many of them are fast-talking hitting wheelers and dealers who succeed in selling ice to the Eskimos or pulling off any number of legendary deals by virtue of their powers of persuasion, pressure and fast talking. Where's the Divine Providence? We all know that so-and-so made millions from crime, graft, or corruption, laughs all the way to the bank, and basks in the Bermuda sunshine this very minute. What's going on here? Where's Divine providence?

The principle of free choice provides the answer to the above question. The Creator conceals His Divine providence in order to give man free choice to do good or evil. "Hashem leads a person in the way of his own choice" (Makot 10b). In other words, Hashem conceals His Divine Providence in order to leave people the free choice to do good or evil and enables that person to proceed in the direction of his/her own choice.

Therefore, when people choose the path of emuna, their livelihoods reach them effortlessly, honestly, and without knocking their brains out or flattering others. In other words, they'll receive their income pleasantly with no sorrow.

But, if they choose the path of arrogance and lack faith, then the Creator will allow them to believe that they are controlling their own destinies. They feel that they are the ones who made the "dream deal" by virtue of their fast talking and wheeling-dealing methods, which of course include high-pressure tactics that oftentimes harm people. We must therefore pray to receive our livelihood with integrity and without hurting anyone.

Even the wheeler-dealer didn't make any more than what was predetermined for him. If he only knew that his income will arrive at the exact time the Creator decides, he'd have much less headaches.

Even if a businessperson decides to make money in a morally or ethically dubious manner, he is given free rein to do so, even to succeed. Since such a person chooses the path of evil, he will now serve as the disciplinary rod to cause anguish to another person, as such: suppose that the Heavenly Court has decreed that Shimon must be cheated out of a thousand dollars. Reuven, the dishonest merchant, sells Shimon an item that is a cheap imitation of a known and reliable brand. The item breaks and Reuven loses his thousand dollars, as was decreed Above. Nevertheless, Shimon will be punished for cheating Reuven. If Shimon would have only had emuna, he would have received the same thousand dollars pleasantly, without causing sorrow to anyone.

Don't Force the Hour, or the Hour Will Force You

The result of impatience and forcing the issue are many. When people try to forcibly seal a deal or make money before the time and circumstances are ripe, they also suffer. Suppose that a merchant forcibly sells an item to a customer who doesn't want it. Since the item is not intended for that particular customer, the customer won't derive satisfaction or benefit from the item. For example, either it won't function properly, or it will be ruined in the customer's domain. The customer may file a complaint or lawsuit against the merchant, causing substantial grief and financial loss. As such, many losses can be traced to a lack of emuna.

It's also possible that the item is intended for that particular customer, but he is destined to receive it at a later date. The merchant who made a high-pressure sale and forced the issue received his money too early and squandered it. The result is that later, when he really needs the money and he was supposed to get it then, he won't have it.

A myriad of details are involved in this area. Forcing the issue, or acquiring money by dishonest means, can sometimes lead to disastrous results for generations to come. Imagine that a person fraudulently acquires a lot of money; this money - in honest means - would have reached his hands and the hands of his descendants over the next three generations. But, since he has greedily swindled to acquire funds that are not yet "ripe" for picking, he has stripped the financial tree whose fruits were intended for the use of the swindler's children, grandchildren, and great grandchildren. There are so many details that are beyond the fathom of our understanding, but we come to one solid conclusion:

"Anyone who forces the hour, the hour forces him" (Berachot 64a). In other words, don't force an issue because you'll end up being forced by a trouble in some way. Be patient, for your personal allotment will reach you in good time.

Here's a golden rule: You don't have to forcibly grab that which is intended for you anyway.

When you believe that God will provide for you, then your life will be calm, pleasurable, and productive. If you think that your fate and livelihood are in your own hands, then life will be a hell-on-earth of strain, pressure, and disappointment strewn with untold obstacles, including the temptation to attain money by dishonest means. The choice is yours.

Gambling

Know full well that on Rosh Hashanah, a person's annual income allotment is determined. It is also determined how much he is destined to lose. For example, suppose it was determined that one's annual income is $150,000 for the coming year. And, it was determined that he'd lose $30,000.

If he does all the tricks in the world and hires an army of statisticians and computer analysts to advise him how to bet on the dice and gamble scientifically, he still won't make any more than his $150,000 annual allotment from Heaven.

But - pay close attention - as far as the $30,000 loss that was intended for him, he can choose to lose more than this, even lose his home and everything he owns, and fall deep in debt.

A gambler will lose either way - if he loses while gambling, he could lose everything that he owns and succumb to debt. But even if he wins money while gambling, he won't get more than was predetermined for him to earn. What's more, the money earned by gambling is devoid of blessings, and he will not be able to enjoy it. Hence, either way he ends up a loser. Who then could benefit from gambling? Could a person change what was determined in Heaven? Better to wait patiently and receive their allotment in an honest and upright manner with dignity.

A Gambler is Cruel to His Family

One is not lord over his money. His money is merely a Heavenly deposit that one should use in accordance with Hashem's will. Most of the money given to a husband and father is intended for the benefit of his family. Without a wife and children, he wouldn't have received the money. What, therefore, gives him the right to gamble the money that Hashem gave him to support his family? By gambling, he is stealing the abundance that belongs to his family - abundance that Hashem gave him to use wisely for their welfare and not to waste on folly and fantasies.

No individual is as cruel to their family as a gambler. Whether he wins or loses, he harms his family. When he loses, he's guilty for the anguish that he causes them. In turn, he'll suffer from the harsh judgments and tribulations that the gambling invokes. Even if he wins, there won't be any blessing in this money. He won't make more than he was destined to, but now he has money from a badly tainted source. Such cursed funds only lead to sorrow and are a source of shame and embarrassment to the family.

The Gambler Thrives on the Suffering of Others

There is a tremendous moral flaw with gambling. In most kinds of gambling, one gains by another person's loss. How could a person with emuna be willing to benefit from money that comes from someone else's suffering? How could anyone enjoy money that is tainted with blood?

Gamblers not only squander loans that they take from partners and friends; if they can't get a loan, they'll obtain the money by other means, including outright stealing.

Even worse, people that run gambling establishments resemble murderers, since they're fully aware that the astronomical profits they make come from the immense pain of those that succumb to gambling. They "assist" the victims by extending them credit so that they can lose more after they've already run out of cash. The gambling institutions help the gambling addict lose his car, home, and business - the very lifelines of the gambler's family, may Hashem have mercy.

In short, gambling and emuna don't mix - a believing person should have no connection whatsoever with gambling.

If a person has an urge to gamble, he should ask Hashem to help him get rid of the lust for money, since gambling is rooted in one's excessive love of money. He should also pray for emuna, because the desire for money and gambling results from heresy, which is the opposite of emuna. This is because by gambling, a person denies that all his income is predetermined by Hashem, and even worse, he believes that it is possible to get rich by gambling, without Hashem's providence, God forbid. Someone who fools himself into thinking that Hashem wants him to make money through gambling should know that Hashem has many better and much more upright means to provide him with the money that he needs.

Lottery Tickets

The only type of gambling that Jewish law tolerates is a lottery, because one's profit is not through someone else's loss.

If a person wants to try his luck in a lottery, the only permitted way is to buy one ticket only. If Hashem wants to use the lottery as a means of sending money, then the person does not have to help Hashem by buying additional tickets.

When a person buys more than one ticket, he is showing that he does not believe that Hashem is the One who determines who will be the winner, but rather chance and statistics are the determinants. Purchasing more than one ticket is squandering the money that Hashem gives him - a foolish deed for which he'll be judged.

The test of emuna here is whether or not he believes that that Hashem determines how much income he will have. With emuna, he need not purchase more than one ticket. Why? If he wins - congratulations! If not, he believes that this too is Hashem's will - for his benefit - and he is not disappointed in the slightest.

An individual who doubts Hashem's providence will think that the more tickets he buys, the greater his chances of winning. He hopes to be "lucky" - his false hopes of easy money turn into disappointment when he doesn't win. Such a mindset is the opposite of emuna.

A Difficult Test

A sudden windfall, such as an inheritance or a winning lottery ticket, is a serious and difficult test of faith. Experience shows that many people who acquired sudden wealth ultimately suffered severe emotional and spiritual maladies, even suicide. Why?

Most people lack the emotional and spiritual gear that's required to successfully deal with more than they're accustomed to. As a result, they become disoriented and arrogant; suddenly, the nouveau-riche husband no longer wants his wife, and vice versa. They entertain fantasies of glamour and grandeur, as if their money entitles them to more. Oftentimes, they use their money imprudently, squander it, or make senseless investments. They fall prey to con artists, greedy relatives, newly-found "friends," or white-collar swindlers such as unethical lawyers, accountants, or investment brokers. Frequently, their new riches are one continuous migraine headache.

Emuna is the only proper and capable spiritual vessel for handling an abundance of wealth. A wealthy individual with emuna knows that money belongs to the Creator and is only a temporary deposit in his or her hands in order to live an upright life and to help make this world a better place. Since they know that the Creator decides who'll be rich and who'll be poor, they do not slip into arrogance. They know that the Creator can take their money away at any instant, so why boast about it? They use their money prudently and in accordance with the principles of emuna. They tithe their net income as they should, giving a minimum of 10% to charity; those on the highest level of emuna give 20% of their earnings to charity. They invest prudently after seeking the Creator's advice. They invest in worthwhile charitable endeavors, especially spreading emuna books to as many people as possible. This type of individual passes the test of emuna and wealth with flying colors, for he is not negatively affected by sudden abundance, whether material or spiritual.

The opposite is true where there's no emuna. Someone without emuna thinks that the money is his to do with as he pleases and with no need to account for what he does with the money. The money drives him crazy; he doesn't know where to invest it to prevent him from losing it. He becomes arrogant, for now he's a rich man! His wife is no longer suitable. He ends up losing his friends and he distrusts everyone, for he thinks that they're all trying to take his money. He's full of worries, suspicion and phobia. Often, he not only loses his windfall, but falls into debt as well - debts that he would never have incurred had he not made the fast buck. His dream of money turns into a nightmare. He fails the test of emuna and his life is ruined by the big and fast profits that he thought would solve all his life's problems.

Happiness or Wealth

As we've shown, the desire for quick money shows a lack of emuna. The gambler looking for the quick profits thinks that money will solve his problems. But those who believe in the Creator know that the quality of their lives doesn't depend on the amount of money they have, but on the extent that they acquire emuna and succeed in performing His will. Prayer, charity, and penitence - as well as a major effort in acquiring emuna - are the only solutions to financial difficulties. If the Creator gives a person the tribulations of financial straits, then money won't solve that person's problems; he or she will only get a different and possibly worse set of tribulations.

Penitence is the only way to end tribulations, since there are no tribulations without transgressions. As long as a person refrains from repenting - even with all the money in the world - he or she will suffer because of his or her uncorrected transgressions. But, with penitence and a clean spiritual slate, people can live sweet and pleasant lives even if they don't have a cent in their pockets. One of my teachers would tell me about his exceptionally happy father-in-law who nonetheless lived in dire poverty. Once, his rich friend told him that he buys his wife and children whatever they want, yet there's never peace in their home. They're never happy. But, since my teacher's father-in-law was always happy, he made his wife and children happy, and they were content despite their needs.

Consequently, a person should be satisfied with his or her lot in life and not strive for riches. Our sages said that the more one has, the more one worries. The truly rich person is the one who is content with his lot in life. In any event, the best and only way to acquire one's needs is prayer, appealing to our merciful Father in Heaven for His Divine blessing and compassion.

Marital Peace - the Main Test

The main tests of a person's faith are in the home, with his wife and children, who unwittingly test his faith from morning 'til night. They make demands on his time, his money, and his nerves. Sometimes they frustrate and humiliate him, and never seem to be satisfied. Emuna is the only way to pass these tests.

The challenges of a marital relationship require a higher level of emuna than difficulties outside the home do. While a person can often avoid friction and confrontation on the outside, it's difficult to escape trying situations at home. Furthermore, a person can change or avoid his friends and associates a lot easier than he can change or avoid his spouse, for a marital relationship is much more obligating.

The true character development of a person begins only once that person marries. Unmarried people normally manage in life without having to invest concerted effort in acquiring emuna. But, the demands of a spouse and children indicate one's true level of emuna and behoove him to earnestly work on attaining emuna.

For example, unmarried people can normally avoid anyone they don't get along with, for in most cases, they're not forced to maintain contact. When a person is able to walk away from a challenging predicament, his or her emuna isn't taxed at all. Where there's no need to cope, there's no test! On the other hand, a responsible married person simply can't walk away from a family. His wife and children are his diagnostic test of emuna. In the framework of a family environment, he must have emuna so he begins to work on emuna.

Here's an example: picture a bachelor who works as a marketing representative of a big company. If one of his colleagues insults him or bothers him in any way, he has a quick tongue and even quicker temper; he's more than ready to heap a double dose of venom on anyone who steps on his toes. Sometimes, he will roll with a verbal punch in order to preserve an image that he wants to create for his customers. It serves his best interests to appear on the outside as a distinguished individual of impeccable character, especially if it helps him seal a deal.

In reality, this unmarried person is short-tempered and ego-centric. In a marital situation, he'd either destroy his wife and children, or end up divorced. To avoid either of these two dismal fates, he must learn emuna; otherwise he'd never pass the tests of a family environment.

The unmarried individual isn't required to give of himself constantly or to listen to or understand anyone else. Contrastingly, the married person must give always, listen to and understand his spouse, yet remain calm and completely tranquil. This is impossible without emuna.

An unmarried person can wear an artificial smile and convince the world that he or she is happy and fulfilled. But, after marriage, the true measure of a person's happiness is revealed, especially when he has to brighten up his household with joy and confidence. A husband can't possibly make his wife and children happy when he himself is miserable. True happiness is impossible without emuna, and marital life is a key testing ground of emuna.

Relationships outside the home, especially in the norms of modern society, are based on mutual advantage. "Scratch my back and I'll scratch yours" is the type of thinking that indicates costumed, self-serving relationships that are designed to attain money, fame, dignity, social standing, advancement, and recognition. But, at home, a person removes the mask of self-serving diplomacy and acts naturally. If he lacks emuna, he'll hate giving without getting - such a person will surely have tension at home, to say the least. If he desires marital peace, he'll have to work on and develop his emuna.

Marital Peace and Emuna are Directly Proportionate

Here's an important rule of thumb: A person's marital peace is directly proportionate to his measure of emuna;

the higher the emuna, the more peaceful the home. Once a person marries, he or she can really attain lasting emuna.

A husband and wife must learn from the outset of their relationship to look at everything that happens in the home from the standpoint of emuna. Almost every daily occurrence between them, their children, their family members, or their respective colleagues at work is a test of emuna. Therefore, they need the constant support system of the three levels of emuna. Emuna, penitence, submission to the Creator's will and profuse prayer are not only the best problem-solving tools in the home; they're the only problem-solving tools in the home.

Happy with Their Lot in Life

The Talmud relates a poignant story (Tractate Taanit, 23b):

Rabbi Manny came to the holy sage Rebbe Yitzchak ben Elyashiv and complained, "I can't stand my wife - she's not at all pretty."

The wise man asked, "What's her name?" The husband said that his wife's name is Hanna. "Then let Hanna be beautiful!" declared the wise man, a holy individual whose every utterance was a surefire blessing.

Hanna became gorgeous. Shortly thereafter, Rabbi Manny returned to Rebbe Yitzchak ben Elyashiv with a new complaint: "Ever since you blessed my wife, she gets more and more beautiful. The more beautiful she is, the haughtier she gets!"

"If that's the case," said Rebbe Yitzchak, "then let Hanna return to her prior status (of ugliness)." The husband came home, and was greeted by a smiling, pleasant, but quite ugly Hanna.

From the fact that Rabbi Manny loved his newly "uglified" wife, we learn that the Creator knows what's best for each one of us. A person must believe that everything the Creator does is the very best for him. This is emuna in Divine providence, the faith that everything the Creator does is for our ultimate individual benefit. With this level of emuna, we're always happy with our lot in life, knowing unequivocally that even life's deficiencies are the product of the Creator's personal intervention in our lives for our ultimate good. He gives each of us what we need to accomplish our mission on this earth.

A couple with emuna is happy with their lot in life, in other words, with each other. They accept each other with all their drawbacks. They know that the Creator gave them the exact partner they need in order to perfect themselves and to fulfill their mission in life.

Contrastingly, a person without emuna has endless complaints. The wife blames her husband for all of her troubles. The husband has nothing but complaints and criticism about his wife and is positive that she's the root of his suffering. Understandingly, their household is a pressure cooker; their children undoubtedly harbor an assortment of emotional maladies. Such a couple flunks the test of emuna.

Consequently, one's entire livelihood, happiness, personal welfare and the welfare of one's spouse and children all depend on emuna.

Get Out of the House!

This section will discuss a test of emuna that most readers will never face. Even so, it shouldn't be skipped, because it explains fundamental principles for life in general, and for married life in particular. These are principals that every married couple should know, and those who are not yet married should also learn them as part of their preparation for married life.

The main tests of emuna are at home. When one consistently fails these tests, he ends up in progressively more difficult situations, as we shall soon learn.

One such situation, a phenomenon of modern times, is that of women evicting their husbands from the home, often using civil law to assist them in doing so. Clearly, this is not a phenomenon that happened overnight; the couple surely had a long history of friction and conflict. If the couple would have worked on emuna, they wouldn't have reached this boiling point of turmoil. They would have awakened long ago to rectify themselves and their relationship.

A husband whose wife has thrown him out of the house must know that although it seems that his eviction was unjust, it's nonetheless from the Creator. Everything the Creator does is justified.

The Creator is the one who really evicted him from his home. If his behavior was damaging himself and the members of his family, it's better for him to be out of the house rather than to do further damage. Even if he feels that his behavior was acceptable, the Creator doesn't do anything without a purpose.

At this point, the evicted husband must implement the three levels of emuna:

The first level is the knowledge that everything comes from the Creator and that this is what the Creator wants. He has to fully believe that the Creator is the one who evicted him from his home, and not think any more about it. There is no place for self-flagellation or for blaming others. Anger, revenge, depression and self-pity are all anti-emuna dark-side emotions. He shouldn't take out his frustration on his father in-law, his mother in-law or his wife's divorcee girlfriend, even though they all encouraged his wife to throw him out. He shouldn't blame the police who believed her (false, in his opinion) allegations and delivered him a restraining order. He must not bear malice toward the judge who signed the restraining order that legally threw him out of his own home. With emuna there's only one thought - **"this is what the Creator wants."**

The second level is the knowledge that the Creator does everything for the best. He should believe that the Creator evicted him from his home for his own ultimate good and for the good of his wife and children. It's a great kindness to remove a man from the whirlpool that has trapped him and give him a time-out to ponder and to try to rectify the situation.

Reality speaks for itself. He and his wife were on a collision course. He hadn't listened to the hints that the Creator had sent him through his wife's complaints. Since he and his wife failed to deal with their problems effectively, the Creator stepped in and separated them for the time being.

Hashem can't evict the wife and mother from the home; that's neither proper nor practical. So, the husband was the one who was evicted. This break in tension gives him and his wife the peace and space that they need to think, to do some serious introspection, to take counsel, understand, learn and to correct their lives. In truth, the Creator has done them a great kindness in that now they have a chance to work on themselves, to take a timeout and to relieve tension without the situation escalating into divorce. The husband should know that everything Hashem is doing is **a great favor for him.**

The third level of emuna is asking: "What does Hashem want from me?" Now, free of the pressures and tension of the home, the husband can work on himself. He can learn what his mistakes were and look for the root of the problems. He can pray about the situation, work on himself and fix whatever needs fixing. If he truly repents, then the one who truly evicted him – the Creator – will send him back home again.

From here, one must learn to deal with problems while they are still small. Especially with difficulties in marital peace, one must immediately apply the three levels of emuna and not wait for a crisis. That way, small problems don't mushroom into major crises. The husband will save himself, his wife and his children tons of anguish, emotional damage and grief.

Listening to the Hints

Usually, it's difficult for an evicted husband to accept his lot with emuna. But the fact that he reached the point of eviction is a sign that he's been far from emuna. Clearly, he wasn't listening to the subtle hints that the Creator was sending him along the way. The husband failed to acknowledge his mistakes and work on his shortcomings. Therefore, he cannot handle the disparagement of being thrown out of his own house because he can't acknowledge the truth...

Hashem always starts off with gentle hints. If we don't pay attention, the hints get louder. If we're still not aroused, we get a slap. A man who got to the stage of being evicted already had many slaps. With emuna, he would have looked for the message that The Creator was sending him via the arguments with his wife and her complaints. He would have listened carefully to his wife's words, tried to get to the root of the problem, and then done something about it. He would've prevented the situation from deteriorating.

It's clear that he didn't pay attention to the hints and now finds himself on the wrong side of the front door. Why? He was always looking at his wife's faults rather than looking at his own and correcting them. As it is, it's hard for him to accept the current situation with faith, because he's now kicked out.

Everything's OK with Me

Sometimes a husband feels that he's behaving fine at home and doing his best. He therefore dismisses his wife's complaints. His self-appraisal is meaningless; his wife's feelings are what counts, and she's not happy - period! Her happiness is his responsibility. If she isn't happy then he must find out why and do something about it.

A mechanic can work hard all day to fix an engine. He may change all the parts and feel that he's done everything he should to ensure its smooth functioning. But if the engine still doesn't work, he hasn't done his job. Can he say that he's done his job, like the surgeon who said that the operation was successful but the patient died? Of course not; until the engine runs properly, the mechanic's job is not over. The Creator runs the world with exacting, individual Divine providence and justice.

So, if a wife is unhappy, her husband still has something to rectify. Blaming her won't solve anything; it will only make the problem worse.

Lack of Emuna is the Only Difficulty

When someone without emuna goes through such a crisis, he gets entangled in a web of mistakes and misery. He may blame his wife and go around angry, thinking how to take revenge. Or he may be very broken-hearted and long for his wife and children, and harbor feelings of misery, loneliness, and self-pity. With emuna, he would have understood that his current situation is entirely for his own good. If he loves his wife, he should make the most of the time that the Creator has given him. He must learn how to avoid upsetting her in the future; how to listen to her, how to honor her; and how to make her happy.

Lack of peace in the home greatly damages children's inner strength and self-confidence - their two main tools in life. An evicted father's love for his children should therefore motivate him to improve himself so that when he returns home he won't repeat the mistakes that destroyed his home previously.

Terrible, Irresponsible Advice

In situations like this, many irresponsible advisors join in along the way - family members, friends, acquaintances - each with his or her warped ideas as to how the evicted husband should behave. One urges him to divorce his wife, the second to stop sending her money. His mother tells him: "You're too good for her. She's taking advantage of your good heart." All this terrible and irresponsible advice leads to one thing only - the destruction of a home that could have been saved, had they followed the path of emuna.

The only true advice for him is to start, from now, to act like a human being. He should be good to his wife and not expect anything in return. He must send her money and make sure that she and the children are not lacking anything. He must maintain contact with the children, comfort them and tell them to listen to their mother. The worst possible thing to do would be to upset his wife, or to use the children as weapons against her.

A New Start

True, one's difficult situation is due to one's own big mistakes. But once the mistake is made, one can start to follow the path of emuna, and to rectify the situation. If the husband now strengthens himself with faith and doesn't get discouraged, he will clearly see Hashem's loving hand of Divine providence and begin to tangibly see how this situation is for his ultimate good.

A Wonderful Gift

The evicted husband now has the time and the quiet that he needs to contemplate and fix whatever needs repair.

Sometimes it's debts that trigger problems in the home. He now has the opportunity to quietly seek a solution to his debt problems, without all the friction that he had at home.

A negative character trait often destroys domestic peace. Maybe he has a quick temper, or is lazy, stingy or ungrateful. Now, he has the time to work on himself and correct these traits.

If he has a serious problem like addiction to drugs, alcohol, or gambling, or if he is violent, now he has the free time he needs to seek help and to try to uproot these problems. With emuna, the evicted husband is undaunted. He sees the current predicament as a golden opportunity to improve his life and the life of his family. He uses his time the best way he can, and he prays hard and long that the Creator should help him to rectify whatever needs rectification.

When the Creator sees that he's doing his part, his wife will too, and this will give her hope. The evicted husband won't have to make any effort to return home, because the wife herself will chase after him to return. When he does return home, and continues to devote serious effort to self-improvement, their relationship will be infinitely better. He'll then see that the "tragedy" was actually an amazing gift from the Creator, an opportunity to make a new beginning. He can only receive this gift properly if he has emuna.

Haste Makes Waste

It's very important that the husband not be impatient and try to return home too soon. Instead, he should believe that Hashem will know when he's ready to return and will send him a sign. In the meanwhile, he must wait patiently for Hashem's salvation and continue to make the most of this opportunity to improve and rectify. That way, when he does return home it will be with his wife's wholehearted agreement.

Even if he thinks that he needs to be at home to deal with certain urgent problems, such as debts and payments, he mustn't return home for these purposes. He should deal with them from wherever he is. Debts and other pressures place a strain on even the best of relationships. The Creator evicted him because He knew that the husband could only effectively deal with his problems outside the home in a quiet environment. He needs to accept this lovingly, using his time patiently and prudently for prayer, soul-searching, penitence and doing what needs to be done.

I Accuse

Understandably, a person with emuna doesn't blame anyone for his problems with his wife. Even if it seems that others are at least partially to blame in such situations, and they incited his wife against him, he doesn't blame them. Maybe his in-laws slandered him to his wife, encouraged her to throw him out and supported her in the process. His wife's divorced friends did the same. It often seems that the whole community plotted against him. It's still up to him to rectify.

Had his wife been happy, she wouldn't have told her problems to anyone else, especially her parents. A happy wife is one who knows that she can turn to her husband for everything, and who is confident that she will get his full support. Such a wife isn't interested in other people's advice. Her husband is her father, mother and best friend all rolled into one. She knows that he is always there, by her side, ready to listen to her, understand her and support her. When a wife feels that her husband is her best friend in the world, nothing and no one can separate them.

Understand full well - the wife must feel that her husband is her very best friend in the world. This makes her feel secure. With a husband like that, she doesn't need to confide in girlfriends, for he is the one who always understands her and always gives her a listening ear. But, when a husband behaves like a state's attorney whenever his wife tells him anything, interrogating her, pointing out her faults and making her feel guilty, it doesn't take much to convince her that she'd be happier without him.

When a wife needs to pour her heart out to her friends, it's a sign that she doesn't feel comfortable telling her husband everything. When she needs her parents' support, it's a sign that she doesn't feel sufficiently supported by her husband, and when she spends hour upon hour on the telephone, it's a sign that she doesn't have her husband's listening ear.

Since we've learned that everything depends on the husband, some of our readers might possibly feel depressed and guilty. This is not our intention, Heaven forbid. Even if you did make many mistakes - depression, despair and self-persecution aren't the way to improve things. The way forward is to learn what mistakes you made and then make a new start. Commit to mending your old ways and pray to the Creator to help you step by step in repairing the relationship with your wife and rectifying whatever was wrong.

A Plan for Recovery

We will now present a recovery plan for an evicted husband, which outlines how he needs to behave in order to successfully pass this test with emuna. This plan works for weathering all trying situations in life successfully.

First, the husband must immediately alter any negative behavior towards his wife. If until now he's been stingy, tight-fisted and cruel, from now on he must give to his wife with an open hand. He should give her more than she needs and even send her presents. If he can speak to her, he should assure her that he takes full responsibility for the situation and is doing everything he can to remedy it. If he can speak to the children he should reassure them that he hasn't abandoned them, and never would, and explain to them that he needs to be away from home for the time being to sort certain things out. He should tell them that he has every intention of returning home and encourage them to listen to their mother and help her. In short, he should act like a responsible gentleman.

Here's our 5-stage plan for recovery:

1. **Emuna**: Once his negative behavior has stopped, the first stage in his work on himself is to pray profusely that he be able to accept everything that's happening to him with emuna, that this is from Hashem and that he should look at no one else, not even himself. This is what He wanted. Such belief leaves no room for blame - whether of himself or of others - nor for anger, depression or despair. When this belief is firmly in place - he strengthens his emuna and is calm and composed - he is ready to progress to the next level.
2. **Learning**: Learn the rules of peace in the home by carefully studying the book "The Garden of Peace", which I devoted to this issue, and by listening to my recorded lectures on this topic, particularly "Respecting Your Wife" and "First Place". The focus should be on learning what mistakes he made with his wife and how he should avoid them in the future. He should learn the book and listen to the CDs repeatedly in order to know what to correct and what to pray for, and not for the purpose of remorse and blaming himself.

3. **Soul searching and repentance:** Designate a time every day to pray about the situation, and to ask the Creator to forgive him for the pain he caused his wife and children. One should assess in detail exactly what he's done wrong according to what he's learned and ask Hashem to instill in his wife's heart a willingness to forgive him and to give him another chance. He needs to put as much effort as he can into these prayers.

4. **Internalization:** One must internalize what he's learned. This means reviewing over and over the points where he was making mistakes, and the new approach that he needs to adopt. He also needs to pray for each point, namely, that the Creator help liberate him from his old negative behavior patterns, and also help him to adopt the new, positive ones.

For example: one of the fundamental rules of peace in the home is to never make any negative comments to one's wife. Fulfilling this requires extensive prayer. Man has a natural tendency to comment to everyone in his environment about whatever mistakes he sees them make, and to point out whatever flaws he thinks they have. Husbands often think that they have an obligation to point out their wife's flaws and mistakes, to help them grow. Such comments don't correct anything. All they do is destroy a wife's self-confidence and bring her to the conclusion that her husband doesn't love her. This causes a wife terrible suffering, because her deepest need is to feel that she is perfect in her husband's eyes.

Therefore, the husband must pray in the following manner:

"Master of the World, thank You for removing me from my home and for giving me the opportunity to correct my mistakes. Please, dear G-d, help me to stand up to the tests in my home. You've taught me that it's forbidden to make any comments to my wife, but I find it so hard to fulfill this. Every time I see my wife making a mistake or doing anything that I don't like, my heart fills with arrogance and I want to tell her what I feel she's doing wrong. This makes me feel superior, that I'm better than her. I behave cruelly and make unfair comments to her. Sometimes I do this without even realizing. Until now, I've always justified myself that it's correct to make these comments to her.

"Please, merciful King, have mercy on me and on my wife and my children and grant me wisdom and understanding to know that comments only destroy, and don't fix anything. Help me to realize that every comment that I make to my wife is an insult that deeply hurts her; and that what I am doing is destroying her self-confidence and positive self-image. My comments bring her to tears, and we fight and argue. This destroys the peace in our home which hurts the children too.

"Please, Creator of the World, have mercy on me and give me the spiritual and mental strength not to make any comments to my wife about anything, ever, in any place or under any circumstances. Help me understand and remember that my wife is my mirror and that any shortcomings that I see in her are really mine. Help me realize that even the things that she really does need to change won't be changed through my comments and rebukes, but only by me giving her more honor and love. Help me identify the root of the problem in myself and pray to You to help me fix it. Help me believe that the more love I give to my wife and the more I honor her, the more she'll change for the good, but only when I refrain from making comments. Help me praise her constantly and sincerely speak to her with words of love, more and more.

"Please, help me to overcome my evil inclination to comment and criticize. Help me rid myself of this cruel trait of seeing my wife's shortcomings and mistakes and commenting to her about them. Help me see all the good she does and her genuine beauty. Help me to sincerely value her, to honor her, to support her and to praise her. Let me prefer to throw myself into a fiery furnace, rather than shame my wife."

In this manner he should pray for all of the fundamental points, for without them, there cannot be peace in the home.

5. Waiting: The "exiled" husband should work on the above four stages for an extended period, and meanwhile do whatever he can for his wife without expecting any acknowledgement or appreciation from her. He must be patient. When the time is right, Hashem will arrange for his safe return home. The crucial point of this test is for the husband to avoid forcing the issue and to believe that only Hashem will decide when it's time for him to return home. Despite his efforts, even if from her side things are only getting worse, he mustn't be discouraged. He should just do his part with emuna and keep going, praying and being good to her. If he truly does all that he can, eventually his wife will herself ask him to return home and they will have peace. Their life together won't be like it was previously; it will be completely new, as if they just got married.

To conclude this section, it's important to stress some of the points that we have learned, which are applicable to all situations in life:

1. Deal with problems while they are still small and don't wait for a crisis.
2. The only way to deal with problems is by applying the three levels of emuna and particularly by applying the element of teshuva.
3. With emuna we see how even the greatest crisis is for our good.

Divorce

This section is a must for those who desire true peace in the home and marital success as well as for those who are contemplating divorce or are about to be divorced. If you're divorced already, then this section will help you plan and manage your life from now onwards.

One of this generation's eldest and wisest spiritual leaders said that the alarmingly high contemporary divorce rate is the result of a pampered generation that doesn't realize that marital success requires hard work and effort. Therefore, following every little spat, they run to divorce court.

The venerable rabbi said: "We also had our share of difficulties, misunderstandings, and quarrels, but we never considered the option of breaking up the marriage. Our goal was to build a successful relationship; we were therefore prepared to invest the needed efforts to reach our goal. Thank G-d, we succeeded in weathering everything. We raised our children and married them off, seeing grandchildren and great grandchildren, all of whom are a source of joy for us. Had we lacked the patience and perseverance required in dealing with all the difficulties in marriage, we wouldn't have reaped all these wonderful fruits."

From here each person must learn to correct the misconception that a good marriage is automatic. Couples with problems look at happy couples as if they've been enjoying a happy marriage from day one; that's far from the truth. Even a marriage between two righteous people of impeccable character is plagued with its share of tension and disagreements. Any human being must learn to compromise and sacrifice in order to make peace and create a happy environment with a second human being.

Marriage doesn't begin and end with the wedding ceremony and reception. A couple must be prepared to learn and to work on themselves. If they do, there's no reason in the world that they should ever reach a situation of divorce. Problems begin when one or both sides are in denial of what they must rectify and aren't willing to invest the needed effort in building a peaceful and loving relationship.

The Eye of Emuna

Since the purpose of creation is emuna, and the Creator wants each of us to fulfill our purpose, He therefore presents us with opportunities to learn and to develop emuna. Marriage is the prime training ground of emuna. Therefore, by learning the principles of emuna, one maximizes the chances of success in marriage.

Conversely, the lack of emuna is the root cause of divorce. A person has tribulations within his home; instead of solving the problems that bring about the tribulations and rectifying what needs rectification, he thinks that divorce is the solution to his ills. He is doing nothing more than trading one set of problems for another. Trading marital problems for divorce problems is not a good deal, for the latter is much more difficult.

As long as a person fails to make amends and rectify past misdeeds, marital suffering is perpetuated. The best marital counseling won't help a person who fails to atone; it's like pouring fine wine into a filthy glass. Without atonement, divorce won't bring relief to a person either.

No one can escape from Hashem. Consequently, divorce without atonement only makes a person's life more unbearable, for since he didn't rectify what he should have and now, his tribulations will further intensify. As Rebbe Nachman of Breslev is quoted as saying, if a person isn't prepared to suffer a bit, then he or she will end up suffering a lot.

Proper Marital Guidance

As long as two people are still married, almost any problem - as difficult as it may be - can be solved with proper marital instruction.

Tens of thousands of couples can testify to the power of proper marital instruction, which saved them from a myriad of marital problems, even divorce, even after they began divorce proceedings. These couples merited the Heavenly gift of proper coaching, and they read my books "The Garden of Peace" (for men) and "Women's Wisdom" (for women), as well as listening to my CDs on the subject. Their lives changed dramatically for the better and they built healthy marital relationships and happy homes.

The power of emuna-oriented marital coaching is so strong that when warring couples come to me, I don't let them tell me their complaints about each other. I simply ask them to first listen to our CD recordings on the subject and to read the above-mentioned respective manuals for men or for women. If they still have problems afterwards, only then should they return to me.

The reality is that no one comes back. Why? Once a person receives proper instruction that includes penitence, guidelines for a healthy relationship and an emuna perspective, he realizes that his complaints about his partner are baseless. He understands the mistakes he made and learns how to correct them and to avoid repeating them in the future. He therefore is not in need of further counseling for he has the tools to build a happy marriage. So many of these people say that they're sorry they didn't learn the emuna guidelines for healthy relationships years before, for it would have saved them tons of suffering...

Wounds of the Heart

A couple who is considering divorce should know what they're getting into - the type of problems that they'll have to contend with. Therefore, we'll mention here briefly some of the tribulations that divorcees must deal with.

Divorcees frequently wake up after the fact, for after the divorce, they can't forget their ex-partner. They have difficulty in starting anew and in building new relationships. Once the divorce is completed, many divorcees feel a gaping wound in their heart. They have difficulty adjusting to their new situation, for the pangs of longing and loneliness give them no rest. When the smoke of the divorce battle clears, they find themselves more miserable without their mate than they were while still married.

One woman told me, "I was looking forward to divorce as if it were a release from prison. But after the divorce, I felt a terrible pain, a gnawing emptiness. I felt as if one of my limbs had been amputated." This woman experienced a true feeling, for the souls of a couple are essentially one; when the two split up, their souls are severed from one another; this is tantamount to undergoing heart surgery with no anesthetic - it's torture...

Loneliness lingers. Before the divorce, people tend to entertain all types of fantasies about the rosy future and the dream second-marriage that awaits them. Once the divorce is over, they discover that their personal value on the mate market is a lot lower than they previously thought. Men aren't standing in line for divorced women, especially those with children. Conversely, women are wary of divorced men. Divorce is a serious stigma that complicates finding a new mate.

Divorcees won't admit it, but many of them regret their divorces and would turn the clocks back in time if they only could.

Remove Anger from Your Heart

There's also the opposite of those who long for their ex; they can't forget and they can't forgive. Their hearts are full of hatred and anger that they harbor toward their ex-mates.

As long as one side harbors hatred, both sides will suffer. Hatred and anger invoke stern judgments both on the person who hates and on the hated. Therefore, from a spiritual standpoint, a divorce solves nothing when hate and resentment linger on afterwards. Sins between man and fellow man are the number one cause of problems in life. Accordingly, the ongoing feud robs both sides of inner peace and any semblance of joy in life until they make amends with one another. So what good has divorce done? That which they should have done while married - namely, to make peace and to forgive each other - they'll still have to do after they divorce.

In short, as long as a person is married - no matter how difficult the situation - things can be corrected. Once there's no more home, there's no love, unity, or base to build upon; problems fester and become worse. While still married, it's much easier to make peace. After a divorce, forgiving and forgetting - a must for both sides in order to rebuild their broken lives - is a most difficult task. Often, the wounds of the heart never heal.

End of the Conflict or the Beginning?

Divorce is not the end of the war, like many think; it's only the beginning of strife that lasts for a lifetime.

New problems and new tensions continually sprout, especially in the areas of educating their mutual children. These are problems that would never had occurred had the couple stayed together in marriage.

Family affairs, such as birthday parties, weddings and engagement parties become nightmares. Preparing the guest list is like walking in a minefield - if you invite this one, then his ex-wife will explode; if you invite her and her new boyfriend, then he'll explode. The arguments and bickering about seating arrangements are enough to cause anyone a migraine. Former spouses are placed in embarrassing situations where they have to encounter former and frequently hostile in-laws. Second wives and husbands are forced to mingle with ex-wives and husbands. As such, divorcees usually dread affairs that married people eagerly anticipate their entire lives.

Every time a divorced couple has to meet again, such as on the occasion of a child's graduation or family affair, old wounds are torn open. Long-forgotten memories return to haunt them. When they see their "ex" with a new spouse, jealousy and bitterness eat away at their hearts. Mixed feelings of anger and revenge rob them of their happiness.

Conflicting interests in the divorced couple's relationship with their mutual children is a minefield of problems. Even with contractual agreement and court orders, visitation always presents practical problems and becomes a bone of contention. Money and child support are even worse; new problems always arise that weren't defined in the divorce agreement, such as who will pay for the child's summer camp or swimming lessons. No one is ever happy. Divorcees are known to manipulate children as weapons. The custody fights, the limited visitations, the misunderstandings and the constant haggling never seem to end. Everyone in the family suffers endlessly...

Divorced couples have extreme difficulty in coping with routine problems - such as a child's health or learning impairment - that married couples take in stride. Such challenges also trigger arguments and accusations, where one side accuses the other of neglecting the children, not loving them, and so forth. Had the couple stayed together, they could have solved the problems so much easier. Their "dream solution" - divorce - turns out to be nothing other than a nightmare.

The Real Solution

Consequently, before taking the irreversible step of divorce, a couple should stop and think: do they want to slaughter their children on the altar of their false pride, or do they want to admit to the truth, that they don't know how to live together properly? With some basic instruction and good will, a person can save his or her own life, as well as the lives of their children. They'll also save tens, even hundreds of thousands of dollars. All they need is to swallow a bit of pride and to express the willingness to start anew. With proper instruction, many couples have made a happy new beginning.

Lack of Knowledge

Most divorces are caused by the husband's ignorance of the principles of peace in the home. For example, a husband who isn't guilty of extreme behavior - he's not a wife-beater or a criminal, makes a living, and is faithful - can still fall on his face in marriage if he criticizes and is constantly finding fault with his wife. He turns her life into a living death.

With even minimal instruction on marital success, a husband will learn that the first rule of peace in the home is to refrain from criticizing his wife, even when the situation is perfectly justified. A woman wants to feel loved and respected; criticism - even the slightest - does the opposite. Even worse, it makes a woman nervous and destroys her self-confidence. Through criticism and finding fault - as justified as it might be - a husband destroys both his wife and his marriage with his own two hands. He should therefore never criticize her.

After criticism, the second culprit behind an unhappy marriage is the husband's unwillingness and/or impatience to listen to his wife. With no mate to talk to or to share the burdens that weigh heavy on her heart, a wife is doomed to frustration and unhappiness. When she sees how her husband animatedly listens to other people, she becomes sorely insulted. Her entire aspirations in marriage were to find a soul-mate who would make her happy and illuminate her soul. With a husband who doesn't respect or cherish her enough to give her minimal attention, she loses all will to stay married.

Children are not even a consolation for a woman who feels unloved, neglected, and disrespected. Even though she has a deep dread of divorce, she'll demand it at all costs when she sees a hopeless future. A woman prefers loneliness to a purgatory of constant criticism and humiliation.

After the wife explodes and demands a divorce, the amazed but ignorant husband shrugs his shoulders in innocence and asks, "What did I do wrong?" He can't possibly know how he broke the rules of marital peace if he never learned them. He must therefore receive proper counseling and instruction immediately.

Licentiousness and Adultery

Many divorces are the result of the husband's lust, which entices him to abandon the wife of his youth and his children for a new woman. The evil inclination paints a portrait in his imagination of the beautiful, enchanting and euphoric life that will be his when he goes off with the new 'love' that he's found. It will surely be like living in the Garden of Eden. What the evil inclination doesn't tell him is that once he does abandon his family and goes after the 'new' love, the 'Garden of Eden' that he expected will turn out to be a fiery furnace of purgatory.

If he begins a relationship with this other woman while he's still married, he'll get a taste of the hell that awaits him: his home will be full of tension and arguments and his children will start to show the signs of the emotional problems that are in store. The Heavenly court is infuriated by such behavior, for the Creator despises immorality, which destroys the world. On the contrary, the Creator loves fidelity, which builds the world. The adulterous husband can therefore expect severe punishments on his body, soul and possessions for the sin he commits against the Creator and against his wife and children.

If the unfaithful husband goes on to divorce his wife and marry this other woman, the image of paradise will soon crumble before his eyes. The sweetness and understanding she showed him will disappear and be replaced by her true character. Now that she has no rival, she has no need to put on a show. Lo and behold, she's a woman like all others. She wants respect, pampering, attention, love and honor. When she's upset, she shouts and insults him. The romance is gone, substituted by her constant complaining that he doesn't give her enough. If he couldn't live peacefully with his first wife, he'll do no better with this one.

Even more so, the Creator's Divine assistance vanishes from the husband who so terribly caused sorrow to his first wife. The pain that he caused her arouses such a severe accusation against him in Heaven that he'll never again be left to enjoy a minute of peace, not in this world or the next.

Note that a husband needn't arrive at such extreme levels of betrayal to ruin the peace with his wife. Marriage is founded on absolute faithfulness. Any and all friendly relationships with other women, however innocent they may seem, damage the relationship with one's wife. When faithfulness is lost, everything else collapses.

Who is the Trouble-Maker?

Sometimes divorce appears to be the result of a relative's meddling that made trouble between the couple. It really makes no difference what the apparent reason or cause was. The bottom line is (except in rare cases) that **the husband is responsible.** If he would live with the emuna that there are no tribulations without prior transgressions, he would repent. This, coupled with learning the rules of peace in the home, would assure him of peace with his wife. Consequently, the people who until now had fueled the crisis between the husband and wife would then either turn around and support them or would fade out of their lives. By virtue of sincere penitence, they would merit a peaceful home.

Trauma of the Soul

Divorce plunges the soul into a deep trauma that requires a long recovery time. Hurt feelings, a sense of failure and painful disappointment about the hopes and dreams for the future that have been shattered fill the divorced person's heart. We frequently encounter divorcees who still carry their pain around with them wherever they go - years after the divorce, their wound still hasn't healed.

The Talmud therefore states that when a man divorces his first wife, the altar sheds tears for them (Gittin, 90b). It's a tragedy when the soul's deepest connection is severed and broken.

It's not Too Late

With all the above in mind, a man should do everything possible, and concede whatever he needs to, in order to save his marriage and avoid divorce.

A man who didn't get this book in time and is already divorced shouldn't think that he has no hope and no way to start anew - not at all. **There is a way to correct the past and prepare him for a new, brighter future.**

Know, dear friend - maybe you've given up hope, but the Creator hasn't given up hope on you. He has a wonderful plan for you, if you'll only choose the path of emuna.

Never forget this important rule of life: **If you believe that you ruined things, then believe that you can fix them again!**

True, until today you made lots of mistakes. You were destructive, both to yourself and to others. But now you're different; you recognize where you went wrong. Put the past behind you and make a new start. Learn to live with faith and prepare yourself for a new life and a new path that awaits you.

Look Forward

A divorcee must look ahead. This is the only way that he will be able to cope with life and build himself anew. Though he's been through a trauma and still must deal with problems from the past, he must accept everything with faith and now focus on what the Creator wants from him henceforth. The Creator expects him to carry on with his mission in life, which is the purpose of his being in this world.

This is a rule for all situations - whatever has happened has happened. Once we've repented and done our best to rectify, we must leave the past behind us and move on. We focus on our next step and how we can continue the journey of our life from this point on with emuna, as the Creator desires.

Forgiving and Asking Forgiveness

One of the first things a divorced couple must do is to forgive one another. Why? As long as a divorced couple harbors resentment or bitterness in their hearts against one another, they won't be able to move forward and rebuild their lives. Sins between man and his fellow man are more severe than sins between man and G-d. The latter are relatively easy to fix by confession, regret and a resolution to not repeat the act. But the former are harder to correct. One is therefore required to appease the person he or she wronged and to go to great lengths to gain their forgiveness.

It's essential that the couple fully forgive one another. If the husband hurt his wife he must do everything he can to appease her and gain her forgiveness. She in turn should not be stubborn; she should be willing to forgive him, even though she was the one wronged, since harboring resentment will only boomerang and prolong everyone's agony.

If you ask: "If she was the one wronged, why should she forgive? And why should her agony continue? She's justified in her anger." The answer is that not forgiving someone shows a lack of emuna and creates a severance with the Creator. If the husband or wife who hurt their partner is now severed from Hashem, they won't be able to live a good life.

Everyone should believe that all suffering in life comes directly from the Creator, to arouse us to repent and atone for our sins. Suffering is never random. Indeed, it's the precise outcome of exact Divine providence. Therefore, we must forgive anyone that causes us pain, for that person who brought about the suffering was only an agent in the Creator's hands.

Remember! Whoever hurt you is an unfortunate person that has been chosen to be a rod in the Hashem's hands because of his sins. Nevertheless, the pain you receive is connected to your ledger with the Creator because of your transgressions. Therefore, when we're not willing to forgive the agent, we are in effect saying that the afflictions came from him or her and not from Hashem. This is heresy. If the agent asks our forgiveness, we should grant it.

Learning from Past Mistakes

A divorced man must accept that what happened until now was the Creator's will and all for the best. He should focus on the present and future and ask himself: "Now that I'm already divorced, what does the Creator want from me? That I should be broken? That I should go around with thoughts of hatred, despair or self-persecution? Or does he want me to put the past behind me, and to start a new chapter in my life, a chapter of emuna and closeness to Him?"

Once he realizes that he still has a life to lead, he can learn from the past to make decisions for the future. He can learn where he went wrong and how he needs to behave now, in order to avoid falling into the same traps. He should ask the Creator's forgiveness for his misdeeds and ask Him to implant a willingness in his ex-spouse's heart to forgive him as well. He should resolve to avoid repeating old mistakes. From now on, he should act with emuna and common sense. He might merit to remarry her, but even if he doesn't, his penitence and prayers will help his future.

Once he has done all this he can pray in the following manner:

"Master of the World, if my ex-wife and I still have a joint mission, help us rectify what needs to be rectified in each of us. Enable us to reconcile, remarry and live in peace and love. Everything is in Your hands and You have many ways to make peace between a man and a woman. And if our correction together is complete, have mercy on us that we should each find a new partner and live lives of emuna, through which we will merit happiness, peace and tranquility."

What Will be with the Children?

One of the extremely difficult problems that divorced couples sometimes face is when the children are put in the custody of the father or mother, who then doesn't take proper care of them, whether physically - as in cases of neglect or abuse - or spiritually, when the parent has abandoned religion and is giving the child an education that goes against the wishes of the other partner.

Apparently, there's no greater problem than this; understandably, the parent who doesn't have custody of the children is broken. But, that's not the way! It's also not truth, for no one should let any problem - as difficult as it is - ruin his life, for that solves nothing. But, with persistent prayer, one can overturn any harsh decree, see all salvations and help others as well.

There's a hair-raising story about the Cantonist Decrees, when Jewish children from the Ukraine were seized from their homes and forcibly taken for a minimum of twenty-five years of service in the Russian Army. Few returned...

Five-year old's, who knew nothing other than their mother's apron, were transported to Russian Army camps, falling into the hands of the cruelest of commanders under the most horrific conditions imaginable. Few ever saw their parents again. Most of those who survived led lives as gentiles, with no remaining traces of their Jewish origin.

Naturally, Jewish parents did everything to hide or smuggle their children away from the Czar's henchmen, who would periodically make surprise searches in Jewish towns and villages, never coming away empty-handed. The alarmed children would be ripped sadistically from the clutch of their parents who wailed and shrieked for mercy, then thrown into wagons like sheep. The parents' cries fell on cold and deaf hearts. The heart of any witness to this tragedy would wither with sorrow.

One woman, whose son was kidnapped by the Czar's soldiers, ran to the local synagogue. She opened the holy Ark of the Torah scrolls and howled like a wounded animal until her soul left her body, Heaven forbid...

The word of the dead mother jolted the village. When the story was told to Rabbi Natan of Nemirov, of saintly and blessed memory, who prayed profusely that this terrible decree should be rescinded, he said: "If she would have come to me, I would have advised her to strengthen herself and set aside daily time to pray for her son so that he should return to her. Her prayer would not only have helped her son, but it would have benefitted other children as well."

We learn from the above story that even when a child is abducted and cruelly forced into the Russian Army, even then, a parent should pray with composure and believe that prayer is the only solution. Daily perseverance in prayer can nullify any evil edict. It will also lead to additional salvations and benefit others as well.

Life Goes On

When children are not in a particular parent's custody and he suspects that they are not receiving proper care, even though the parent's worry is justified, he or she must decide: "I'm doing all that I can for my children. I'm providing for them financially, I'm visiting as much as I can and I'm giving them attention and love. Apart from praying for them, which I do every day, I can't do any more. Nerves or loss of temper won't help me." The parent should pray for the health, success and happiness of the children every day for a fixed amount of time, and then turn his attention to other things. Waging wars with lawyers and the like will only make the situation worse.

Prayer is the only advice for such a parent, and his or her prayers will help more than anything else. I know many people who came from broken homes who turned out to be successful, happy, capable people in the merit of the prayers of one of their parents.

With prayer we can achieve anything. A divorcee should entrust his children into Hashem's loving hands and pray to Him, saying:

"Master of the World, even if the children were still under my care, I would need to pray for Your mercy that they should grow up properly. And now that they aren't in my care, I'm placing them in Your hands. I believe that wherever they are, You are watching over them. Please have mercy on them and instill in their hearts to follow the right path. Keep them away from bad friends. Give them good friends and bring them close to You. Let them find favor and grace in Your eyes and in the eyes of all who see them. Fill their hearts with pure and simple emuna, and help them to grow up with good character traits and to lead upright, righteous lives," and so forth.

Emuna is the cure for all sorrows, whether before the decree or after it. Happy is the one who lives his life with perfect faith.

Child Education – Personal Example

Personal parental example is a vital aspect of child education. A couple once came to the "Chofetz Chaim" in Radin, Belarus asking him to bless their newborn baby that he should grow up to be a righteous scholar. He asked why they were so late in coming. The couple was bewildered. Why late? The baby's only a month old! The "Chofetz Chaim" told them that they should have come to him twenty years earlier. Again, the couple didn't understand; twenty years ago, they were only toddlers. The "Chofetz Chaim" was in effect telling them that they won't be able to give their child anything that they don't possess themselves. If they want their child to be an upright Torah scholar, then they must be sincere upright lovers of Torah who do their utmost to observe Hashem's commandments.

The couple frowned, obviously disheartened. "Don't worry," the "Chofetz Chaim" consoled them. "I wanted you to internalize an important principle. If from this day on, you do the very best to polish your character traits and grow in love of Torah and awe of Hashem, your reward will be double: You'll see success in your own lives, and you'll derive gratification from all your offspring, who'll grow in the path of righteousness."

The foundation of educating our children is educating ourselves. Whatever we desire to impart on our children, "If we live it, we can give it". We therefore can properly educate our children only after we've educated ourselves.

Education is Love

Our sages say (Avot 1:12), "Love your fellow human beings and bring them close to the Creator." The way to bring others closer to the Creator is with love. Since our children are also "fellow human beings", the only way to bring them close to the Creator is with love.

A child who is loved is a child that will grow in self-confidence. He loves himself and believes in himself, for these are the traits that become the basis of good character. Since his soul is healthy and happy, he has the power to give to others, to understand others and to yield to them. A person without these capabilities that were attained by virtue of parental love won't act with courtesy or consideration toward other people. As such, parental love is the key to a child's success in every area of life, his entire life long.

Education with Emuna

The most important aspect of child education is parental personal example, which means good character traits - the result of emuna. Education with love is therefore possible only when a parent is pleased with his or her lot in life. If not, the parents won't be happy, they won't love their own lives and therefore won't be able to love their children. Consequently, loving one's children is dependent on the parental level of emuna. Once parents educate themselves in emuna, they'll be able to truly love their children and teach them emuna.

Cruelty is not Education

A common and unfortunate mistake that many parents make is confusing criticism and chastisement with education. According to their warped view, one must be cruel to a child and humiliate him in order to teach him a lesson. They also compare him to other children, saying, "Why can't you be like him?" The outcome of such "education" is tragic. The child loses his positive self-image and the power to be good; so much so that there are children who'd prefer to terminate their lives, for they have no power to keep on living. No words can describe the damages that these skewed methods of so-called education cause to children.

Many of these types of mistakes result from the parents' desire that their child behave like a miniature adult. They forget that the child is but a child and that his childish mischief is totally healthy and normal. If they would only remember that they were once children, they could tolerate their child's mischief and allow him to enjoy his childhood with joy.

Therefore, if a person knows how to educate - to love, to rejoice and to inculcate good desires and self-confidence in the child as well as love for himself and the desire to improve and achieve - then indeed, let him educate! But if he doesn't know, and his entire approach to his children is negative - full of admonition, humiliation and yelling - then he shouldn't be the one who educates his children. The damages he'll do are worse than no education at all.

Here's an ironclad rule - if you don't know how to educate properly, don't educate! You won't do any good - you'll destroy. Better that the child should grow up with no education at all than to receive an "education" that destroys his soul, rendering him devoid of the needed tools to navigate life with joy and good.

Prayer

My own teachers taught me that a child's success depends on the parents' prayers, even more than their efforts in other areas. Just as a person needs profuse prayer for any material request, he must all the more beseech the Creator to help him educate his children. He must pray to be an upright personal example. Even if he has all the resources of money and ability to invest in his children, he must still pray for their proper education for the contemporary world is full of dangers; prayer provides a shield of protection. Parents' prayers instill emuna and the awe of the Creator in children.

Root Treatment

Educating children entails many tests of emuna: a child that doesn't listen to his parents; a child who is cruel to his siblings; a rowdy child; a child who refuses to eat or to wear the clothes that were laid out for him; a child who does anything that the parents consider improper behavior, and other such situations that test the parents' emuna.

Proper education of children obligates the parents to adhere to the three principles of emuna. One must know that the Creator directs the world in a measure-for-measure fashion - He uses the children to show parents what they need to correct. For example, suppose that a son doesn't listen to his father; it's probably because the father doesn't listen to his Father in Heaven, or else he didn't listen to his own parents when he was young. If a child is cruel to others, then the parent probably is/was as well, and so on in each matter.

Practically, a parent should be stimulated to improve himself when he sees a shortcoming in his child. When the parent corrects himself, the child will be corrected automatically. Rebbe Nachman of Breslev teaches (Likutei Moharan I:141) that a parent's heartfelt teshuva and remorse for wrongdoing directly affects his/her child's heart, for the Torah says, "And Hashem your God will circumcise your heart, and the heart of your offspring" (Deuteronomy 30:6). Parents' self-improvement consequently has a major and direct influence on their children.

Yet, in order for a parent to influence his children, his self-improvement must be a "root treatment" and not superficial and cosmetic alone. A parent's sincere efforts at improving himself are the core solution to rectifying a faulty characteristic in the child, especially one that torments the parent. Nothing else - especially force - will solve the problem, which will only grow as the child grows.

Even in the most trying situations, such as that of a cruel sibling who torments his other siblings, which are difficult to accept with emuna, the parent must nonetheless believe that this too is from the Creator. This is what the Creator wants. There are no tribulations without prior transgressions. As difficult as it may be, one must nullify his own desires to those of the Creator. He must believe that the Creator is doing everything for the ultimate best and avoid becoming angry. The root treatment is his only solution. The root treatment entails daily personal prayer where the parent asks the Creator to help him understand what he needs to correct in light of his child's cruelty. Maybe he himself was once cruel or acted cruelly and so forth. He should pray for his child and that the Creator should instill in the child the good sense to act properly and to succeed in life. Don't forget that a person always pays for the evil he does; therefore, the parent must pray that his child doesn't wrong a single human on earth.

The Difficulty of Delinquency

There are situations that break parents' hearts, especially when their children veer from the path of upright conduct. The child might be dating outside of the fold, toying with drugs or falling under the influence of terrible friends, Heaven forbid. We need not list many other difficult situations, all of which break parents' spirits and rob them of their joy in life. These parents must know that they are undergoing a test of emuna and understand that - despite the heartbreaking circumstances - sadness, depression, blaming each other or themselves and bickering are not only unproductive but only make things worse. Why add marital and health problems to the challenge already at hand?

Frequently, delinquent children were beaten cruelly or humiliated when they were younger. Anger and threats won't work with them now. The preferred way is to shower them with love. If the parents reinforce their own faith that everything is from the Creator and for the very best, while implementing the principles that we've learned while trying to rectify themselves and investing as much as they can in prayer, the Creator will have mercy on them and save their child. They will merit seeing their child return to the upright path. Such parents will earn a high score on their test of emuna. If they continue their efforts in prayer and self-betterment even after the situation improves, their child will attain even higher achievements.

On the other hand, a person who doesn't view such challenging situations through eyes of emuna is destined to see yet further deterioration of the situation. He'll fail the test of emuna and will succumb to sorrow and despair. If a person claims to be a believer, then he must believe that the Creator can do anything, including rescuing his child from delinquency, if he only turns to Him in prayer.

Prayer, Personal Example, and Penitence

There are two ways to insure effective parenting. The first is prayer, asking the Creator to lead the child on the right path, to distance him from negative influences and bad friends, to give the child wisdom and understanding and help him learn. The parent should pray that the Creator open the child's heart to the truth, to good character traits and to genuine emuna. The parent should also pray to be a positive role model whose own actions are upright and worth emulating. Such prayer is necessary even if there are no special problems in educating one's children.

The second way is required when a person encounters a challenge in educating his children, when prayer alone doesn't suffice. A parent must seriously repent for whatever transgression that he or she might have committed as indicated in their child's misbehavior. When they do, they are assured that the problem will be solved since they are doing all that they can.

With all the above in mind, only emuna enables parents to properly educate their children. They see educating their children as part of their own relationship with the Creator and understand that child education is simply applied emuna and penitence.

A Worthy Soul-Mate

One of life's tests that many have difficulty with is the area of one's soul-mate. This is a test of emuna that lasts from the time one is searching for a mate until way after the wedding, throughout their entire lives together.

In the test of emuna that finding a soul-mate entails, there are several points that need strengthening. One is the long waiting period until one finds his soul-mate. Don't forget that the Creator's precision individual Divine providence is tailored to one's spiritual correction in this world. As long as one is still single, this is his Divine-sanctioned optimal situation for the meanwhile. This is the best way for him to get closer to the Creator at this time. The same goes for any other deficiency a person has at the moment; one's deficiency is his perfection, for this is the best way for him or her to get close Hashem at this time.

A person's task during this interim waiting period is to focus on his current mission - to attain emuna and to pray for a soul-mate. Each prayer he prays will directly influence his subsequent married life. Therefore, he should pray for each detail. In other words, he shouldn't merely pray to get married, but pray for his soul-mate as well, that they live in harmony and that they will agree on all matters and especially in serving Hashem. He should pray that they both enjoy fertility, that their families get along with one another and all other relevant prayers for those things that help build a proper marriage.

Someone who ponders his mission on earth doesn't rush into marriage. With emuna, his life is full of contentment. His main incentive in getting married is his knowledge that he cannot attain true emuna on his own. Married life is the climate that stimulates a person to climb higher in emuna. He therefore trusts the Creator to send him his soul-mate at the exact proper time. He is happy with his lot in any situation. This person earns a high score in emuna, for he accepts any delay in getting married with love and with joy and does everything that he needs to do. His life is already pleasant in this world and he will surely merit a worthy soul-mate as well as rewards in the World to Come.

On the other hand, the person without emuna blames his delay in getting married on all kinds of natural factors. He knocks his head against the wall in trying to find a soul-mate and falls into hopelessness. He doesn't realize that when it comes time for him to get married, the Creator will send his soul-mate right to his front door; he won't stay single for a split-second more than is destined from Above. Yet, he loses his self-confidence and succumbs to sadness and depression. Therefore, he should pray for emuna and ask, "Master of the World, grant me emuna, that You decide when I'll get married and that You haven't forgotten me. Remind me that You love me and that all the delay is for my ultimate benefit."

Another test is in choosing a soul-mate. A person with common sense knows that he can't possibly know who his designated soul-mate from Above is. He knows that he can't truly know the character traits of the person he has now met until they're living together as one in marriage. He therefore doesn't attempt to investigate too deeply, yet depends on the Creator, and asks: "Master of the World, You know that I can't possibly recognize who my true soul-mate is. Have mercy on me and help me find a suitable mate, so I can get married without unnecessary delays and confusion."

The most important thing is to rely on the Creator and to pray profusely. Those who do will be spared of tons of sorrow and aggravation; they'll merit to get married and to live a life of happiness in marriage.

Social Life

A person undergoes many tests of emuna in the course of his social life: at work with colleagues and superiors; in the army, with his buddies and with his commanders; in school, with friends and teachers; at home, with parents and with siblings, and so forth. There are tests in every area: in monetary matters, when a person is robbed or cheated or when others use his property without permission; with status, when a person is demoted or fails to be promoted, or when he suffers an affront to his dignity.

A person must utilize the three principles of emuna in each and every one of life's tests and believe that everything that is happening to him comes from the Creator. Others are only sticks in Hashem's hand whose purpose is to stimulate us to seek more emuna. One who is aware of this and lives this spiritual fact of life will enjoy inner peace and tranquility; he'll get along with everyone and he'll have a high score in the World to Come.

The unfortunate individual who lacks emuna suffers insult and sorrow so badly that it's difficult for him to be consoled. He is consumed with thoughts of revenge against those who harmed him. He plots all types of responses, but in the end, becomes paranoiac for he thinks that others are pursuing him. He has no peace of mind and is full of anxiety, fears, bitterness and anger. He doesn't seem to last in any job, for he always thinks that the grass is greener elsewhere. This is all for one reason only - he perceives that other people have hurt him.

Don't forget that other people are sticks in the hands of the Creator. Hashem uses them to awaken that person, for as it is written in the Book of Proverbs, "Save the rod and spoil the child"; also, "He shall chastise those whom He loves". Rebbe Nachman of Breslev explains that when a person veers from the upright path, he enters a spiritual labyrinth of wrong roads and dead ends in life that create a degree of confusion and malcontent that make it difficult for him to find his way back to the right path. But, the Creator calls out to him to return, each person according to his or her individual inclinations. To one person, He calls subtly; someone else gets a loud and harsh wake-up call.

When a person with emuna encounters hardships, he examines himself to determine what he must rectify; he attributes his difficulties to his own misdeeds and lack of emuna. He knows that if he turns to the Creator, he'll receive help in correcting whatever he needs to correct. Therefore, he repents and merits salvation. He lives a good life in this world and rewards await him in the next world. But the person without emuna blames his troubles on others; he looks at what other people need to correct as if he himself has already attained perfection. His sorrow is therefore double: he can't rectify the other person and he continues to suffer himself, since he doesn't do what he should. He continues to think that he is suffering because of other people.

The hard-core rule is that whenever we suffer from anything or anyone, **emuna is the only consolation!** There is no one but the Creator, so we must extend our antennae to receive His messages and understand why we are experiencing difficulties. Then, we must act in accordance with the three principles of emuna and pray profusely. Then, we'll succeed without a doubt in our social interactions.

Trust

Hashem directs a person in accordance with that person's level of emuna. If the person believes that Hashem is **the** physician, provider, matchmaker and the source of all abundance, then **the Creator oversees that person with complete individual Divine providence**. But if a person thinks that things depend on him, then the Creator withdraws His individual Divine providence. Hashem leads a person on the path that the person chooses (Tractate Makkot 10b).

When a person trusts in his own prowess, powers and efforts, the Creator removes His Divine providence from him; this is the cause of his failure.

A Chassidic story tells the significance of trusting in and depending on Hashem for everything:

The Baal Shem Tov asked Rebbe Yitzchak of Neshchiz to bring him wine from Bessarabia. Rebbe Yitzchak made the journey, delayed there for the entire two months of the local wine-making season, the months of Elul and Tishri. He closely supervised every phase of the winemaking, without a moment of being sidetracked in any way. He carefully guarded the grape harvest, the crushing of the grapes and the fermentation process, making sure that everything adhered to the strictest level of Kashruth.

The fermentation of the wine continued until after Succoth before the wine was fit to transfer to kegs. Now, with the cold weather and the rainy season setting in, Rebbe Yitzchak encountered untold difficulties on his way back to the Ukraine. Despite rain, sleet, snow, muddy and pock-holed road and sleepless nights, he never let the wine barrels out of his sight. Each mile travelled required total dedication. He finally arrived in Medziboz, the Baal Shem Tov's hamlet, and ran to tell him the good news that he had arrived with the wine.

At the very moment, just as the horses and wagon with the wine kegs on board stood in front of the Baal Shem Tov's house, a Cossack policeman arrived and starting yelling, since transfer and transport of alcoholic beverages was forbidden back then. The policeman – a gentile – inspected the goods while inserting his stick and tasting the wine of each keg, rendering it not kosher (see Shulchan Aruch, Yorah Deah 132:1).

Rebbe Yitzchak's sorrow was beyond description; all his efforts and suffering in fulfilling his holy master's wishes were down the drain. He came into the Baal Shem Tov's room, wailing and heartbroken, asking: "Holy Rebbe! What did I do wrong to deserve this misery and disappointment? I literally gave my life to do the mitzva of making perfectly kosher wine for you. And now, it's all for nothing!"

The Baal Shem Tov replied, "You accrued this punishment because you thought that you were the one who guarded the wine. Understand that no human has the power to guard anything. Sure, you were dedicated and you almost gave your life because you thought that it was up to you. You forget that Hashem is the only Guardsman - everything is in His hands. Sure, your efforts were warranted - you did what religious law required of you. But, you should have prayed, turning to Hashem from the bottom of your heart and asking for His assistance. King David said, "If Hashem doesn't guard a city, the watchman guards in vain" (Psalm 127:1).

We learn from the above story that in every matter of life and in every worry or concern, a person must know that beyond his basic efforts, he has no control over anything for it's all in the hands of the Creator. A person is sorely limited; he therefore must not try to fulfill the function of the Creator. In every endeavor, he should bind himself to the Creator and seek His guidance, channeling all his worries into prayer.

Guard my Children

For example, there are parents who constantly worry about their children and fear for them. They are troubled with fantasies of what might occur to them, Heaven forbid - that they'll be run over by cars or be kidnapped and the like. They feel compelled to be over-protective. Children suffer from such parents. These children learn heresy, as if all their protection comes from their mother or father. They also lose their self-confidence.

The bare truth is that parental worry adds nothing to the children's safety; it only hurts them.

The advice for over-protective parents is to strengthen themselves in emuna, and particularly in the belief of Divine providence. Parents must be aware that the Creator watches over their children every single moment. Beyond their basic parental responsibility and necessary efforts in protecting their children, they should pour their love and worries into prayer, leaning on the Creator with complete trust.

Protect Me on the Roads

Many people have fear of traveling. Every trip fills them with worry and trepidations. They often hound their driver, or they themselves are driving but lack self-confidence. They must know that safety depends on many factors in addition to the driver, such as the other drivers on the road, the extent to which the roads are maintained and the weather conditions. Even if their driving is perfect, they have no control over other vehicles that are liable to collide with them. There are also many wonderful drivers who committed tragic split-second mistakes that caused accidents. On the other hand, there are mediocre drivers who have never been involved in the slightest accident. The conclusion is that only Hashem can guard a person on the road. One's entire worry and fear should consequently be channeled into heartfelt prayer, asking the Creator to protect them on the way and to reach their destination safely.

Between Heaven and Earth

Trust in the Creator is the only thing that can help a person who fears air travel. On a natural level, the fear of flying seems justified, when a person is suspended between Heaven and earth. But, when a person has emuna and trust, he has no fear, for he knows that his fate is in the hands of the Creator.

Certain transgressions cause fear, such as slander, both the person who speaks badly about others and the person who listens to the slander. Anything connected to promiscuity also invokes fear. Those who expose themselves to fearful and violent books and movies also fill themselves with scary thoughts and images.

These of course are only lone examples. One may apply the same principles to anything that causes him anxiety and worry.

Trust in One and Don't Fear

A person's entire trust should be in the Creator and in no one else. As soon as someone trusts anything other than the Creator, he becomes subservient to the factor that he trusts. For example, if a person thinks that he can only enter a certain place if the guard lets him in, then he becomes subservient to the guard; he'll try to placate the guard or to flatter him. And, if he tries a different approach and threatens the guard, the Creator will only harden the guard's heart so that the person will not be allowed to enter. But, if the person believes that everything is up to the Creator, he'll first pray to the Creator and ask Him to let him enter. If afterwards, the guard allows him in, it's a clear sign that this is the Creator's will. And if he isn't allowed entrance, that too is a clear sign that Hashem doesn't want him to enter.

Suppose a person has a meeting with a clerk or bureaucrat, such as in a bank or an employment agency. Maybe the person is looking for a loan or for a job. If he thinks that the fulfillment of his request depends on clerks or bureaucrats, the Creator most certainly will harden their hearts and the person will go away empty-handed. One who trusts the Creator will therefore pray before his meeting at the bank, the employment office or wherever else he needs to arrange something, for then he'll be emotionally prepared for anything, even a negative answer, for he knows that this is what Hashem wants. **For a person with true emuna, there is no difference between a positive answer and a negative answer, for this is what the Creator wants.** The individual believes that he is in good hands and whatever the Creator is doing is the very best for him. The familiar expression says that when Hashem closes one door, He opens dozens of others instead...

Here's a beautiful example in a touching story about Rebbe Akiva from the Gemara in Tractate Berachot, 60b:

Rebbe Akiva was traveling on the road with his three possessions - his donkey that he rode on, his rooster that served as his alarm clock, and his candle that illuminated the darkness for him. He entered a town looking for a place to rest but couldn't find an inn in which to sleep. Rebbe Akiva didn't try to plea to anyone. Nor did he use his status to try and forcefully convince anyone. He simply sought a place to sleep in a field outside of town, gleefully accepting that whatever the Creator does is for the very best.

A wind came and extinguished Rebbe Akiva's candle, so that he was left in the dark. He simply said, "Whatever the Creator does is for the very best." A cat came and ate his rooster. Again, he said, "Whatever the Creator does is for the very best." A lion came and ate his donkey. Once more, Rebbe Akiva, now left with nothing, said: "All that the Creator does, He does for the very best," despite the fact that there was no logical reason to say that these occurrences were for the good.

That night, enemies entered the town where Rebbe Akiva wanted to sleep and took all the residents into captivity. He was saved specifically from the calamities that had befallen him the previous night. Had he slept in the town, he too would have been taken into captivity. Had his candle burned, his rooster crowed or his donkey neighed, he too would have been discovered.

Rebbe Akiva placed emuna ahead of logic. Logically, good things were not happening to him. It surely would have been more comfortable to sleep in a nice hotel in town rather than sleeping in a field. Sitting by candlelight is certainly better than sitting in the dark. Having a rooster to wake you up is better than over-sleeping. And of course, riding a donkey beats walking on foot. Yet, Rebbe Akiva believed without understanding. He **discarded his intellect** and lived in emuna. Emuna says that everything is from Hashem and all for the very best, **even when it appears to be otherwise**. Anyone who truly follows this path will merit seeing with his own eyes that everything is truly for the very best, just like Rebbe Akiva did!

Living in Sanctification of Hashem's Name

Many people harbor the misconception that they are allowed to be angry or upset in the performance of a mitzvah; they think that they can even trod on people for the purpose of doing a mitzvah. Such delusions are none other than the evil inclination's tricks. The EI will be happy to let a person do a mitzvah as long as that person is also committing serious sins on the way.

Robin Hood is not an emuna character; we are not allowed to steal from the rich in order to give to the poor like he did. By the same token, our sages explain that one is not allowed to steal money to build a succah or purchase tefillin, for a mitzva may not be accomplished by committing a transgression. In light of this principle, one must not incorporate anger in the performance of any mitzvah, for anger is worse than stealing; our sages teach that it is comparable to idolatry. Even though stealing is a serious offense, our sages don't compare it to idolatry.

Sadness and depression are also serious transgressions, stemming from the sitra achra, or "dark side" of spirituality, the opposite of holiness, which Hashem cannot stand. How can something that Hashem cannot stand be used to perform any of Hashem's commandments? What's more, making other people sad is a transgression of Torah, a breach of the mitzvoth between man and fellow man, which is much more serious than a breach of the mitzvoth between man and Hashem and much more difficult to rectify.

These misconceptions stem from a lack of emuna. How? Those who become angry or sad when they encounter obstructions in the performance of a mitzvah don't realize or believe that those very obstructions also come from Hashem. Hashem is testing those people to see if they will lose their temper or not or whether they'll trample people or not on the way to doing a mitzvah. Prayer is the only way to overcome obstacles. A person who tries to muscle his way past the obstacles is acting in the "might of my right hand" heretical mindset, because he thinks that everything depends on him and he doesn't see Hashem at all. Such individuals try to force their will on others by way of anger, shouting or outright physical violence. The mitzvah they wanted to do turns into a dozen or more serious transgressions, Heaven forbid.

Not only material matters are in Hashem's hands, but spiritual ones as well. Only Hashem decides if anyone will have the privilege of performing a mitzvah or not. Beware of the evil inclination, which utilizes a person's arrogance and forcefulness in tricking that person into committing numerous transgressions while forcing his way to do a mitzvah.

Leibel'e the Shoemaker

To further illustrate our subject at hand, here is a Chassidic story from some 240 years ago:

It was Passover Seder night. The holy tzaddik Rebbe Aaron the Great from Karlin, of sacred and blessed memory, was a wise man and a revered spiritual leader who served the Creator with all his heart. Tradition held that when he sang songs of praise to the Creator, even the angels would descend to earth in order to listen. On holidays, his pupils would gather around his table to join in his singing and to bask in the light of his wisdom. The joy and enthusiasm around Rebbe Aaron's table were indescribable.

Rebbe Aaron led the Seder according to the Kabbalistic tradition of the Ariza'l. His disciples felt like they were in paradise, as if in those very moments, they were leaving Egypt with Moses and the Children of Israel, seeing all the miracles of Passover with their own eyes.

Suddenly, Rebbe Aaron stopped singing and closed his eyes in what appeared to be deep meditation. His chassidim too became silent, waiting for their mentor to do or say something.

Ultimately, Aaron "awoke" with a knowing smile on his face from something that obviously caused him gratification. The pupils asked their mentor why he's smiling. The wise man said, "My pupils, you certainly felt elated, as if we had reached the portals of Heaven with our Passover Seder. True? Well, you should know that we haven't reached the spiritual shoestrings of Leibel'e the Shoemaker, whose singing jolts the Heavens and brings the greatest joy to the Creator."

"Leibel'e the Shoemaker!" they gasped, "we surely don't make fun of any human being, but Leibel'e is nothing but a simple person." How can his Passover Seder possibly compare to that of Rebbe Aaron the Great?

"Go to his house and see for yourselves," Rebbe Aaron told them. The chassidim went to Leibel'e's run-down shack to see what's so special about his way of serving the Creator. They peeked in his window and witnessed the following:

Leibel'e had not yet started to eat his holiday meal. He stood with a tray full of food in his hand in front of his wife and said, "Beloved wife, my crown, come let us begin our Passover Seder. Such an occasion occurs only once a year, so let's not miss the opportunity."

Leibel'e's wife was afire with anger. She snatched the tray from his hand and screamed, "No! You shall not eat a thing today!"

"Dear wife," said Leibel'e gently, without a trace of negativity, "I just want you to know that you are the greatest gift the Creator could give someone - there is no one like you in the whole world! Come, let us begin our Passover Seder; we'll sing the songs you like and tell your favorite stories. Let's not miss this once-a-year opportunity. This will give us renewed strength for the entire year."

"I told you!" she screeched, "there won't be any Seder tonight!" She stomped away to the kitchen with tray in hand.

Leibel'e prayed quietly, "Master of the World, may Your Name be blessed, thank you for all the obstacles. Everything is from You; please have mercy on me so that I may celebrate the holiday according to Your wishes. I know that you are preventing me from making this festive meal, not my wife. Please forgive me for my transgressions, Master of the World."

Leibel'e's wife returned from the kitchen and yelled at him, "What are you looking at me like that for? You always sadden me; what a mistake I made by marrying a fool like you."

"Dear wife," said Leibel'e lovingly, "you have no idea how much I love you. I cherish you more than anything in the world. I would do anything to make you happy - I'll buy you whatever you want. But please - allow me to carry on with our Seder. It will make you happy and you won't feel any sadness at all. It's getting late. Come, my beloved, and let us make our Seder together in joy."

Leibel'e tiptoed into the kitchen to bring the tray once more, all the time praying under his breath, "Blessed Creator, let me know that this is a test of my faith from You, to determine if I truly believe in You, or if I will succumb to any negative feelings toward my wife, by thinking that she controls my fate and not You, Heaven forbid. Let me know that there is no one but You. Help me contain my temper, and even if she doesn't let me make a Seder, I shouldn't be angry. Enable me to accept everything with complete emuna, that whatever is happening is Your will only."

Leibel'e placed the tray on the table. Again, his wife grabbed it and returned it to the kitchen. Once more, she yelled at him and disparaged him. Undaunted, Leibel'e once more spoke to her lovingly, while continuing in his heart to plead to the Creator: "Dearest Creator, please help me! Don't let me lose my temper or my patience for even a split second, for if I do, no penitence will help me. Give me the right words to soften my wife's heart and to relieve her sorrow. Give me the spiritual awareness to see only You. Help me avoid any negative emotions and know that everything - including my wife, my Seder and me - are all in Your loving hands. Have mercy on me and in Your infinite compassion, help me make her happy and to make a proper Passover Seder."

The tray volleys back and forth between the kitchen and dining room table for six entire hours! Leibel'e incessantly speaks words of love to his wife and simultaneously prays in his heart while his wife yells at him, belittles him and curses him. Suddenly, with no explanation whatsoever, she does a complete turnaround, smiles, and calls her husband to the table. "Come, darling! We must eat - the food is getting cold... "

They had to rush through the meal, for daybreak was almost upon them. Leibel'e the shoemaker made an entire Passover Seder, ate, drank wine and sang Passover melodies while his wife faithfully served him.

Rebbe Aaron's chassidim watched this spectacle with suspended breath. They left their observation post at the window and let out a deep sigh of relief. They didn't believe that there could ever be such a happy end. The simple shoemaker had taught these scholars a lesson in emuna. They understood how his Passover Seder, the product of his impeccable character and unshaking faith, brought the Creator so much gratification.

Fulfilling the Creator's will by overcoming hardships is much more laudable than doing it with ease, especially when one accomplishes his goal by way of prayer and penitence rather than acting forcibly and aggressively. When a person endears others in a considerate and conciliatory manner, he knocks down walls of resistance. Leibel'e, as such, attained a lofty spiritual level that night with his innocent and pure faith in the Creator. He could not have done this if everything in his life would have gone smoothly, devoid of obstacles.

A Mitzva Attained by way of a Transgression

The above story teaches us that anger and sadness - especially insulting or harming another human - have no place in the fulfillment of Hashem's commandments. One cannot earn a good deed by doing a bad deed. Unlike Robin Hood, one may not rob the rich to give to the poor. While giving to the poor is certainly a worthy deed, one is not permitted to touch a cent that is not his. Therefore, one must not insult or yell at others even if they are transgressing and he wants to correct them; such "outreach" is the product of the evil inclination. The evil inclination often conceals itself within an apparent good deed in order to trick a person into committing such outright sins as getting angry at and humiliating others.

With the above story in mind, one may think that a once-a-year mitzvah like the Passover Seder, having invested so much time and effort in preparing for it, is a legitimate reason to get angry and force the wife into doing what she should. The evil inclination loves situations like this: "Hey, she's not doing what Hashem wants! Look how insolent she is! Put her in her place - this is the Creator's honor!" May Hashem save us from giving Him "honor" like this...

People think that they're allowed to steal money in order to purchase matzah or food for Shabbat. No way! By the same token, one may not lose his temper in doing the Creator's will, for losing one's temper is just as bad as stealing.

The angry person forgets and ignores the principles of emuna and severs himself from Hashem. So, how can one possibly do Hashem's will by severing himself from Him? What a ridiculously senseless notion! Anger is a statement that a person is displeased with the Creator's way of running things. Sadness and depression make the same statement. The anger or sadness-plagued individual cannot possibly do the Creator's will, nor can a person who harms others, for the sins between man and fellow man are difficult to rectify.

People make such mistakes because of a lack of emuna. They don't believe that the obstacles that hinder them in doing the Creator's will are also from the Creator. Hashem is testing them; will they lose their temper, or not? Will they harm others, or not? The only way to overcome obstacles, especially in serving the Creator, is by way of prayer. One who believes in "the might of my right hand" and attributes his success to himself is far from Hashem. Both the material and the spiritual sides of our life require emuna that everything is from the Creator. But, the evil inclination tries to sever one's connection with Hashem by tripping him up with arrogance and the illusion of self-dependence.

The illusion of self-dependence, as if things depend on us and on our efforts, is none other than a gross lack of emuna. If a person would have emuna, he'd heed the voice of the good inclination that says to him: "The obstacle in your way comes from the Creator, for there is no one but Him. You may not overcome the obstacle by committing a transgression, and certainly not by causing harm to another human being."

Just as one may not repay a debt (good deed) by stealing (bad deed), one may not overcome a human obstacle to doing a good deed by anything other than peaceful means. If one doesn't succeed, then he should resort to prayer, for the Creator Himself is responsible for the obstacle.

People aren't aware of the seriousness of harming and bringing sorrow to others. Such self-righteous people think that their duty to fulfill a commandment takes precedence over another human's feelings. Who gave them the right to perform a good deed at another person's expense?

People don't regard anger and depression as transgressions, for they think that certain situations justify angry reactions or feelings of sadness. Anger and sadness are not only transgressions; they negate the truth and emuna and are therefore heresy. In many respects, they are worse than many outright sins.

Between the Hammer and the Anvil

Suppose that a person wants to fulfill one of the Creator's commandments but he is hampered – this is a test from

Above. Will he become angry or depressed? Will he lose heart? Or will he pray for Divine assistance in removing the obstacle while clinging to his desire? At any rate, if for the time being he still cannot fulfill the good deed, he certainly may not harm another person in attempting to remove the obstacle. The Creator has no complaints against those who are coerced and prevented from doing His will. Our only obligation is to try our utmost and then cling to our desire.

One who is prevented from doing a good deed should pray as follows:

"Master of the world, You put me in a difficult position. From one standpoint, I am obligated to do Your will; from the other standpoint, I cannot do what I must without losing my temper or embarrassing/harming/yelling at someone else. If I do that, I'll be transgressing Your will. Please have mercy on me, Creator of the world, and help me do Your will without committing the slightest trace of a transgression. Remove the obstacle in my way. Help me cling to emuna and to avoid anger, which is outright heresy. Help me avoid doing anything wrong to the person who is standing in my way, so that my good deeds should cause no harm to anyone in the world. Let my priorities be clear and help me realize that a good deed cannot be built on the foundation of a bad deed. Help me uphold all of Your commandments between man and fellow human and enable me to treat every other human in the world properly.

"Please, save me from sadness, which is total heresy that You despise, and help me to do Your will. Come to my aid in this difficult moment and remove the obstacle from my path. May I find favor in Your eyes so that even my adversaries will reconcile with me."

Don't give up praying ever and hold on to your desires. Eventually, you will succeed. Your obstacle will completely turn around as it did for Leibel'e the shoemaker.

The greater your desire and dedication, the more valuable each tiny action of serving the Creator becomes. Things that come easily cannot be compared with accomplishments that were attained with dedication, desire and sacrifice, the sign of a heart that burns with love for the Creator. With this in mind, Aaron the wise man wanted his pupils to witness the difficulties in life of a seemingly "simple" soul, Leibel'e the shoemaker, who exhibited phenomenal desire, patience and commitment in fulfilling the Creator's will against all odds.

Be Killed but Don't Transgress

One of the Torah's commandments is to sanctify Hashem's Name. Within the bounds of this mitzvah, known as the mitzvah of Kiddush Hashem, if a person is given a choice between performing idolatry or being executed, he should choose the latter, and not deny G-d, Heaven forbid. This seems strange - why get killed? Maybe it's better to commit idolatry one time and then to live on to perform many additional good deeds for years to come. Must a person lose thousands of potential merits just to avoid transgressing our emuna, our belief in the One G-d, even one single time?

The answer is yes. The Creator doesn't want us to let go of our emuna for a single second, for this is not only the foundation that our lives stand on; emuna is the foundation that the whole universe stands on!

This is not just some hypothetical discussion. Oftentimes, we are faced with an obstacle in doing the Creator's will. The obstacle is liable to anger us. Since our sages teach us that anger is tantamount to idolatry, then it's better to refrain from forcibly doing something - even a good deed - if it will bring us to anger. In effect, a person who for the time being gives up a mitzvah that he strongly desires to do in order to avoid getting angry is sanctifying Hashem's Name.

According to the Torah, a person must delay doing a mitzvah for the time being if he will become angry in the performance of it.

The performance of mitzvoth is designed to enhance our emuna. If so, why transgress our emuna in order to perform them? Just as it is a mitzvah to give one's life rather than commit idolatry, even at the expense of all the mitzvoth that person could have performed had he lived longer, it's a mitzvah to forfeit a mitzvah if it will bring a person to anger, which is tantamount to idolatry.

We hereby learn a necessary lesson for all areas of life: emuna is our most important asset. Nothing - even doing the loftiest deed - is worth compromising our emuna. If we can't do something important without getting angry or transgressing in some other way, we should meanwhile refrain from doing the deed and channel our efforts into more prayer and desire, just as Leibel'e the shoemaker did.

Leibel'e succeeded because he guarded his emuna; this enabled him to be phenomenally patient with his wife and steadfast in prayer. Never once, did he insult her; not a word left his mouth that he regretted afterward. Eventually, his wife not only came around, but was happy too.

Enduring Everything with Emuna

When a person finds himself in a trying situation, he must remember - this is what the Creator wants! This is a test of faith! Prayer is the only way to overcome - not by anger, not by violence and certainly not by sadness. If a person acts in accordance with emuna, he'll merit Divine assistance. Really, who is standing in his way? It's Hashem Himself. If he understands that and acts according to the principles of emuna that we have learned, then the obstacle or hardship will dissipate. He'll accomplish what he wants with no anger, no arguments and no bitterness.

The story of Leibel'e the shoemaker is an excellent example, showing us the way one should react to obstacles and challenges in life. In trying times, we should remember the way he handled his difficulties. In doing so, and in passing the test of emuna, a person earns a stronger connection with the Creator. He also avoids needless arguments and strife with his human antagonist, whether it's his spouse, his boss or a neighbor. He keeps the peace and avoids slander and many other transgressions, and therefore saves himself from potentially harsh decrees. What's more, he attains a higher spiritual level. Nothing is more wonderful than passing the test of emuna!

I Must Go!

Suppose that a person wants to attend a regularly-scheduled Torah lesson or to speak to the Creator in his daily personal prayer session, but his wife doesn't want him to leave the house for any reason. If he gets angry and goes out against her will, he will fail his test of emuna. At any rate, he won't reap much benefit from the good deed that he wants to do, because he has more than likely lost his self-composure and he can't focus properly. What's more, if he loses his temper with his wife, Hashem will be upset with him because of the sorrow he caused her.

But, if on the other hand, he is wise enough to act according to the principles of emuna, he'll realize that Hashem is standing in his way, not his wife. He'll submit to Him, assess himself and repent for anything he might have done wrong. Quietly, he should pray for Hashem's help so that he will be able to perform the mitzvah that he planned. Of course, he should neither lose his temper nor say anything hurtful to his wife. Indeed, he should listen to her and empathize with her. This is what Hashem wants him to do now, as well as to strengthen his desire to do His will and to get close to Him. His patience will most certainly pay off. Once his wife receives the proper treatment and attention she desires, she'll undoubtedly let him attend his Torah lesson or fulfill his other plans. In the meanwhile, he has accrued the dividends of additional prayer and successfully passed the test of emuna, which is the main thing.

Into the Fog

In every aspect of life, when a person faces an obstacle, he or she should believe that it's Hashem standing in their way and no one else. Rebbe Nachman explains (Likutei Moharan, I:115):

"Hashem conceals Himself within the obstacle, for Hashem loves justice, and He also loves His people Israel. Yet, His love for His people Israel is greater than His love for justice. Therefore, when the accusing forces of stern judgment complain that someone is not worthy of proximity to Hashem...and Hashem loves justice, so He must listen to the accusers and therefore agree that a person is obstructed from getting close to Hashem, according to that person's misdeeds and according to the force of justice, For Hashem cannot dismiss justice for He loves justice.

"But, since Hashem loves Israel, and this love is greater than His love for justice, He must therefore agree to the obstacles as the forces of justice demand, and He agrees to that demand, but since He loves Israel and wants to bring them close to Him, He conceals Himself within the obstacles. In truth, there are no obstacles at all. By way of these obstacles in particular, one can get close to Him. That's what the Torah indicates when it says, 'And Moses approached the fog' - in other words, the obstacle - '...for the Lord is there.'"

With the above in mind, anytime a person faces an obstacle in the fulfillment of a mitzvah, he shouldn't be angry or sad. He should remind himself that whatever or whoever is standing in his way is acting according to the way Hashem wants. So what good is it to fight the obstacle? Can one defeat Hashem? One should appeal directly to Hashem and ask for the privilege of fulfilling the desired mitzvah. Meanwhile, one should be patient and merciful toward whoever is obstructing him. Don't be disappointed or depressed, just believe that it's Hashem who is causing the obstruction. This is all to test to determine whether a person will act in according with emuna or not. If one so merits, he'll choose emuna and earn a high score in emuna. That way, he'll attain a higher spiritual level and live a pleasant and tranquil life.

Just as we are commanded to die in sanctification of Hashem's Name, we are required to live in sanctification of Hashem's Name.

Life's Many Tests

Until now, we've given examples about tests of emuna, which a person can apply to other areas of life:

Buying or selling a house or apartment - even when the purchase or sale of your home goes smoothly, this is no easy process. One needs considerable patience and emuna, for many problems are liable to arise on the way. Sometimes the contract signing is delayed or cancelled altogether. Meanwhile, one may have bought, sold, or rented a new house or apartment. Maybe the other side is late with a payment, causing you to be delinquent on your new payment schedule. The numbers of things that can go wrong defy description.

One must believe that all the difficulties are exactly what Hashem wants, and therefore refrain from getting angry, nervous, or depressed. Hashem sends difficulties as an indication that we have something to correct, so we should utilize our energy in trying to understand Hashem's messages by devoting time to personal prayer and introspection. Strengthening emuna will also save us from bickering and falling into needless legal battles that will only deplete our time and money. As soon as a person realizes that difficulties are from Hashem and reacts with prayer and teshuva, the difficulties amazingly work themselves out.

Feuds with neighbors - relations with neighbors are catastrophic when based on power and not on emuna. Some feuds last for years. But, with emuna, neighbors readily compromise and bridge gaps, so everything turns out for the best.

Disputes - Rebbe Nachman of Breslev teaches (see Likutei Moharan I:258) that when people gang up against someone, they can make him fall from his spiritual level and ruin his emuna, Heaven forbid. We can therefore understand what King David said in Psalm 119, "Many have persecuted, but I have not wavered from Your laws." Despite King David's many opponents and enemies, he never veered in the slightest from his service of Hashem.

Having people against you is a difficult test of faith. A person with weak emuna will succumb to feelings of hatred, vengeance, and a burning desire to retaliate. Such negative emotions will only distance him further from Hashem. But, with emuna, a person will pray to Hashem and let Hashem fight his battles. Eventually, the enemies fall by the wayside.

Finding Employment - this is a challenge that's often accompanied with frustration, disappointment, insult, and bitterness. But, when a person looks for a job and applies emuna to his search, the process becomes simple and pleasant. He knows that any rejection is from Hashem because that particular place of employment would be detrimental in some way.

In general - life throws many tests of emuna in our path. In fact, **every single difficulty in our lives is a test of emuna.** One needn't feel blame or feelings of inadequacy. Therefore, there's no need to persecute yourself. Accept that your difficulties are all from Hashem to facilitate and to stimulate your spiritual growth, and all for the best. Every time a person successfully passes a test of emuna, he or she moves up another rung on the spiritual ladder, assuring a better life in this world and in the next.

A Substitute for Suffering

There's a way to mitigate or to altogether neutralize our suffering and tribulations in this world, as we'll see in the following example:

A father punishes his son. If the son is stupid, he bears malice in his heart toward his father and hates him.

If this son has some sense, he understands that he was punished for a reason, even though he doesn't like the punishment. When he realizes what he did wrong, he admits his wrongdoing, expresses his remorse, apologizes, and promises to improve his ways. Even if he doesn't understand exactly what he did wrong, he asks his father's forgiveness in a general manner and says, "I'm sorry for upsetting you, Dad - help me to avoid making the same mistakes in the future."

A truly intelligent son realizes that his father loves him and that the punishment was for his ultimate benefit. He therefore willfully accepts the punishment, turns to his father and says: "Dad, I know that your intent was to wake me up and to bring me closer to you. Thanks so much for paying such close attention to me - that really means a lot to me. Dad, please explain to me what I did wrong and help me improve..." Once the father shows the son his mistake, the son expresses remorse, admits the mistake, asks his father's forgiveness, and makes a firm resolution to do better in the future.

The third son is on a lofty level of spiritual awareness. He appreciates tribulations since he recognizes that he has deficiencies that need correcting.

Then again, there's a fourth son who surpasses all of his three brothers. He doesn't wait to be punished in order to improve his ways. Every day, he does a thorough process of self-evaluation where he weighs everything he did that day and asks himself if his deeds are really upright in light of his father's requests and standards. He then speaks to his father every single day and says, "Dad, by virtue of the wonderful education you gave me, I was fortunate in doing such-and-such good deeds. Thanks so much. On the other hand, I don't think my speech or behavior in a certain situation today was the way you would have wanted. I'm really sorry and I'll try my best to strengthen this weakness..."

The father of such a son glows with satisfaction and gratification. "What a beautiful human being! What a sensitive, considerate, and humble son! He doesn't wait for me to punish him - he's always trying to improve. Even if he were to do something seriously wrong, how could I punish him? He's constantly evaluating himself; he's always striving to fulfill my wishes. So, even if he does make a mistake, I'll just give him a gentle hint. With his sensitivity, he'll surely understand." The father will want nothing more than to fulfill this wonderful son's wishes.

Continuing to ponder his sons, the father says, "I wish my other three boys would come and speak to me on their own initiative every day. If they only realized how much I loved them, they'd ask for whatever they want and I'd be happy to give it to them. Even my son that bears malice toward me would realize how much I love him if he would only speak with me every day."

The Beloved Son

Imagine a loving son or daughter that thanks a parent profusely every single day for every little amenity that he or she received. Imagine that the same son or daughter always confesses wrongdoing without having to be reprimanded. If that's not enough, the son or daughter always seeks more and more of the parent's love. If this were your child, how in the world could you ever punish him?

We can now understand how to be Hashem's beloved sons and daughters. All we have to do is to set aside an hour a day for prayer in solitude, whether out in the field, in the office or in the kitchen at home, and speak to Hashem - our beloved Father in Heaven - in our own words. We take stock of everything we did in the previous twenty-four hours since our last session of hitbodedut, or personal prayer in solitude. We judge ourselves on three levels - thoughts, speech, and deeds. We rectify our wrongdoings and resolve to improve. We ask Hashem to bring us closer to Him. Such a process of personal prayer frees a person from stress, worry, sadness, and all other negative emotions. Even better, when we judge ourselves, Hashem doesn't let the Heavenly court judge us, and we save ourselves untold anguish and severe judgments. We don't wait for painful wake-up calls from Above, for we wake up on our own initiative.

Pay Attention

One who devotes an hour a day to personal prayer is on an even higher spiritual level than a person who accepts his tribulations with joy, for the former doesn't wait to be aroused by tribulations; he seeks to serve Hashem more and more on his own accord.

The Gemara says (tractate Berachot 7), that one measure of self-discipline is more effective than a hundred lashes. As such, the self-disciplined person saves himself limitless troubles in life.

When a person arouses himself to rectify his wrongdoing, he saves himself untold tribulations. Plus, one's own initiative in doing teshuva is much more effective than tons of tribulations.

Dear reader, stop and think about the wonderful gift that Hashem has given us by enabling us to speak to Him whenever we want to, any time of day or night. We can now begin to understand what Rebbe Nachman of Breslev meant when he said that hitbodedut - **personal prayer -is more virtuous than literally anything else**!

The Power of Simple Prayer

An hour of hitbodedut and soul-searching is so cogent that it can protect the entire world. Rebbe Nachman of Breslev once said (Rebbe Nachman's Discourses, 70), "How do we allow Hashem to bring harsh decrees to the world? We must call Hashem away from all His other tasks. We must draw Him away from decreeing harsh decrees to the world. We must tell Him to put everything else aside and listen to us, for we want to ask Him to draw us close. For when a person wishes to speak to Hashem, He casts aside everything else. Evil decrees are even set aside at this time. **Hashem puts aside everything and only listens to the person seeking His presence.**"

The amazing meaning of the above discourse is that any person - man, woman, or child, regardless of their current spiritual status, even the lowest and most contemptible person on earth - has the basic right to approach G-d and to speak to Him! Not only that, but Hashem listens! And who knows - maybe this very minute, some terrorist's or tyrant's evil designs are being foiled because the local street cleaner is talking to Hashem. If people would be speaking to Hashem round-the-clock, there could be no harsh decrees in the world.

Before the outbreak of World War II, a group of students in the Lubliner Yeshiva in Poland had a twenty-four hour personal prayer vigil. One of the young men would always be engaged in hitbodedut. For some reason, the police detained one of the boys and the chain of continuous personal prayer was broken. On that day, the holocaust began...

The above story sould be an incentive for each of us. Dear reader, hitbodedut is both pleasant and gratifying. It's not difficult, either. Could there be anything more ideal than speaking to the all-powerful King who can give you anything you want?

Imagine that the leading and most prestigious matchmaker in the vicinity calls a single young man for an hour's conversation. Who would refuse such a meeting? Imagine getting an hour's audience with a Bronfman or a Rothschild, or some other multi-millionaire that might be in a position to help you financially. Who would be too lazy to meet such a person? Imagine giving a sick person the opportunity to seek the advice of the world's leading doctor. What daft person wouldn't take advantage of such a chance?

Our hour of solitary personal prayer is an hour with the all-powerful King and Master of the World, Physician of all flesh, in whose loving hands are life, livelihood, our soul-mate, or anything else we need! Speaking to Hashem is one-stop shopping for all our aspirations, needs, and all our heart's wishes.

For those of our readers that have not yet experienced the joy of personal solitary prayer, we'd like to emphasize that it's tailor made - that's why it's called **personal** prayer. You can speak to Hashem anywhere, anytime, and in any language. Use your local slang and speak in any way that makes you comfortable. You can stand or sit, or even lie in your bed under the covers. Make yourself comfortable and speak your heart out. You can tell Hashem anything you like.

Put Everything Else Aside

If that's the story, then why isn't everyone talking to Hashem? Why are there so many obstacles to something so beautiful and natural?

The answer is that the Yetzer Hara, the Evil Inclination knows the value of personal prayer. He knows that it's the ultimate expression of emuna and the fulfillment of our very purpose on earth! He knows that a person who does daily hitbodedut will attain a full soul correction and overcome the obstacles and difficulties of life in this world. For that reason, the Evil Inclination does his utmost to weaken a person and discourage him from doing any solitary personal prayer. He tells you, "What, are you crazy? What do you think you'll accomplish by wasting an hour and talking to the trees? Besides, since when do you have a spare hour?" The Evil Inclination gives you one-hundred eight different reasons for not talking to Hashem in personal prayer.

Our wise readers will surely conclude that no matter what, we have to drop everything else and designate an hour for personal prayer. Daily personal prayer is a new lease on life, a special sweetness! As in the previous example of the four sons, Hashem's greatest gratification is when His beloved sons and daughters approach Him daily with personal prayer, self-evaluation, and requests for everything they need. Even if they don't succeed in rectifying everything they need to, Hashem waits patiently and doesn't punish them.

One of the most important items on our daily personal prayer agenda is asking Hashem to help us strengthen our emuna, as in the following sample personal prayer:

Please Hashem, give me complete emuna. Help me believe that there's no evil in the world, that everything is in Your hands and that everything is for the best. Give me the emuna that You love me just the way I am, and that You derive gratification from me.

Give me the complete emuna that there is no one but You, in other words, anything that distresses me is simply a rod in Your hand in order to arouse me to seek Your proximity. Give me the complete emuna that there's no one to blame for my troubles - not my wife, nor my in-laws, nor my boss - my moments of displeasure in life are all wake-up calls from You, beloved Father.

Give me the complete emuna that there's no need to torture myself and to tear myself down. Help me direct my energies into the positive endeavor of prayer and help me believe in the power of my prayers. Beloved Father, help me feel that You are with me - there is no greater gift or feeling. Help me scrap my bad habits and to do Your will. Give me the desire to pray and help me realize that all my spiritual and material deficiencies are merely the result of insufficient prayer.

Give me the emuna that everything is in Your hands, Hashem. Let my principle efforts be channeled in the direction of prayer and let me depend on Your magnificent loving kindness and not on my sorely limited ability and aptitude. Let the prayers flow forth from my heart, soul, and lips always...

Rabbi Levi Yitzchak Binder of blessed and saintly memory told me that when a person ascends to the Heavenly Court after his one-hundred-twenty-year go-round on this earth, the Heavenly Judges will open a big book - the story of that person's life, where every thought, utterance, and deed is recorded. Each page represents a day in that person's life. On every page where it's written that the person did an hour of personal prayer, the page is turned and that person is not judged for anything he may have done wrong on that day. But, on a day with no hitbodedut, the person is meticulously judged for every thought, utterance, and deed of that particular day.

Now we know why the Evil Inclination puts up such a fight against personal prayer. Every day is a new war for our hour of hitbodedut. For that reason, we have to be courageous and not give in. Hitbodedut is the gate to connecting with Hashem!

In light of the above, let's drop everything else and seize the rare opportunity to get close to Hashem and to solve all our problems. No wonder Rebbe Nachman of Breslev said, "Hitbodedut **is the ultimate virtue greater than anything else**!"

Chapter Four:

The Way of Teshuva

In this chapter, we'll learn the way a person can rectify himself and do teshuva. The Creator wants us to do teshuva - to return to Hashem and get close to Him always. When a person commits to doing teshuva, as we shall learn, with Hashem's help, he nullifies all stern judgments and accusations; he merits a tranquil life that's beautiful and meaningful.

24 Heavenly Courts

There are 24 Heavenly Courts that judge a person every single hour of every single day. A person that does good deeds receives a positive verdict; the soul immediately reacts to a positive judgment in the Heavenly Court with optimism and happiness. The opposite also holds true; one who incurs an unfavorable verdict that resulted from a negative action feels sadness, pessimism, and a heaviness of the spirit. This is what our sages say in the Mishna (Tractate Eduyot 5:7), "Your deeds shall bring you close, and your deeds shall push you away."

Rosh Hashanah, the New Year of the Jewish calendar, is the annual Day of Judgment that determines whether a person will live or die, how much annual income he or she will have, and other general factors. This doesn't contradict the fact that a person is judged every hour of the day. For example, on Rosh Hashanah, it's decided that a person will earn two thousand dollars on January 8th; on the morning of January 8th, it's decided how that person will earn the money, whether in joy or in sorrow.

The following Chassidic story further explains the concept of daily and annual judgment:

The Baal Shem Tov met an elderly water-carrier on the way and asked him how he was. The water carrier smiled a semi-toothless smile and praised G-d for giving him once more the strength to earn a respectable day's living.

A few days later, the Baal Shem Tov met the same elderly water-carrier. This time, the old man barely moped along under his yoke and two buckets, as if he were carrying the entire world on his shoulders. With a long face, he complained to the Baal Shem Tov how difficult his lot in life was.

The elderly man's extreme change of mood surprised the Baal Shem Tov. After a moment's contemplation, the Baal Shem Tov smiled and thanked the water-carrier. "My friend, you've just answered a difficult question I had while learning tractate Rosh Hashanah. The Mishna says that a person is judged on Rosh Hashanah, yet the Gemara says that a person is judged every day and every hour. The question in my mind was, if a person is judged on Rosh Hashanah as to the outcome of the entire year, why be judged again every day and every hour?"

The Baal Shem Tov then explained that the hourly and daily judgments determine the way a person will receive what's been predetermined in the beginning of the year; if one's actions are favorable, they receive their lot happily that particular hour. If their deeds are otherwise, then they get what they deserve with sadness, depression, or aggravation on that particular day and hour.

The day that the water-carrier was happy and optimistic was a day when his actions received a favorable judgment in the Heavenly Court. He didn't earn any more than he did on any other day, nor did he toil any less. Yet, he felt gratitude to Hashem and joy in his heart. A few days later, having apparently received an unfavorable judgment from the Heavenly Court for less than desirable deeds, his mood plummeted and his work became torture.

In reality, there was no change in the water-carrier's predetermined income from Rosh Hashanah. He was destined to make his living by carrying water. But, whether he'd attain his daily wage in joy or in misery was something that depended on the hourly judgment.

In any event, a person can change that which has been predetermined on Rosh Hashanah by teshuva, prayer, and charity.

Pay Attention to the Subtle Hints

The story of the Baal Shem Tov and the water carrier explains how our moods, situation, or circumstances can change from hour to hour. You've most probably experienced how you're getting along famously with your spouse or with your superior one hour, and then all of a sudden, out of the clear blue, you're being yelled at and chastised in a manner that logically makes no sense at all. When you take hourly judgments into consideration though, everything makes sense; one hour's favorable judgment manifests itself into successful and gratifying events and good moods, while another hour's severe judgments turn into all types of headaches and hassles.

Everything that saddens a person, even the tiniest cause of mild anguish such as a small itch, is the result of a

Heavenly-Court decision. Every tiny hint of discomfort or undesirability should prod a person to self-assessment and subsequent teshuva. Don't attribute anything to nature, fate or chance.

In Tractate Chulin 7b, the Gemara teaches, "Rebbe Chanina says: a person can't lift a finger down here below unless it has been declared Above, for it states (Psalm 37:23), 'It is from Hashem that a man's strides are determined.'"

The Gemara also teaches (see tractate Arachin 16b) that every tiny anguish in life comes under the heading of Heaven-sent tribulations, such as trying on a garment that doesn't fit properly or reaching in your pocket and pulling out a quarter when you wanted to pull out a nickel. By internalizing the knowledge that these moment-to-moment happenings in our life are the products of Heavenly-Court judgments, we greatly enhance our spiritual awareness, our emuna, and our connection to Hashem. We realize that everything is directed from Above in absolute justice, each individual according to his actions.

Hashem is Righteous and Just

When tribulations befall a person, and he blames nature, luck, his shortcomings or other people around him, he's making an unfortunate mistake that only leads to frustration and bitterness. Not only that, but it triggers displeasure with him from Above. It's like a son that misbehaves and subsequently receives a punishment from his father. Instead of correcting himself, the mischievous son now blames his misfortune on his younger brother and picks a fight with him. Now, the father is doubly perturbed: not only has the mischievous son failed to correct his behavior, but he's now started a fight with his little brother, who had nothing to do with the punishment!

An additional error people make is when they believe in Divine providence but they think that Hashem is acting unfairly with them. This is what Rebbe Nathan of Breslev calls, "spoiled justice," for when a person feels that Hashem's judgments are unfair, her or she develops a warped sense of justice that impairs honest self-evaluation and soul-searching.

Rebbe Nathan writes (Likutei Halachot, Choshen Mishpat, Nezikin 5), "One develops a warped sense of judgment from the mistaken notions of the world. Most people yell that Hashem doesn't deal fairly with them, and that their tribulations are beyond their capability of withstanding. They also say that they have no time to serve Hashem, because of the demands of making a living. They therefore believe that Hashem makes impossible demands."

The truth is that Hashem doesn't demand anything that a person is not capable of.

The key to inner peace is the internalization of the fact that Hashem is righteous and that His decisions are just. Hashem doesn't make idle demands of a person or complain about them; He doesn't ask anything that a person is uncapable of doing. Hashem knows that our main test of faith is to make time for Torah learning and Divine service despite our demanding work schedules. Our sages said, "He who upholds the Torah from poverty will eventually uphold it from wealth."

No matter what happens to a person, we must believe that this is from Hashem and that Hashem is just and righteous. Hashem runs the world, does everything for the best, and has a specific purpose for everything

He does. Just as one believes that everything comes from Hashem, one must believe that all of Hashem's judgments are not only righteous, but merciful and compassionate as well. Since Hashem's Judgments are merciful and compassionate - even though they might not seem that way sometimes - they are always for our ultimate personal benefit. The trials and tribulations that Hashem sends us are designed to bring us closer to Him. But, spiritually-unaware people regard those same tribulations and suffering as unjust, and accuse Hashem of acting unfairly with them, Heaven forbid.

Just as we are required to believe that everything is from Hashem, we must believe with complete emuna that Hashem is just and righteous, and there is no such thing as Divine injustice, Heaven forbid. Everything He does is just and merciful, whose entire purpose is to bring us closer to Him and not to push us away.

The Creator's Tremendous Mercy

The road to righteousness is a long one - a person doesn't become a tzaddik overnight. Yet, many people shy away from making teshuva since they're afraid of "paying the price" for past sins. Sooner or later, everyone will be making teshuva; does that mean that they all will have to go through an odyssey of torture as a process of atonement?

The answer is no. There's a way to beat the rap. Hashem doesn't allow double jeopardy. Therefore, as Rebbe Eliezer teaches us in the Midrash Raba (Devarim 5:5), "When there is judgment below, there is no judgment Above." In other words, when we judge ourselves, the Heavenly Court is not allowed to judge us.

The Zohar teaches that where there's judgment below, there can't be judgment above. In other words, when we judge ourselves, the Heavenly Court is not allowed to judge us. Practically speaking, this means that when we regularly confess our wrongdoings to Hashem, seek forgiveness, and resolve to improve, then Hashem doesn't allow the Heavenly Court to judge us; Hashem judges us himself.

There's a vast difference between Hashem's judgments and those of the Heavenly Court - whereas the Heavenly Court judges in exacting, hair-splitting precision by the letter of the law, Hashem's judgments are merciful and forgiving. When the Heavenly Court tries the case, the defendant is almost always found guilty. When Hashem tries a case, the defendant is always declared innocent.

So, if we want to avoid suffering and tribulations, we should set aside sixty minutes a day for self-evaluation and personal prayer, where we judge ourselves in front of Hashem. If we find ourselves guilty of wrongdoing, all we have to do is confess, ask for forgiveness, and commit to do better. The Heavenly Court subsequently is not allowed to touch the case and to try us even for the worst crime, providing that we've confessed to Hashem and are truly making Teshuva at our own initiative. Where there's judgment below, there can't be judgment above.

Traversing Life with a Smile

A person who spends an hour a day in personal prayer and self-evaluation is bound to win a favorable verdict on the critical annual judgment day of Rosh Hashanah. What's more, after his 120 years on earth, he'll depart unblemished from this world and walk right into Gan Eden.

A. Confession - telling Hashem what we've done wrong.

B. Remorse - we should feel sorry for going against Hashem's will.

C. Asking forgiveness - we ask Hashem's forgiveness like a child would ask forgiveness from a loving parent.

D. Commitment - we commit to do our utmost to improve in the future, and not to slide back to our old ways.

Anyone who follows the Rambam and confesses his sins every day fulfills the mitzvah of teshuva and will be rewarded accordingly. The most important thing is that all his transgressions are forgiven. Since there are no outstanding judgments on such a person, he won't have tribulations.

Complete Fear of G-d

We just learned how simple the mitzvah of teshuva is. That notwithstanding, most of the world is far away from teshuva because they lack proper guidance and don't realize how readily accessible this mitzvah is. Hosea the prophet said, "Take your words with you and return to Hashem" (Hosea 14:3). In other words, speaking to Hashem comprises the main part of teshuva - confessing, expressing one's remorse and praying to do better. Since people lack hope, optimism and self-reinforcement in their service of Hashem, they lack self-composure and their fear of G-d is incomplete. Sadness and depression that seeps their way into one's service of Hashem result from a lack of spiritual awareness. That's what Eliphaz the Yemenite says to Job, "Your fear of G-d is foolishness" (Job 4:6). Therefore, in this chapter while we're speaking about teshuva, we'll learn some important principles that will enable us to attain complete teshuva.

Get to Know Yourself

The first principle and the most important and vital condition for rectifying yourself is to realize who you are! Know that you have an evil inclination - that's an unavoidable fact.

Even though we might not like it, we must accept the fact that we have an evil inclination just like we have two arms and two legs. We don't ask Hashem he created us with two ears and two eyes, so we don't need to ask Him why He created us with an evil inclination - this too is "factory-supplied" equipment from the Divine Manufacturer. Without the evil inclination, a person lacks free choice between good and evil. We are people, not angels; we therefore need not be upset and discouraged by the fact that we have forces within us that gravitate toward negative character traits and bad habits. That's ridiculous! Hashem created it.

The worst evil inclination is complaining to Hashem for giving you an evil inclination. Self-persecution is the worst evil inclination, so don't persecute yourself or fall into depression because of your drawbacks, lusts and bad habits. Simply get to know yourself - the whole package including lusts, unfavorable character traits and bad habits. Be honest with yourself. Simply ask the Creator to help you overcome your evil inclination and help you fulfill your potential and life purpose.

A person who loses heart every time the evil inclination overcomes him will never be able to rectify himself. He must first be honest with himself and recognize that on his current spiritual level, he still has a strong urge for evil. Don't be in denial, don't fool yourself and don't entertain fantasies that you're on a higher spiritual level than you really are. The spiritual map is just like a road map - if a person doesn't know where he is, he won't know how to find his way to his destination.

Since the "map of self-rectification" is difficult to read, one must be totally honest with himself and identify his true present spiritual station. Self-perfection is a long and difficult road with ups and downs, triumphs and setbacks. One's lusts never give him rest. And, in the meanwhile, he still must deal with life's day-to-day challenges such as making a living and raising a family.

The Greater a Person

Fact - each one of us is fighting a war against the evil inclination until the day we depart from this physical earth. Like any other war, sometimes we win and sometimes we lose. Sometimes we overcome and other times we are overcome. Just like two people fighting one another, when one gets the upper hand, the second fights even harder. Rebbe Natan writes in Likutei Halachot (Choshen Mishpat, Hona'a 3): "The general rule is that when a person seeks the proximity of Hashem and to return in teshuva, he must endure thousands of ascents and descents beyond measure."

Another phenomena that defies nature characterizes the war against the evil inclination. As a person fights the evil inclination, it is neither weakened nor reduced. As a person grows spiritually, so does his evil inclination, for our sages say (Tractate Succah, 52a): "The bigger a person, the bigger his evil inclination." After making spiritual growth, many people make the mistake of thinking that they've finally overcome their evil inclination. Sorry, but now it's even stronger.

Rebbe Nachman explains (see Likutei Moharan I:72): When a person contemplates teshuva, all his good deeds at that moment destroy the evil inclination that he had up until now. He then receives a new and stronger evil inclination in accordance with his new and higher spiritual level. If he doesn't make a concerted effort to overcome it, the new evil inclination will overcome him. As such, one must gird himself with renewed and greater strength against the new evil inclination that has come to him.

Elsewhere, Rebbe Nachman writes (ibid, I:25), that when a person ascends from a lower level to a higher level, the stronger negative forces of the higher level overcome him. As such, many pious people, upon seeing that their lusts and lewd thoughts have reawakened, think they've suffered a setback in their service of Hashem. That is not true! Indeed, since they are now at a higher level, the forces of opposition at the higher level are also stronger. Now, he must overcome them and continue his ascent.

In light of the above teachings, if a person falls into sadness and disappointment every time his evil inclination overcomes him, then he'll be depressed his entire life and he'll lose the war with his evil inclination. He therefore must reconcile himself to the fact that this is his reality - he has an evil inclination that he must always fight - for this is what Hashem wants and this is what gratifies Hashem. Once he knows this, he can really fight, and he'll win. Hashem has joy simply from seeing a person fight against his evil inclination.

Know Your Evil Inclination

Once a person recognizes that he has an evil inclination, he can learn how to fight against it. The evil inclination's objective is to fill a person with heresy. The only weapon the evil inclination has against a person is heresy, for as soon as a person loses his faith, he's easy prey. But, as long as a person clings to his emuna, his evil inclination is neutralized. Practically speaking, a person with emuna is a person with a defunct evil inclination. Such an individual can live with the Creator, confide in Him, consult with Him about everything in life and ask for all his needs, material and spiritual.

The evil inclination is cunning, though, with different strategies at its disposal. Sometimes, it injects a person with total heresy, inciting him to deny the Creator, Heaven forbid. Other times, it won't tell a person to totally deny the Creator, only to doubt the concept of personal Divine providence or the validity and relevance of one of the Torah's commandments. It also incites a person with lust; satisfying such lust would mean violating the Ten Commandments, which too is heresy. It injects a person with negative desires, all of which can be traced back to heresy.

Suppose there's a person that has overcome all the above temptations. He has complete belief in Hashem and in the Torah; would he still have an evil inclination?

The answer is yes - he might be inclined toward arrogance and smugness, thinking that he is on a higher level than he really is. If so, any small setback would trigger a process of self-persecution and depression.

Let's explain:

A person has free choice, which is basically desire: if he desires, he does; if he doesn't desire, he does not. The evil inclination is always poised to pounce on a person and trip him. There are two stages of its battle with a person.

Stage One: The evil inclination does everything in its power to make a person transgress. A person's defense at this stage is to strengthen himself in emuna and remember that he has the power to overcome, but that he is helpless without Hashem. He should therefore pray and enlist the Creator's assistance, Who will be more than happy to help those who seek Him. He should also learn as much as he can from the holy books and take the advice of tzaddikim, for they will give him the right outlook and perspective for making the right choices.

At this stage, the evil inclination is still comparatively small as long as a person composes himself and realizes that he can easily overcome. One must be careful, for the evil inclination will then try to inject him with arrogance and prevent him from seeking the Creator's help by telling him to be independent and to bravely fight his own wars. At this dangerous point, a person must remind himself that he is powerless without the Creator.

Since the evil inclination is a spiritual force, no physical weapons can overcome it. One needs the Creator's help; the evil inclination will make every attempt to fool a person into thinking that he's master of his own destiny. A person who forgets Hashem and his own futility without Hashem begins to take action and make decisions on his own - without consulting Him - and then he falls down hard. His mistake began with arrogance and ended up with heresy, when he forgot about the Hashem. Without prayer means without the Creator.

Stage Two: This is the dangerous stage when a person considers himself a pious individual who has already overcome his evil inclination. Such a person is in grave danger, for any fall or setback will devastate him. From his state of arrogance and smugness, he is in grave danger of falling into a state of self-persecution and depression!

The Evil Inclination's Real Gain

Rebbe Nachman of Breslev said that more than the evil inclination desires the transgression itself, it desires the sadness and depression that neutralize a person after the sin has already been committed. As for the transgression itself, teshuva with love will turn it around into a great merit. For this reason, the evil inclination doesn't suffice by tricking a person into committing a sin, because that's not yet enough to spiritually and emotionally paralyze a person. All the sinner has to do is to make teshuva; that way, he or she not only escapes the evil inclination but is deemed a tzaddik as well. To "knock a person out", the evil inclination injects him with the venom of sadness and depression - that's evil's big gain, for as long as a person is depressed, he can't pray a word or serve Hashem in any other way.

The "primary" evil inclination incites a person to sin. The "secondary" evil inclination, which knocks a person down in sadness after the sin, is in effect much more dangerous. This sadness is heresy. Why? After a person sins, he should know that Hashem is waiting for him and expecting him to do teshuva. Hashem loves him! All he needs to do is to talk to Hashem and to tell Him the truth. "Hashem, I fell! Help me get back on my feet again..."

The Prosecutor's Claim

The nasty prosecutor - the evil inclination - not only tempts a person before the sin but afterwards represents the prosecution in the Heavenly Court. Its first claim is, "The person had free choice; why didn't he choose to do good?" The prosecutor not only files the claim Above, but hounds a person incessantly below, convincing him that he's obviously evil and worthless, otherwise he would have done good. That way, the EI weakens a person's soul by wearing him down so much that he lacks the power to resist evil anymore and he continues to spiral downward. This is the trap of self-persecution. One needs a large measure of Divine mercy to put an end to his or her self-persecution.

This is the secondary EI, the EI after the sin has been committed. It's sly and dangerous, just like a snake. A person must combat this enemy with every weapon he or she has at their disposal. A person's entire teshuva depends on his or her ability to avoid the trap of depression and self-persecution. At all costs, they must strengthen themselves in their desire to continue striving to get close to Hashem. Rebbe Natan would always say that a tzaddik's spiritual level was determined by the measure he'd strengthen himself whenever the evil inclination tried to overcome him, especially during times of setbacks. The greater the self-strengthening in the face of difficulty, the greater the level of the tzaddik.

As long as a person has not yet made complete teshuva, he'll still suffer from setbacks and failures; for that reason, he must learn the correct way to make teshuva, namely, to stay happy and to hold on at his current spiritual rung without falling into the abyss of despair.

The more he'll strengthen himself in the face of his challenges, the higher he'll ascend. This is what Rebbe Nachman referred to when he said that if a person wants to do teshuva, he must know how to act during times of expansion, when things are going good, and during times of contraction, when the world seems to be crashing down on him. If during the "down" times he continues to desire Hashem and refuses to give up, he'll see tremendous spiritual gain (see Likutei Moharan I:6).

Hashem Desires Teshuva

After a person transgresses, taking into consideration the dangerous second type of evil inclination, he or she now faces a more difficult test than before the transgression. The EI does everything to knock the individual down in despair and depression to the point of frustration where he persecutes himself. Those negative feelings are heresy! Why? Hashem's mercy is infinite and He is always ready to accept a person's sincere teshuva. We say thrice daily in the Shmona Esrei prayer, "Blessed are You, Hashem, Who desires teshuva." As such, the EI's inciting him to persecute himself and the subsequent peril of depression and self-persecution is even more dangerous than the original sin, for the person is liable to lose hope altogether and to fall into the trap of heresy.

In light of the above, Rebbe Natan of Breslev would pray (Likutei Tefillot, 60):

"Do not despair, Heaven forbid, saying that your sins can never leave you, they bury you and you wither from them; don't say that there's no way back from your foolish ways. Have mercy on yourself and on the few days that you're allotted in this world, which passes like the blink of an eye; these things you say are worse than the original misdeeds themselves. These negative thoughts are destructive and they anger the Creator more than all the sins and misdeeds you committed ever since you came down to this earth. There's still hope, every hour and every minute. There is no end to Hashem's compassion, ever. You cannot fathom the magnitude of His mercy for those who seek to come back to Him in sincerity. Even though they haven't come back yet, Hashem's entire desire is for those who seek, anticipate and yearn to find refuge in and return to Hashem, even though forces beyond their control obstruct them every moment and prevent them from returning to their Father's home for days and even years. Even so, Hashem's compassion overcomes them in a way that defies description and even thought. If all the seas were ink and all the river-reeds pens and all of humanity scribes, they would not suffice in describing one iota of the loving-kindness that Hashem bestows on every generation, especially on the downtrodden and the suffering people who look forward to returning to Hashem in truth. Therefore, strengthen yourself at every moment and begin to serve your Creator in truth while turning away from the path of evil, contemptible thoughts and the pursuit of folly. Connect to Hashem and don't return to foolishness. Look upwards and return to your soul's original love. Arise, my soul! Open your mouth and let your words illuminate."

Don't ever forget that depression is worse than all other transgressions, as the above prayer alludes to. The depressed person is in effect making a statement that Hashem does not desire teshuva, Heaven forbid, as if Hashem is incapable of sending him salvation, Heaven forbid. The truth is that there is no despair in the world and that Hashem desires our teshuva. Hashem always wants for a person to make a new beginning, to do teshuva for the past and to improve his ways from this moment on. Hashem can do anything, so be strong in your belief and ask Him for everything!

Arrogance Precedes Failure

To further our understanding of tests of faith and setbacks, we must first understand why we were born. The entire purpose of our being created is to teach us humility; in other words, so that a person can realize that he or she is nothing without Hashem. The truth is that there is no one or nothing but Hashem - ein od milvado. Anything else is a lie. One who fails to live with the truth that he is nothing without Hashem lives a life of falsehood. This began with Adam and Eve, when the serpent injected them with the spiritual venom of arrogance, where they felt like they were on the same level with Hashem.

The first test of faith of Adam and Eve's offspring - Cain and Abel - was arrogance and self-persecution after the sin. This is what tripped Cain. Abel had humility, he knew he was nothing; he didn't even think he was worthy of bringing a sacrificial offering to Hashem. Yet, despite his feeling that he wasn't worthy, he wanted to bring gratification to Hashem so he brought the very best offering he could. He thought, "If Hashem accepts my offering - wonderful! And if not, no big deal because I'm not worthy anyway. But, I want to give it a try - maybe Hashem will have compassion on me and accept my offering."

Consequently, Abel did the very best he could. He was even prepared to lovingly accept a rejection. He could do so because of his humility. He had no expectations and no sense of entitlement, for he knew that everything is a free gift, the product of Hashem's compassion.

A person should pray like Abel. From one standpoint, he should have the "holy boldness" to ask for his needs and desires, but with no expectations or sense of entitlement. Yet, he should trust that Hashem will surely do what's best.

Cain on the other hand had an evil inclination of arrogance. This is the only evil inclination that leads to heresy, for arrogance is tantamount to heresy. It's the feeling that a person doesn't need the Creator, doesn't need to pray and doesn't need to seek His advice. Cain didn't learn the lesson of humility that Hashem was teaching when He sought the opinion of the angels. Therefore, Cain brought a contemptible offering, worthless scraps that were unfit to set before the Holy One.

How could he do such a thing? He was so arrogant that he thought he was doing Hashem a favor by bringing Him an offering. Cain was expecting a thank-you from Hashem, positive that He would accept the offering. It's like a person who has respect for someone greater than him - he'll present the latter with the very best gift he can. But, if the giver is arrogant and he feels superior to the receiver, he'll dig up something that's buried in the bottom of his closet - something that he neither needs nor uses - and present that as a gift...

That's exactly what Cain did. No wonder Hashem didn't accept his offering. So what should Cain have done? He should have been ashamed. He should have humbled himself. A setback should teach a person humility. OK, he had a setback, but why? It was his arrogance that prevented him from praying. If he would have had humility, he would have prayed and he would not have failed. People with humility don't ever fall; they feel like they're no higher than an ant, so there's nowhere left for them to fall. Humility means that a person truly knows that he is nothing without Hashem. "Without Hashem" means without prayer, for without prayer a person can't overcome the feeblest evil inclination.

Will You Eat More Garlic?

Clearly, a person fails because of his arrogance. So, if he's had a setback, he should tell himself, "I sinned because I forgot that I'm powerless without Hashem. I was smug, so the evil inclination was able to trip me." The solution is therefore to humbly seek the Creator and pray for His help because the setback was the result of his lack of prayer and his failure to see that he's powerless without Hashem.

But what happens to a person after a setback? He falls into even greater arrogance with despair and depression, for he continues in the lie that he is able to contend without the Creator and is therefore devastated when that misconception slaps him in the face. He adds the sin of depression to the sin that he committed. The old adage says that instead of freshening his breath after eating garlic, he simply eats more garlic. In like manner, after committing the sin of arrogance, he commits the greater sin of despair and depression.

The arrogant person persecutes himself because he thinks he should have overcome the evil inclination on his own, without Hashem and without prayer. A spiritual fact of life is that a person cannot overcome the evil inclination without the Creator's help. We must therefore realize that we need the Creator at our side always. Each of us should always have a prayer on our lips such as, "Hashem, please help me overcome my evil inclination. Help me overcome the urge to covet what's not mine. Guard me from self-persecution, laziness and bodily appetites that destroy both body and soul. Protect me against laziness, selfishness and cruelty. Help me remember You always." Prayer means clinging to the Creator, the best thing a person can do.

If Hashem loves us so much, then why does He let us fail? Failure is a reminder that we are nothing without Him. Our loving and compassionate Creator wants us to be close to Him, yet our arrogance is an iron curtain that separates a person from Him, for when a person is arrogant, Hashem leaves him. One can't succeed without Hashem; therefore, after a setback, a person should make an enhanced effort to strengthen and renew his connection with Him. As such, failure is a gift in disguise to bring us closer to the Creator and to help us repel arrogance.

What is arrogance? This is the feeling that one can manage without prayer and Divine assistance. The antidote to arrogance is remembering that we are futile and virtually nothing without the Creator. A person who clings to Hashem and seeks His advice on every matter prays all the time. Such a person doesn't fail. But even if he would fail, he'd thank Him for bringing him closer and for reminding him that he's nothing without Him. He would express remorse for every moment that he forgot the Creator and for every tiny endeavor that he did or tried to do without prayer.

Indeed, after a setback, a person must really thank Hashem. "Thank You, Hashem, for bringing me back to reality and reminding me that I'm nothing without You. Thank You for putting me in my proper place. I'm sorry for the past, for not living in emuna and in humility. I hereby do teshuva and ask You to help me realize that I am nothing without You, Hashem. Forgive me for my arrogance and help me cling to You always from now on, to pray for everything and ask for Your assistance." Then, the person should do teshuva on the particular transgression he committed, in the order that we previously learned.

Sadness is a Revolt Against Hashem

Cain failed to learn from his mistake. He became even more arrogant. The Torah says, "And Cain was very incensed, and his countenance fell." Then Hashem asked him, "Why are you so incensed and why has your countenance fallen?" (Genesis 4: 5-6). Hashem is saying - what's wrong with you, Cain? You fouled up and you're angry? What for? Are you upset that you've discovered that you're nothing?

Imagine if the king's servant dropped a tray with the king's expensive crystal wine goblet, which crashed into smithereens on the floor. The servant gets angry and throws a tantrum: "This whole palace can jump in the lake! I hate it here and don't want to work here anymore!" What an affront to the king! Instead of asking the king's forgiveness, the servant becomes angry, arrogant and insolent in the worst way. Instead of atoning and trying to do better, he quits. He'd be lucky if the palace head butler says, "Listen, fool! Grab a broom and dustpan and clean up your mess. Be grateful that you aren't being thrown into the dungeon for your nasty attitude and insolence."

Could the above parable be talking about each of us? Our evil inclination is not failure; that's our miniature evil inclination. Our major evil inclination is the bitterness, despair and self-persecution after a setback which is nothing other than arrogance. What could be greater insolence? One's failure should have brought him to humility, but no - instead, he gets angry, falls into depression and "quits" the Creator.

The more dangerous evil inclination - the one that follows a setback or failure - is much worse than the failure itself. Failure breaks a person's ego. Many people have difficulty accepting the fact that they're "nothing" without the Creator; even though the setback or failure is proof, the evil inclination won't let them acknowledge that fact and cast their inflated ego aside. Rather than clinging to the Creator, they cling to the fantasy that they determine their own fate.

The penitent - the one who does teshuva - is in effect confessing that he is nothing without the Creator. The beauty of teshuva is his recognition of this fact. No wonder our sages said that the righteous cannot stand on the same level with those who have done teshuva (Sanhedrin 99a). A baal teshuva - one who does teshuva - must redirect the post-failure negative emotional energy of sadness and depression into the positive spiritual energy of teshuva, which lifts himself higher than he was before the setback.

So, when the baal teshuva admits and acknowledges that he is nothing without Hashem, he surpasses the righteous person who never sinned. Although this seems illogical, because the righteous person never sinned or felt arrogant in the first place, he doesn't feel his nothingness with the same intensity that the baal teshuva does.

A person who overcomes the post-transgression evil inclination of sadness attains major spiritual growth. This is what Hashem promised Cain when He said, "If you better your ways", you'll climb tremendously high. Hashem tells Cain that he should have first overcome his evil inclination of arrogance and then he wouldn't have sinned at all. But now that he has sinned, and the evil inclination wants to bring him down even more in sadness, disappointment and depression, he must now confront this second, stronger evil inclination. By becoming a baal teshuva and overcoming it, he'll even surpass his brother Abel who was completely righteous.

The wondrous works of the Omniscient One

Rebbe Natan of Breslev lauds the lofty virtues of teshuva (see Likutei Halachot, Basar Shenit'alem min Ha'ayin, 4):

"Teshuva is effective in rectifying even the worst transgressions in the world. Even though a person blemished what he blemished and ruined what he ruined, teshuva is nonetheless effective. On the surface, this defies comprehension. Sins are destructive, both to the individual and to the world. How can penitence and remorse rectify damage that has been done? Even though the soul of the sinner becomes liable for severe punishment, Hashem's greatness and compassion are beyond our understanding and He prepared a remedy for the world - teshuva. Even though the sinner deserves the most severe punishments, if he does teshuva, Hashem forgives in a way we cannot fathom.

"As soon as a person does teshuva and commits to refrain from misdeeds, etc., Hashem immediately has mercy on him and shines an illumination of rectification from

Above on him, from a place where there is no ruination. Indeed, great rectifications are attained.

"Therefore, one must pursue a path that never transgresses anything against Torah, Heaven forbid, for no matter how he acts, Hashem will help him. He who doesn't do teshuva will suffer his bitter outcome.

"But if Heaven forbid, the evil inclination ensnared him in its trap, and he succumbed be it accidentally or willfully, even if he repeatedly transgressed against the entire Torah, Heaven forbid, there is still no despair in the world at all as we've explained several times, for our sages say that nothing stands in the way of teshuva. After a person did whatever he did, he must arouse and strengthen himself in teshuva and depend on Hashem's mercy, for Hashem will shine rectifications from Above and everything will turn around for the very best. This is the aspect of sins turning into merits by way of teshuva.

"But, a person cannot rely on this if he desires to repeatedly sin intentionally and then make teshuva, for he won't be enabled to make teshuva. He who says, "I'll sin and then I'll repent" is using his trust in Hashem's mercy as a license to sin; therefore, Hashem will remove His mercy and take away His Divine help for the person to do teshuva. But, if he ultimately overcomes despite the difficulties and does make sincere teshuva, that too will be good, just that he won't benefit from Hashem's assistance." These are the teachings of Rebbe Natan osb"m from Likutei Halachot.

There's Always a New Choice

A person should not misconstrue the notion of Divine providence and say, "Everything is preordained from

Above. It therefore doesn't matter what I do, whether I make an effort to withstand tribulations or not, or to act morally or not. The Creator knows anyway what'll happen, because it's already been preordained if I'll be a good person or an evil one. Therefore, I'll do whatever I want, for I can always say, 'That's what Hashem wants'..."

The above attitude isn't faith - it's total heresy. A person has free choice, period. The Creator made the world so that a person would have a free choice between good and evil or emuna and heresy - no one can complain of coercion. The Torah says, "Behold, I place before you today life and good and death and evil...you shall choose life" (Deuteronomy 30:19) - this is an explicit command for a person to do everything in his power to do good, to conduct his or her life in a responsible and upright manner and not to transgress even the tiniest sin. If a person does not choose to do good, no excuse will help him Above. The Torah says that every person has free choice and that is how he or she is judged.

Suppose, after the fact, someone makes a wrong choice; that's not the end of the world! He can make a new choice at any given time. Self-assessment and penitence enable him to chart a new course and return to Hashem. His virtue will be even greater, for our sages say that the tzaddik cannot stand in a place where baalei teshuva - penitents - stand. That way, a setback will turn into a triumph, as Rebbe Nachman said, "There is a concept that everything turns around for the best!" A person can choose between the renewed vigor of a new and good choice or the anger, despair and self-persecution of failing to start anew.

Everyone makes mistakes from time to time. But what happens afterwards? Those who climb back on their feet after a fall are stronger than those who never fell. With repentance and new choices, one turns mistakes and setbacks into new growth opportunities.

Rebbe Nachman of Breslev explains in Likutei Moharan I: 261 that spiritual setbacks, like everything else in life, come from Above. Sometimes it seems like Hashem is pushing a person away, but in truth, He is bringing him closer, for the person's setback triggers a greater effort to reinforce oneself in emuna and seek the Creator with greater desire. Everyone should therefore learn to make new beginnings every day of their lives and not be discouraged from anything...

If a person reacts properly after a fall or setback, he or she will certainly go far. We of course prefer going through life without making mistakes, but those very mistakes help us fulfill our mission in life, improve and attain perfection.

There is no Evil Inclination

The moment a person recognizes that once he sinned already, the door of teshuva is still open and that he can always improve, then his mistakes and setbacks become springboards for new growth and enhanced proximity to Hashem. By using his transgressions as catalysts to improve, he neutralizes the evil inclination. The evil inclination, which is essentially heresy, wants him depressed and upset with himself after a sin. Once again, we are speaking about after the sin, once it has been committed. What was done is done. But, as we learned, before the sin, one must do everything to avoid committing it. After the sin, the choice is to do teshuva and improve one's ways and not fall into a self-persecution mode.

Self-persecution has nothing to do with teshuva - it's the opposite of teshuva. After a sin, one must realize that he or she is powerless without Hashem's help. This conclusion brings a person to humility and is conducive to getting closer to Hashem. Self-persecution, on the other hand, is the epitome of arrogance, when a person is angry that he or she did not succeed without Hashem's help.

Where does it say in Torah that teshuva means despair and wailing? Teshuva, as the Rambam teaches us, is simply confessing, expressing remorse, asking the Creator's forgiveness and resolving to do better in the future. With that said and done, one can turn the page and start anew! The Zohar says that sadness and depression are from the dark side, and Hashem despises them.

Before doing something, we try to do our very best and to make the right choice. But once the deed is done, we can rectify a mistake or a sin by returning to the Creator in repentance, which brings us to the awareness of what we did wrong and to the good character traits of humility and honesty.

A person who lives his life with emuna doesn't deal with the evil inclination. He doesn't persecute himself after making a mistake and he accepts everything that happens in his life with the faith that this is what the Creator wants. He says to himself, "OK, if Hashem wanted me to have an evil inclination, then I must fight it. And, if the evil inclination gets the best of me, then I must find out where I went wrong, repent and seek Hashem's help." Such a spiritually pragmatic attitude provides a person with a mode of constant spiritual growth and improvement.

Really, a person doesn't even need to confront his evil inclination as long as he lives with Hashem's Divine providence: before committing a transgression, he learns religious law, prays and asks for Hashem's help in making the right choice. But, after committing a transgression, Heaven forbid, he should do teshuva and learn the lesson of his setback, thus learning to make the right choices in the future.

A person who recognizes his mistakes learns humility. Since prayer and penitence follow his mistakes, the evil inclination has virtually no power over him! This is a true servant of Hashem, even after a failure or a setback.

Teshuva from Love

Rebbe Natan also writes in Likutei Halachot (Tefilat HaMincha, 7) that a person who believes in the real tzaddikim and strengthens himself in their teaching that no matter what, a person should strengthen himself even in the most difficult times, then all setbacks turn into ascents and success.

A person with emuna doesn't fall into depression and despair when he makes a mistake. He's not worried about bolts of lightning coming out of the sky to hit him on the head. He looks at himself, assesses his wrongdoing and simply takes the proper steps to make teshuva and rectify, rather than falling into despair and self-persecution because of his misdeed, This is called "teshuva from love", because he has no depression or discouragement from his misdeed.

This is what our sages meant when they said that a person who does teshuva from love merits that his willful misdeeds turn into mitzvoth (see Yoma 86b). If he doesn't fall into depression and self-persecution, but he's jolted into action because of the terrible thing he did and he arouses himself to do teshuva, then his bad deed becomes the catalyst for his teshuva; it turns from a serious demerit to a merit.

Maybe a person is in spiritual slumber, sleeping his life away. He had a lust or a bad habit that he didn't consider to be so serious. Yet, once he transgressed in this area and did something seriously wrong, he awakened to the fact that he must improve. Therefore, for the type of person who does teshuva with love, even his mistakes turn into merits for they bring him to better himself and his ways.

Human nature is that people don't usually learn a lasting lesson until they make a mistake in that particular area. Why? Failure is a wonderful teacher; it triggers self-assessment, new conclusions and stronger second efforts. Failure, when accepted in a positive emuna-oriented manner, is a step to higher growth. Yet, when failure leads to depression and despair, it's the tool of heresy.

We have no control over the past. But we must do everything in our power to secure a good future.

Truth

As long as a person fails to see his limitations and that periodic failure is a part of everyone's path in life, then he's far from the truth. As long as a person fails to recognize that he is nothing without Hashem, he'll keep on failing until he learns his proper place and proportions. One must always request emuna from Hashem and seek to strengthen his connection to Him.

Success means remembering Hashem constantly, that we are nothing without Him, and asking for His help. But let's not fool ourselves; we must recognize that we'll make mistakes in the future. We therefore must always ask Hashem for emuna and that we won't forget Him for a single moment, knowing that Hashem personally is enabling every breath and heartbeat and we are nothing without Him. We must therefore ask His help in guarding us from transgressing.

People fool themselves into thinking that everything will go smoothly, for two reasons:

The first reason – Rebbe Nachman of Breslev writes (Likutei Moharan I:79) that there are two sides of teshuva. One is the "weekday-style teshuva", where sometimes a person is pure and sometimes spiritually contaminated, sometimes worthy and sometimes not. This is the teshuva categorized by ups and downs, falls and setbacks. Yet, there is the second, or "Sabbath-style teshuva", where a person enjoys rest from all temptation and the evil inclination has no power over him. Only a few special individuals in each generation attain this level.

Most people, including those of spiritual prominence, are holding at the level of weekday-style teshuva. This is remindful of the comedian who put on a show for the guests at the wedding of one of Rebbe Nachman's daughters: he came out on the stage dressed as an angel, then a minute later came out again dressed as a priest and repeated this several times. When Rebbe Nachman saw this, he told his students in Yiddish, "It's just like all of you – a mol a malach und a mol a galach – one minute you're an angel, and the next minute you're a priest."

Who did Rebbe Nachman tell this to? Were his students people on our level? No way! We can't even fathom the greatness of Rebbe Nachman's students. Notwithstanding, Rebbe Nachman put them in their place so they wouldn't think that they had already attained the level of "Sabbath-style teshuva". They were still in weekday-style teshuva with its ups and downs and frequent setbacks, just like the comedian acting on the stage.

We too should know and recognize our true spiritual level, that we'll still be facing setbacks and failures on our way in life.

The second reason - Rebbe Natan of Breslev, Rebbe Nachman's prime disciple and loyal student, said to his students: "You see me, that things are going smoothly in my old age, is because all my life, I prayed profusely for everything. So now, in my old age, all my prayers are coming together to help me in the service of Hashem."

Apparent in Rebbe Natan's above expression is that until he reached his final days on earth, nothing was easy for him. He had extreme highs and lows, for on his level, he still lacked the needed prayers for a spiritually smooth life. We should only merit to pray like he did...

So what can a person who barely prayed for all that one needs to pray for possibly expect? We must pray for guarding our eyes, guarding our tongue, guarding our time, for learning Torah, for praying properly. Have we done so sufficiently? Only a person who fools himself can expect a setback-free life.

I Ate and I'll Continue Eating...

One who knows that he is prone to sin again is more inclined to pray profusely and seek Hashem's assistance in guarding him from future wrongdoing. But, if he fools himself into thinking that he has already attained angel status, he won't notice the pitfalls that are liable to ensnare him and he won't pray.

Rebbe Menachem Mendel of Kotzk osb"m explains Hashem's apparently surprising question to Adam: "Where are you... did you eat from the tree that I commanded you not to eat from?" (Genesis 3: 9, 11). Adam answered, "...the woman that You gave me gave me the fruit of the tree and I ate it" (ibid.). The Midrash says that Adam was telling Hashem, "I ate it and I'll continue eating it." The Kotzker Rebbe asks, "Isn't this unprecedented insolence? Hashem asks if you ate from the tree, and instead of confessing, showing remorse and committing to rectify your misdeeds, you tell Hashem that you intend to continue sinning?!"

The Kotzker Rebbe answers his own question and says that there is no insolence here. Why? Hashem's question to Adam, "Where are you", means where are you holding? What level are you situated on after the sin? Are you capable of controlling your evil inclination? Adam answers that he cannot. He's on a level where his evil inclination is stronger than he is. He's not fooling himself that he won't sin anymore.

This is the answer to what many people ask: everything's well and good if I would really sin no more after I made teshuva. But the reality is that I will make more mistakes and I will sin again. How can I turn to Hashem again and ask forgiveness, when I know that I'll sin again?

Here's your answer: sure, it's embarrassing to keep on sinning, but that notwithstanding, a person must be honest with himself. Yes, he has an evil inclination that is difficult to overcome. If he doesn't pray profusely and ask for Hashem's assistance, he'll undoubtedly fall and fail repeatedly. He therefore must strengthen himself and be happy with his lot in life, including his spiritual lot. And he must know that despite his repeated efforts in teshuva, he'll still have setbacks. Nevertheless, Hashem cherishes his desire to do good and get closer to Hashem. Indeed, his embarrassment of continued sinning is part of his teshuva.

Confess and Move Forward

A person needs emuna to repent properly. Simply speaking, emuna is being happy with our current lot in life, both material and spiritual. Sure, we all want to improve. But meanwhile, even if we've had a setback, we just move forward, repent and do our utmost to get close to Hashem. We accept our shortcomings with love; rather than be depressed about them, we strive to improve them.

Know full well that if we don't accept our shortcomings with love, we'll never overcome them. Accepting them with love means to accept them with emuna; emuna connects us to the Creator, and with His help, we can accomplish anything. How can a person improve, repent or do anything for that matter without Hashem's help? If he tries on his own, he ends up blaming himself for his setbacks and he comes to all kinds of mistaken conclusions. But he doesn't blame himself of the proper accusation:

I didn't believe in Hashem and I didn't ask for His help. I depended on myself...

Only a person who recognizes and acknowledges his shortcomings shows that he lives with emuna, for he understands that Hashem wants him to improve. Such a person readily prays to Hashem and seeks His help.

Know Your Creator

Rebbe Nachman of Breslev teaches us that a person should look for his good points and rejoice in them. Even if he has fallen, he should hold on tight to the good he can find in himself for it will prevent him from falling further. If he follows this advice, he will merit in making teshuva with love and then his transgressions will all become mitzvoth. No matter what, a person should not let himself despair in any way; indeed, he should strengthen himself in the knowledge that Hashem's mercy is limitless.

The Creator knows you intimately. He knows that you have an evil inclination that you cannot overcome without His help. So stop persecuting yourself! No matter how low you fell or whatever you did wrong, Hashem does not want you to be depressed. Make a new beginning! After you strengthen yourself and return to the optimistic mode, you can now do effective teshuva on whatever you slipped up on.

Don't ever forget that Hashem loves you always! He wants to help you. He created you in order to have mercy on you and to do good for you. You enjoy endless mercy that suffices for life's most difficult situations. Hashem's good and mercy never terminate. That's what we say every day in the Amida prayer, "You are good and Your mercy never diminishes, You are merciful and Your compassion never ends, for we have always yearned for You." Ask Hashem always to have mercy on you and to help you make teshuva.

The Holy One Helps

Since we can't overcome the evil inclination on our own, our task is to pray and enlist the Creator's help, asking Him to help us refrain from and avoid transgressing. As our sages said, the evil inclination overpowers us every day and without Hashem's help, we cannot prevail.

A person's main task therefore is to strengthen himself against the evil inclination by way of prayer, praying daily and asking for Hashem's assistance in avoiding sin. Also, one must learn Torah for this gives a person added spiritual strength and stamina.

There is no room in our lives for anger, depression and self-persecution - they accomplish nothing. Those who fail to understand this important principle continue to harass themselves every time they do something wrong; that way, they rectify nothing. Sadness and depression drain a person and leave him powerless to do anything.

Rebbe Nachman of Breslev in his classic teaching (Likutei Moharan I:282, known as "Azamra") writes that sadness and depression keep a person far away from Hashem, for the attitude of self-persecution prevents a person from praying to and seeking the Creator.

Understand that those negative emotions all come from the evil inclination that is trying to keep a person from seeking the Creator. Therefore, advises Rebbe Nachman, a person must focus on his good points and rejoice in them, building on them to thank and rejoice in the Creator, and then he will surely return to Him and rectify that which needs rectification.

What Hashem Demands from Us

The Gemara (Avoda Zara, 3a) teaches that Hashem doesn't harbor baseless complaints about His creations. He knows exactly who they are and what they are capable of and therefore does not make demands on them that they cannot fulfill. Hashem therefore speaks to each of us and says:

Listen, My son, My daughter! I can't tell you not to sin, for there are commandments that you won't be able to fulfill until you refine your negative character traits. But you can certainly pray for the future and desire to improve; that, you can do!

At the dawn of history, Cain offered an undesirable sacrifice to the Creator. When it was rejected, Cain became depressed. The Creator chastised him, "Why has your countenance fallen?"

Pay attention that Hashem didn't chastise Cain for sacrificing a few handfuls of flax seeds, his cheapest crop. Hashem also didn't complain that Cain didn't pray to Him or seek His Divine guidance. The Creator chastised Cain for the way he received his setback - "Why has your countenance fallen?" "Cain", Hashem was asking, "what do you expect to achieve with your depression and self-persecution? Be pro-active; move forward and then you'll be able to rectify everything."

A person who accepts setbacks in the right way merits the gift of humility. He realizes that he can't succeed without Hashem. Therefore, from here on, he seeks to cling to Him. He strengthens his desires and therefore his setback turns into a major triumph. He attains an ultimately higher spiritual level than he would have if he never had the setback or if he would have succeeded with his first effort. Our sages tell us that a baal teshuva – a penitent individual – is actually on a higher spiritual level than the righteous person who never sinned in the first place.

If a person knows his place and admits to himself that although there are things that he does not yet have the power to uphold as the Torah requires, the path of teshuva is nonetheless open to him and if he begins the process of self-improvement and spiritual growth in a proper and pleasant manner, he'll merit to rectify everything. The important thing is to avoid the pitfalls of depression, self-persecution and other negativity, which are none other than the evil inclination's ploys to immobilize him and break him down.

The Creator's principle complaint against a person is, "Why are you sad? Why don't you learn from your setbacks? Why don't you realize that you can't overcome the evil inclination without My help?" Those who don't awaken from the spiritual slumber of depression continue to persecute themselves. Let's not be like that! Turn to the Creator for help and go forward.

Don't ever forget that Hashem knows that you are incapable of overcoming the evil inclination without His help. All He expects from you is that you acknowledge that fact. Learn from your setbacks that you can't overcome the evil inclination without Hashem in your corner, so start praying for His help. The only thing that perturbs Hashem is when people deny the fact that they need Him; that's exactly why they end up persecuting themselves when they fall, because in their lack of emuna they believed that they could prevail over their evil inclination on their own.

That's why we all must wake up. Set aside an hour a day for personal prayer and ask Hashem to help you overcome your evil inclination. Get started!

Teshuva is Joy

A third important rule is that teshuva is only possible when done in joy.

Rebbe Nachman of Breslev teaches that a sad person loses control over his thought process. He cannot attain a measure of mental composure where he can take stock in himself. A person must compose himself and ponder where all the bodily lusts and the extra-bodily lusts, such as honor, are taking him. Once he is happy, he can properly assess himself and will certainly come back to Hashem.

Yet, melancholy subdues his ability to control his mind as he desires. That's why joy is the key that releases him from his mental and emotional prison, for the prophet says, "For by joy, you shall go out," (Isaiah 55:12). As such, by way of joy, he is a free man and no longer a slave to the evil inclination. Joy terminates his emotional exile.

In addition, Rebbe Nachman writes that without joy, even the fear of G-d is diluted with foolishness, for it is written (Job 4:6), "Your fear of G-d is foolishness." Only by way of joy, can a person attain genuine spiritual awareness. One cannot function properly without joy.

Joy is necessary to confess a sin and repent for it, says Rebbe Nachman (see Likutei Moharan I:178). Why? Without joy, it's difficult for a person to speak mundane things; all the more so, confessing sin and speaking to

Hashem. This can only be done with the joy of performing a mitzva, since teshuva is certainly a lofty mitzvah.

Rebbe Nachman testified that even if he would commit the worst sin in the world, he wouldn't fall into despair and depression. He'd simply pick himself up, repent and go forward in joy. We conclude that joy is a vital prerequisite for teshuva. As long as he is not in a positive mindset, he shouldn't even begin to judge himself.

The lack of joy, more than anything, prevents people from dealing with their setbacks and failures. Rebbe Nachman's advice is once again to focus on the good that we find in ourselves, for there's no one alive that doesn't have good points. This helps us uplift ourselves in joy and enables us to set out on the path of teshuva.

Unfortunately, much of the above advice falls on deaf ears. Many who want to implement this advice fail to do so. Why? They don't believe that it's possible to be happy after a sin or setback. They suffer from a gross misconception about teshuva. They think that they must torture themselves about the sin they committed. That's ridiculous! Why torment yourself, because you have an evil inclination? Remember the two mindsets we've spoken about: before doing something, we do our best to do the right thing. But after the deed is done, that's what Hashem wanted. Indeed, we should be happy that we are upset with ourselves, for that shows that we want to repent.

People still ask, "How can I be happy? OK, if I knew that I wouldn't sin anymore, I could be happy. But I know that I'll foul up again and again. How can I be happy?"

Once again, the answer is that is soon as you remember your real situation in life - that you're a mortal with an evil inclination, and you're not yet an angel - you can be happy! Hashem loves you and has infinite mercy on you and is always ready to welcome you back with open arms. With that in mind, be happy and make a new start! If you still doubt what you're reading, go back to the beginning of this chapter and review it carefully.

Summarizing the Three General Rules

Rule 1 - a person becomes discouraged because his evil inclination overcomes him in some way, either with a bad habit or with lust of some sort. He does not yet recognize his own reality and he harbors the fantasy that he is expected to be, or capable of being totally good with no bad ever. That's simply not correct. The evil inclination is a part of his nature, so it's no surprise that he has lust, negative character traits and so forth.

Rule 2 - Not only do you have an evil inclination, but you are incapable of overcoming it! So what are you upset about? This is a law of creation, that the evil inclination is stronger than a person. Our sages say explicitly that every day, the evil inclination rises up to overcome a person, and if Hashem doesn't help, he cannot prevail on his own.

Rule 3 - Be happy with your lot in life. Know that it's not your job to be perfect; simply strive to learn Torah and pray as much as you can. Invest an hour of daily personal prayer, where you assess yourself in a calm and composed manner and repent for anything you might have done wrong in the last 24 hours since your previous personal prayer and self-assessment session. Ask Hashem to help you overcome your evil inclination. Don't be disappointed in yourself when you repeat a wrongdoing. Simply share with Hashem what's happening in your life and turn to Him sincerely in teshuva because He is always waiting for you with open arms, no matter what you've done wrong. Never give up your desires and never stop praying - the more the better - and you will certainly avoid sin. And, if you're upset that you still commit sins, simply pray more and more and ask for Hashem's assistance - there is no better advice.

Judging Oneself

The principle of justice is one of the most important foundational principles of humanity. Justice differentiates us from the animals, which function according to instinct. Humans have an intellect that is capable of making choices and rectifying mistakes. Justice and intellect are the tools that the Creator embedded in the human soul so that people would be able to assess themselves. The human conscience with its sense of right and wrong sets man above the animal kingdom.

Judging oneself is a natural human phenomenon. People judge themselves constantly, but oftentimes according to warped standards that bring them to self-persecution, self-pity, lack of self-confidence and low self-esteem. These warped standards cause a person to feel that he's a failure. No wonder he's sad and depressed, for he's unwilling to forgive himself.

Something is terribly wrong with concepts of self-judgment that cause negative emotions and sever a person from the Creator, to the extent of heresy, Heaven forbid. Remember what we've stressed - the evil inclination cares much more about the post-sin despair than it does about the sin itself.

Transgressions, in addition to their inherent damage, distance a person from Hashem. Yet, sadness and depression distance a person from Hashem much more than the sin itself. For this reason, a righteous individual is not necessarily the one who doesn't sin; he's the one who sins but gets back on his feet fast. He is strengthened by his setbacks. If he judges himself properly, he'll be closer to Hashem after his sin and resulting repentance. What's more, he'll succeed in both improving and rectifying himself rather than allowing the setback to knock him down in despair and disappointment, Heaven forbid.

The Rules of Judgment

There are seven rules that provide the proper perspective of an individual's personal-judgment system:

1. **Hashem desires teshuva, not sadness.** A person must clarify in his mind, first of all, what does Hashem want? Does He want me to be depressed? Or does He want me to strengthen myself and repent? For sure, He wants the teshuva.

2. **Confession.** A person should confess his wrongdoings according to the four stages that we learned from the Rambam: confession, remorse, apology and resolution to do one's utmost to avoid sinning in the future. Since a person knows that he lacks the strength to remain sin-free, he must move on to the next rule:

3. **Hashem doesn't test a person with a level of difficulty beyond his capabilities.** Hashem doesn't give a person a test that he can't pass. He should therefore learn and pray, thus rising to subsequent challenges. This, therefore, is his resolution – he will pray to Hashem and

learn what he must learn in order to avoid sinning in the future. Specifically, he should request Hashem's help in helping him implement what he learned. Meanwhile, we should understand that any shortcoming we have is the product of Divine providence, to stimulate personal improvement and rectification. This brings us to the next rule:

4. **Learning.** One should earmark daily time to learn about the area in his life where he is vulnerable to sin and therefore needs rectification. This can include reading relevant books on the subject, listening to CD lessons or seeing online classes. Review and internalization are important components of learning. Prepare a notebook and keep notes on all the salient points of the problematic area that you need to rectify. Learn the subject well so that you'll know how to make comprehensive teshuva in that particular area until the permissible and forbidden become crystal clear in your mind.

5. **With prayer, one can accomplish anything!** One should set aside time for daily personal prayer and believe that by way of prayer, he can accomplish anything. His prayers should be detailed, asking Hashem to help him implement everything he learns. He should be patient and tenacious in prayer, for prayer is not instant coffee! He should be steadfast, without expecting immediate results. He should also avoid falling into a sense of entitlement after he prays, relying on the following rule:

6. **I don't deserve a thing!** A person should realize that the Creator owes him nothing. From his very first prayer to his last prayer on earth, a person must request a free gift; that way, he won't be impatient and he

won't lose hope. Asking for a free gift that we don't deserve enables us to pray profusely. Voluminous prayers correct everything.

7. **Gratitude.** To pray profusely, one must thank the Creator daily for the privilege of praying. Taking nothing for granted, one must thank Him for every single blessing in life - every heartbeat and every breath - leaving no stone unturned. Such expressions of gratitude are major contributions to happiness and emotional strength. One must also thank the Creator for his setbacks in life and for everything that doesn't proceed according to his plans. Nothing in the world mitigates stern judgments like such expressions of gratitude, for they express a person's staunch faith in Divine providence.

In effect, gratitude is not only the seventh rule of self-judgment, it's the first as well, for these seven rules are like a circle rather than linear. Our expressions of gratitude to the Creator should precede everything we do.

The Desire for Teshuva

A person who desires to get close to the Creator must learn and internalize the above seven rules of self-judgment and pray to be able to implement them. Without them, the same desire for penitence and rectification could reduce a person to negative emotions and distance him from Hashem, Heaven forbid.

Without the seven rules of self-judgment, learning can be dangerous. Why? When a person discovers what Hashem really wants from him, he sees his shortcomings much more. If he doesn't know how to judge himself according to the above seven guidelines, he's liable to fall into severe depression, for he thinks that penitence is self-punishment or self-flagellation. He also loses hope that he can ever change and improve.

Such thoughts of course are products of the evil inclination. But, with our seven rules of self-judgment, we know that any shortcoming we have is the result of Divine will and providence, as a catalyst for self-betterment. We approach our shortcomings in a positive and productive manner, with prayer. That way, we succeed in rectifying anything and everything.

Let's work our way through an example to see how to practically apply the seven rules of self-judgment to our daily lives. Suppose a person has an anger problem that he wants to rid himself of; here's how he should put the seven rules into practice:

1. What does Hashem want from me? Every time he judges himself, or loses his temper, he should ask himself: Does Hashem want me to be depressed or to persecute myself? I'll just get knocked down further and for sure won't be able to correct anything. Wouldn't Hashem rather me strengthen myself in joy, emuna and in hope? Then, I can move forward and do good as much as I am able, including trying to overcome my anger problem. Hashem surely wants me to maintain my joy in life, so I'll do everything in my power to do just that.

We can now continue to the next point:

2. Teshuva and confession. Proceed according to the Rambam, namely, confession, remorse, and ask forgiveness. When arriving at the stage of resolving to do better, one should be honest with himself and

not resolve that he'll never again lose his temper, because he cannot promise such a thing. Therefore, he should proceed to the next point:

3. Believe that Hashem doesn't give a person a test that he can't pass. This means that he should believe that he has the power to overcome his anger streak by way of learning and prayer. This brings us to the next point:
4. Learning. One should earmark daily time to learn about the area in his life where he is vulnerable; in the example at hand, anger. This can include reading relevant books on the subject, listening to CD lessons or viewing online classes. Review and internalization are important components of learning.
5. Prayer. Daily, he should pray to overcome his anger. One must believe that with prayer, he can rectify anything! With perseverant prayer, a person literally feels how his spiritual awareness is heightened, and in places that he used to have temper flare-ups, he doesn't lose even a bit of his self-composure any more. He should never lose hope in prayer, for many have overcome anger by innocently and simply following these guidelines.
6. Ask for a free gift. Even after one has prayed profusely but still loses his temper, he should remember that Hashem owes him nothing. He should appeal to Hashem's mercy and ask for a free gift and neither lose patience nor become discouraged. In the end, if he doesn't give up, he'll rid himself of anger completely, as many others have done by following these steps.
7. Gratitude. He should thank Hashem daily for the privilege of praying for character improvement,

particularly, overcoming anger. He should thank Hashem for every test of anger that he succeeds in passing. And, even if he didn't completely pass the test but merely reacted less violently than he usually does, he should still thank Hashem, for this too is meaningful progress. The more he thanks Hashem for every little gain, the more Hashem will be happy to help him further.

Start Walking

Some friends went on a hike together. When they came to a crossroads, they saw a man waiting there. Seven days later, they returned to the same crossroads and found the same man still waiting there. They asked him, "Why are you waiting here?"

He answered, "I'm waiting for a ride to Jerusalem." They asked him how long he had been waiting already, and he answered, "Eight days." They told him that Jerusalem was only twelve miles down the road. He could have reached it already even if he was crawling...

The above parable tells us a lot about ourselves. We all desire to rectify, but we procrastinate. In the end, we get nowhere. If we'd "begin to walk", we could have reached our destination long ago.

An old folk expression says that the thousand-mile journey begins by taking the first step. Oftentimes, a person has a long way to go in order to reach his goal or destination; but he'll never get there if he doesn't take the first step.

The first step toward self-rectification is to set aside a daily hour for self-assessment and prayer. A person who wants to better himself must seek Hashem's assistance in strengthening every weak character attribute. He shouldn't forget to thank Hashem for what he has succeeded in improving thus far, and to ask for help in moving forward. This daily hour of prayer and self-assessment is the wind in your sails of perfecting yourself.

A person who wants to rectify himself and make teshuva yet doesn't set aside time for prayer and daily self-assessment, is like a person who desires to reach a certain destination yet doesn't take the first step in that direction. The two most vital tools for self-improvement are prayer and daily self-assessment.

A person shouldn't suffice with the three daily prescribed prayers from the siddur (prayer book). Few people are capable of maintaining proper intent during prescribed prayers. And, even if a person does maintain proper intent, his request for a certain area will only be a few brief lines. How can he hope to make a significant change with only a few lines of prayer? What's more, since a person's needs change from time to time, his prayers must be personal and flexible. Not everyone has similar needs either, further necessitating personal prayer. For example, a married person doesn't need to pray for a soul-mate but a single person doesn't need to pray for marital peace (yet). Also, people face different types of tests and tribulations that they must seek Hashem's help in dealing with. All these things necessitate augmenting the prescribed prayers.

The great tzaddikim of all the previous generations prayed profusely beyond the three daily prescribed prayers of Shacharit, Mincha and Maariv, even though they prayed them word-for-word in fervent intent. They added additional prayers for personal rectification and for the general welfare of our people. If they prayed like that, we certainly must.

The famed "Chafetz Chaim", Rabbi Yisroel Meir Kagan of Radin osb"m writes (Likutei Amarim 10:47):

"...if we would pray and pour our supplications before the Holy One, blessed be He, they certainly would not come back empty. A person should not suffice with praying Shmona Esrei thrice daily, but periodically throughout the day, he should pour forth his prayers and requests to Hashem from his own home and from the depths of his heart."

To Pray for Prayer

The daily hour of prayer and self-assessment is a wonderful gift that no one should take for granted. Imagine the privilege of talking to the King whenever you wish! Therefore, we must pray to Hashem - first of all - that we'll be able to set aside this daily hour for personal prayer.

We should preface our personal prayer session with a five-minute prayer request that we should merit having a proper personal prayer session, asking Hashem to put the right words in our mouth and to help us sincerely and candidly express our innermost feelings. We should thank Hashem for all our blessings in life, taking nothing for granted. Finally, we should ask Him for all our needs, for the main reason for deficiency is lack of prayer.

Here is a useful prayer to add to your own daily prayers: "Master of the World, help me believe in my power of prayer. Help me believe that my prayers are capable of invoking all the salvations that I need, and that they have the power to help me improve myself and overcome all of my character flaws and shortcomings. Help me judge myself properly every single day. Let me thank You profusely for each of the multitude of blessings in my life and believe that everything is the product of Divine providence and all for the best. Help me believe that there is no challenge in my life that I am incapable of dealing with. Help me remember that the only advice in solving problems is to turn to You in prayer. May I always seek whatever I need from You as a free gift, with no sense of entitlement whatsoever…"

You'll be amazed how readily such prayers as the above one are answered, and you truly will merit your daily hour of personal prayer and a sweet life.

Any new venture should be prefaced with prayer. No one should depend on their own strength and prowess, for that is the seed of arrogance. Our prayers and our dependence on Hashem not only help us to be humble but enable us to cling to Him. The more we cling to Him, the more we see and feel His many blessings in our lives.

A person doesn't receive a "visa" to enter the gates of true and lasting success unless he has prayed for it profusely. That way, he can climb higher in life without becoming arrogant. The fortunate individual who attains what he wants by way of prayer attributes his success to the Creator and therefore avoids the pitfalls of vanity and conceit; this is true success, knowing that there is no one but Him.

Secret of the Good Life

We already referred to what Rebbe Nathan of Breslev said, "Wherever I see deficiency, I see lack of prayer or insufficient prayer!"

Rebbe Nathan's above remark is the secret of a good life: Since lack of prayer is the cause of deficiency, with prayer, we can attain literally anything and fulfill all of our needs, both material and spiritual. Yet amazingly, most people don't pray at all! They claim that they lack the time for prayer. Earlier in this book, we told the story of the disheveled and ragged prince sleeping on the park bench; when one of the King's ministers found him and asked why he doesn't turn to his all-powerful father for assistance, the prince answered that he didn't have the time...

The person who neglects prayer goes through life with deficiency upon deficiency - problems in marriage, in finances, with bad character traits, with laziness, depression and many more. They ask him, "Why don't you ask your Father in Heaven for what you need?" He answers that he doesn't have time to ask...

The fortunate person that discovers the secret of the good life can't go for a day without prayer. Indeed, those who discover the power of prayer can't go for a few hours without feeling a thirst for prayer. The more one prays, the more one attains proximity to Hashem. The closer we are to Hashem, the more He illuminates our souls. The more He illuminates our souls, the happier we feel. That's the secret of the good life in a nutshell. We should therefore pray for all our needs - spiritual and material.

By judging ourselves daily in self-assessment, we turn all our setbacks into springboards that catapult us closer to Hashem. What's more, we gain "not guilty" verdicts in our daily judgments in the Heavenly Court. And, after one's 120 years on earth, he or she walks right into Heaven without seeing anything of purgatory.

Chapter Five:
Attaining Emuna

With Hashem's help, this chapter will present advice for attaining emuna.

The Right Address

A person must ask Hashem for emuna.

Once, a person complained to me about his trepidations and worries. I told him to strengthen his emuna. He argued that he already had strong emuna.

I elaborated: "You believe there's a Creator of the world, but you don't believe He personally takes care of you. When we have emuna in Divine providence and recognize that everything the Creator does is for our very best, we don't worry. Worries and trepidations originate in negative thoughts that things will be bad; that goes against emuna, for with emuna, we know that everything Hashem does is good. That way, we're not worried about anything - no person or no evil eye, no lack of income or anything else - for we place ourselves in the Creator's hands, and He does everything for the best."

He asked, "In that case, how do I build emuna?"

I answered, "Ask Hashem to grant you emuna and to help you believe that everything He does is for the very best; pray for the awareness that there are no tribulations without prior transgressions. Ask Him to withhold severe soul corrections as long as you are trying your best to correct yourself."

"What, can I ask the Creator for emuna?"

"Do you have a better address?" I asked in return. "We ask Hashem for all of our material needs, so why not ask for our spiritual needs too? He won't give us material things which we don't need or would be detrimental to us, but He always gives us what our souls need. So, if you ask for emuna, you're sure to get it! Ask Hashem to help you believe that He's the address for everything - health, livelihood, material needs, your safety, and spiritual needs."

King David says (Psalm 16:5): "Hashem, You are my portion and my cup, You **determine** my fate." The "Metzudat Tzion" elaborates 'determine' as, "You stimulate me to believe in You." King David knew that Hashem was the only address for attaining emuna. Therefore, every person must know that if he or she has emuna, they must thank Hashem accordingly. Conversely, if they lack emuna, they must ask Hashem to give it to them.

Every creation has a spark of emuna. Prayer, particularly personal prayer - speaking to Hashem in one's own words - has the ability to fan that spark into a brightly-burning flame. If our emuna is weak, we must ask for more. We must also thank the Creator for every measure of emuna that we attain.

The pious Rebbe Natan of Breslev osb"m composed an entire collection of personal prayers that are a mere sampling of the huge amount of personal prayers he poured out to Hashem. A close examination of these prayers show that they all rotate around a central theme, the request for emuna. When one builds emuna, all prayers are subsequently answered.

Even more noteworthy is the fact that Rebbe Natan was a scholar and a righteous individual. Despite his remarkable piety, he never failed to ask the Creator for more and more emuna.

Personal Prayer

Personal prayer is the key to your personal, intimate relationship with Hashem, for the words you utter aren't printed in any prayer-book - they come straight from your soul. Therefore, personal prayer is one's individual discourse with the Creator, in one's own language, one's own accent and one's own slang. The wonderful attribute of personal prayer is that it's truly personal - one needs no prescribed text, time, or place to speak with Him. Personal prayer is also the greatest expression of emuna there can be.

Personal prayer is the key to building emuna for the following reasons:

1. Speaking to Hashem on a daily basis instills emuna in a person's heart.
2. Having one's personal prayers answered greatly reinforces emuna.
3. Personal prayer is a cogent tool for personal improvement; by overcoming negative traits, one builds emuna and vice versa.
4. Hashem shines truth and emuna in the hearts of those who thank Him on a daily basis.
5. By confessing one's transgressions to Hashem daily in personal prayer, one attains the cognizance that everything He does is for the very best, which is the essence of emuna.

Tangible Emuna

The "Chazon Ish" osb"m asks how a person can attain tangible emuna in Hashem and answers: "Anything you need, request it from Hashem. If you need new shoes, stand in a corner of the room and say, 'Master of the World, look at my torn shoes and please give me the money I need to buy a new pair' - and the same for everything else. Accustom yourself to recognizing and feeling that Hashem gives you everything. That's the way to attain tangible emuna!"

The "Chofetz Chaim" osb"m would advise a person to stand alone in an isolated corner and pour his heart out to Hashem, like a son speaking to a loving father; ask for your needs simply and that Hashem should have mercy on you and act with loving-kindness. That way, Hashem will certainly hear your request.

Rebbe Nachman said (Rebbe Nachman's Discourses, 233) that one must pray for everything. In other words, if his garment is torn, and he needs a new garment, he should pray to Hashem for a new garment to wear; the same with everything else, no matter how big or how small. One should get used to praying to Hashem for all his needs.

Even though it's most important to pray for what's most important - one's service of Hashem and to get close to Hashem - one must also pray for all one's material needs as well, even the seemingly insignificant. If one does not - despite the fact that he has a roof over his head, an income, food and clothing - he lives with the spiritual awareness of a mule. Remember, a mule also has a barn roof over his head and food to eat. The mule has a basic animal soul, but a human has a higher level Divine soul.

Anything acquired without prayer provides no vitality for the Divine soul.

Rebbe Natan once needed a button for his coat. Rebbe Nachman told him, "Pray to G-d for it." Rebbe Nathan was astonished to learn that one must even pray to Hashem for such seemingly trivial things. Seeing his surprise, Rebbe Nachman asked, "Is it beneath your dignity to pray to God for a minor thing like a button?"

To build emuna, we must pray for everything, even the most trivial things. By praying for the little things in life, we learn to take nothing for granted and build the emuna that everything comes from Hashem. The foundation of emuna is the cognizance that Hashem is the source of everything and that we are dependent on Him for all our needs - every breath and every heartbeat - every moment of our entire lives. **This is the main lesson of emuna - to know that there is no one but Hashem.**

When people insist on believing in their own power and abilities, they expose themselves to tribulations that are designed to reveal their futility. Oftentimes, feelings of complacency invoke problems almost immediately. Therefore, we should pray for everything and that way, we attain emuna.

"Good for Everything"

Important rule - one must pray to Hashem for everything!

Emuna is synonymous to prayer, for the Torah says, "And his hands were emuna" (Exodus 17:12). Unkeles translates that the hands of Moses were "uplifted in prayer".

Emuna brings a person to prayer, as King David teaches, "Hashem is good for everything and merciful on all His creations" (Psalm 145:9). "Good for everything" indicates prayer, when a person believes that Hashem can and does provide all his needs. With such a level of belief, a person's main efforts are devoted to prayer. Without emuna and prayer, people run all over the place trying to attain what they need; sometimes they succeed and sometimes they don't. Yet, Hashem is good for everything. By praying for everything in life - income, health and all our needs, great and small - we learn to take nothing for granted and we build the emuna that everything comes from Hashem; He is the source of everything and that we are dependent on Him for all our needs - every breath and every heartbeat - every moment of our entire lives. There is no one but Him, as the Torah says, "Who is like Hashem our G-d in everything that we call upon Him" (Deuteronomy 4:7); in other words, Hashem is always there for us in everything we ask from Him.

The only one who can help us in any situation is Hashem. A person who lacks adequate income, marital bliss or good health must seek Hashem. If he wants to sell his house, if he has a problem at work or with the neighbors, Hashem is the One to turn to. His main efforts in coping with any challenge should be prayer, both in material areas and in spiritual endeavors.

Going with The Torah

From everything we've written up to this point, we can conclude that the most important thing we can pray for is emuna.

A person must be specific in prayer and elaborate to Hashem exactly what he or she needs or wants. One parable tells about a weary pedestrian who has no more strength to walk. He asks Hashem for a donkey but forgets to ask for a donkey that he can **ride on**.

While he prayed, a caravan passed by. One of the caravan's donkeys gave birth to a baby donkey that slowed the whole caravan down. The wagon master heard the pedestrian praying for a donkey, so he happily cast the newborn foal in his direction and called out, "Here mister - you can have this for a gift!" The caravan quickly departed.

The weary pedestrian was dumbstruck. The Creator answered his prayer in the blink of an eyelash; on the other hand, that wasn't the type of donkey he intended. Not only could he not ride on the foal but he'd have to carry it on his back...

Our sages teach that a person must be specific in his prayers. One must elaborate exactly what he seeks, and repeatedly at that. Therefore, when a person requests emuna, he should do so over and over. He should also be specific, and ask for the various facets of emuna, such as emuna in financial affairs. Such a prayer is more befitting, more complete and more acceptable. A person can always make his own prayer nuances and pray as long as he or she wants.

Our abundance is in accordance with our prayer. People often wonder why we need prayer at all, for Hashem reads our hearts and minds; He surely knows exactly what we need! Very true, but He gives us the power to pray so we'll seek Him and develop emuna. If our needs were fulfilled automatically, without ever having to ask for them, we'd never seek Him or strive for emuna, and our souls would wither. As such, the more we pray and speak to Him with many voluminous and varied personal prayers, the more we connect with Him and the more we receive exactly what we want.

Learning in Order to Fulfill

In order for a person to pray sincere, cogent and effective prayers, he should have a strong desire for whatever he's asking for. He should therefore learn about whatever he's asking for. For example, the more he learns about emuna and the advantages of emuna, the stronger he'll yearn for it and the more he'll pray for it. His prayers will be full of yearning and desire. That's the importance of learning this book and praying to implement each of its teachings. The more one learns this book in depth, the more he or she will have the desire for emuna and to pray for it, until they merit to live wholly in emuna.

For example, when learning about emuna, we should ask Hashem to help us internalize each stage of our learning. Once we've learned about the first stage of emuna, namely, that everything in the world is a product of Divine will, then we should incorporate that in our prayers. We should ask Hashem to give us the complete emuna that everything is from Him and all a product of Divine providence. We should pray for total awareness that all of our trials and tribulations are exactly according to Hashem's will. For example, if a person's wife is yelling at him, he should pray for the emuna that it's not her, but Hashem is talking to him. At work, he should see Hashem and not attribute anything to natural causes and the like.

And, after learning the second stage of emuna, namely, that everything that the Creator does is for the very best, we can create a new receptacle of Divine abundance by praying to implement this too. A sample prayer in this case would be, "Master of the World, help me realize that everything You do is for the very best, and even if I fail to understand how or why, help me believe strongly that everything in my life is for the very best. Let my emuna be so strong that I can even thank you for my headaches in life, knowing that You are doing everything for my ultimate benefit. Hashem, enable me to cast logic aside and believe that everything is from You and all for the very best, and that there is no bad in the world."

This principle should also be applied when we learn the third stage of emuna as well, that everything is a message from Heaven to accomplish a specific purpose. Especially when it comes to the tests of emuna, a person must pray for Divine assistance in every challenging situation, knowing full well that there are no tribulations without prior transgression. After learning each new principle and each chapter of this book, one should pray to internalize it and be able to implement it in his or her life. We should all pray for Hashem's mercy and His help in our quest for emuna.

One should also reiterate the advantages of emuna and its importance to Hashem, for such prayer is conducive to attaining emuna. He should talk to Hashem about the losses that his insufficient emuna causes him, as well as any other ideas that come to mind. All of us must pray to implement what we learn. Prayer designed to implement our learning is a cogent spiritual vessel. We should therefore ask Hashem repeatedly to help us implement what we learn, especially what we learn about emuna.

Full of Favor

Prayers that result from one's learning are full of favor and readily accepted. Such prayer is the core fulfillment of Torah and proves that a person wants to fulfill what he learned with all his might. We ask Hashem because we know that He can deliver the goods, but we ask in a pleasing and humble manner, not by demanding and banging on the table.

Rebbe Nachman talks about the wonderful aspects of creating prayers from our learning and says (see Likutei Moharan, II:25):

"It is wonderful to make prayers from Torah learning. In other words, when a person learns a particular Torah treatise and makes it into a prayer, namely, to plead to Hashem that he'll be able to uphold and implement everything in that treatise. He who desires truly, Hashem will lead him in the path of truth. The person will merit understanding the inner dimension, how to act in this respect, so that Hashem will bring him close. Especially when he makes prayers out of his Torah learning, he creates immense pleasure Above." This is exactly what Rebbe Natan did from the treatises of Likutei Moharan when he composed his compendium of prayers, "Likutei Tefillot."

Additional Advaice for Attaining Emuna

Crying out to Hashem

Rebbe Nachman of Breslev teaches that when a person lacks emuna, he or she should cry out to Hashem. Such a cry doesn't have to be audible at all; a silent cry from deep down in the heart is very good. The fact that one cries out to Him is proof of the spark of emuna in their midst, for without this spark, they wouldn't cry out at all. The spark in turn becomes a glowing flame of emuna.

Speaking Emuna

Emuna depends on a person's speech. Whether a person wants to strengthen himself in emuna or recover from a breakdown of emuna, he can do so by speaking words of emuna, as King David said, "I will tell of Your emuna with my mouth" (Psalm 89:2). When a person feels like he's clouded in darkness, and has difficulty feeling the Creator's presence, then he should speak words of emuna out loud, such as: "I believe in Hashem, that He's the One and Only God, and He protects me and watches over me every minute of the day my entire life, and He always listens to my prayers. Hashem loves me and cares about me unconditionally, and He always listens to my prayers."

One should continue to speak words of emuna in whatever area one needs help, as follows: "I believe that the Creator sustains all His creations. He will surely send me my livelihood;" or, "I believe that Hashem is the physician of all flesh. He will surely send me a cure." Before an important exam or negotiation, we enhance chances of success by saying, "I believe that success comes from the Creator. I've done my best to prepare, please Heavenly Father, help me succeed!"

By speaking words of emuna, we arouse the spark of emuna within us, as King David says, "I believed because I spoke" (Psalm 166:2). Speaking words of emuna kindles a bright flame of emuna which not only warms the soul and illuminates the darkness within us but invokes Divine compassion.

Just as speaking words of emuna does wonders for the soul, we should consequently be careful to avoid saying anything which contains the slightest hint of heresy, even in a joke. Words of heresy or agnosticism extinguish the spark of emuna and render a person's soul cold and dark, Heaven forbid.

Judging Ourselves

A wonderful way of attaining emuna is by self-evaluation - judging ourselves daily as to the quality of every single thought, utterance and deed during the last 24 hours since our previous session of self-evaluation. One who judges himself reinforces the belief that Hashem sees, hears and knows every single thought, utterance and deed. This creates a high level of awe of the Creator, to the extent that the individual will not want to leave any blemish uncorrected.

By evaluating ourselves every day, we are reminded of our relationship with God. Four wonderful things happen when we judge ourselves on a daily basis: First, we remind ourselves of the Creator and of His commandments. Second, we make decisions to correct that which needs correcting, and therefore don't accrue spiritual debts which lead to stern judgments. Third, when we judge ourselves, the Heavenly Court is not allowed to judge us. And fourth, daily self-evaluation reminds us there is a Creator in the world; when we contemplate whether our actions are in accordance with His will, we contemplate Him. By thinking of Hashem, we enhance emuna.

A person who doesn't judge himself daily makes the statement that he is not afraid of Divine judgment. Such a person lives a life devoid of emuna.

Fear of punishment is therefore not only entrance level fear of Hashem, but entrance level emuna as well. A person with a fear of Divine punishment will assess and judge himself; ultimately, his daily self-assessment will bring him to the lofty level of exalted fear. He'll also attain steadfast emuna.

Dear readers, don't let your assessment of yourself knock you down. Believe that everything, including your setbacks and shortcomings, are all part of your mission on earth. Hashem simply wants you to pray, and He desires to bring you close to Him. Judge yourself happily, for Hashem is so loving and merciful. It doesn't matter how many blemishes we have; it matters what we're doing to improve ourselves.

Why Not Start from the Beginning?

Be very careful to avoid philosophical texts that deal in logical investigations of the Divine. These are destructive to the simple and wholesome emuna that is the foundation of Judaism. Those who engage in these types of texts become agnostics and even heretics. Why? Since everyone is born with an incline toward evil, people gravitate toward evil, lust, bodily appetites and the enticements of this world. The awe of G-d and the fear of punishment shatters lust and enables a person to walk in the path of Hashem. But, when he engages in philosophical and theological investigation, Heaven forbid, the poison of doubt and heresy awaken the evil in his nature (see Rebbe Nachman's Discourses, 5).

A person may not read any books, magazines or newspapers that contain heresy or investigation as to the existence of G-d, for they are devastating to emuna.

Rabbi Leib, the son of the Chofetz Chaim, related that when he was young, he took an interest to investigative theological writings, but his father was against his doing so. Once, the Chofetz Chaim caught him reading "The

Guide to the Perplexed" by the Rambam, a classic Jewish investigative work, and took it away from him. Rabbi Leib wondered and asked his father, "Who is greater than the Rambam, yet he engaged in investigating the existence of G-d. Also, our sages tell about our forefather Abraham who attained emuna by way of theological investigation?!"

The Chofetz Chaim answered his son that whoever looks for proof of emuna in investigative works shows that his awareness of Hashem is blemished, for he harbors doubts and contemplations. Also, the Rambam and Abraham are not proof, because the Rambam wrote "The Guide to the Perplexed" for the confused agnostics of his generation. Also, Abraham lived in a generation of idolaters; as the first believer, he came to the awareness of Hashem by way of an investigative process. But for us, everything is clear. Hashem revealed himself to our entire nation of Mount Sinai and they all heard the voice of Hashem speaking to them. So, we need not "discover the wheel" and start from the beginning.

The Gemara tells us in Tractate Sanhedrin 90a that all of Israel shares a portion in the World to Come. Yet, there are those who forfeit their share, such as those who doubt the truth of Torah, the revival of the dead and that the Torah is from Above. Rebbe Akiva adds that those who read "external books" - the works of philosophy and heresy - also forfeit their share in the World to Come.

In addition, hearing expressions of doubt and heresy are also destructive to emuna. One must keep a safe distance and even avoid those who speak words of doubt and heresy. Also, one must not expose himself, his family or his home to media that broadcasts doubt and heresy, for that's just like having a heretic present a lecture in your living room...

If a person has slipped up and has read such philosophical works, he should do teshuva and ask Hashem's forgiveness. He should resolve that from this day on, he won't engage in reading about or dealing in theological investigation in any form. That will be beneficial in his guarding his share in the World to Come.

Learning Torah

The light of Torah destroys the darkness of heresy and doubt in a person's heart.

People construe heresy, or epikorsis, as total denial of Hashem; that's not true. One can believe in the existence of Hashem yet still harbor many thoughts and opinions that negate emuna. These opinions are the heresy that blocks him from seeing the existence of Hashem and His Divine providence. Learning Torah nullifies heresy and brings a person to a proper outlook that enables him to attain complete emuna.

Torah leads to emuna only when a person subjugates his own intellect to the wisdom of the Torah. In other words, he lets the Torah override and overwrite his own intellect and desires. This is what's called learning purely for the sake of performing Hashem's will and not for the sake of personal gain. By learning Torah in order to implement Hashem's will, one attains emuna.

When a person toils to understand the Torah, he is rescued from spiritual darkness. Indeed, he merits an aspect of the Divine countenance and the illumination of Torah that nullifies the evil within him that blocks Divine light (see Likutei Moharan I: 101).

By invoking the light of Torah in the world, we invoke a higher level of Divine providence on ourselves, each person in accordance to his connection to the Torah (see Likutei Etzot, Talmud Torah, 21).

"Guarding the Covenant": Personal Holiness

Nothing preserves emuna like guarding the holy covenant, when a person is meticulous in guarding his or her personal holiness. But first, let's elaborate on what constitutes a breached or blemished personal holiness, for nothing destroys emuna like lewdness and licentiousness.

The Torah tells about Jacob's grandson Err (see Gen.38:7), calling him "evil in the eyes of God". Rashi explains that Err would spill his seed so that his wife wouldn't become pregnant and her beauty would be preserved.

The Code of Jewish Law states (Shulchan Aruch, Even HaEzer 23:1), "It is forbidden to spill one's seed in vain, and this transgression is worse than all the sins of the Torah. As such, one may not thresh on the inside and sow seed on the outside. Those guilty of masturbation who spill seed in vain, not only have they done a heinous violation, but they are subject to excommunication." Even though today's religious courts no longer excommunicate people, when a person commits a transgression that is subject to excommunication, Hashem turns a deaf ear to that person's prayers. What's more, Isaiah the Prophet refers to the evildoers and says, "Your hands are full of blood" (Isaiah 1:15), comparing the licentious to those who murder souls.

The holy covenant means that we use our reproductive apparatus only in the performance of a mitzvah, which is either procreation, insuring marital bliss, or both. The guarding of the holy covenant, or Shmirat Habrit, is probably the most conducive factor in attaining and preserving emuna.

Kedusha, or holiness of thought, speech, and deed, is the best way of guarding the holy covenant. The more we immerse ourselves in Torah and the less we expose ourselves to the influences of today's lewd and permissive society, the better we guard the holy covenant (See Shulchan Aruch, even Ezer 23:25). Practically, one should marry at as early an age as possible, for this is most conducive to personal holiness.

The Torah commands, "You shall not stray after your heart and after your eyes" (Numbers 15:39). Our sages elaborate that straying after one's eyes refers to harlotry. This is our source for learning that looking at any other women - married or single - other than one's wife constitutes a heinous transgression of Torah. Rebbe Nachman says that idolatry begins with the eyes (see Likutei Moharan I:7).

The Code of Jewish Law specifically and emphatically requires us to avoid "even at a woman's pinky finger" (See Shulchan Aruch, even Ezer 21:1). Our sages teach (see Rambam, Laws of Teshuva, 4:4) that merely harboring the image of a strange woman in one's brain is tantamount to mental adultery. People think, "What's the big deal about looking at a woman? I didn't do anything..."; such an individual fails to realize that the eyes kindle desire and that negative desires both lead a person to forbidden acts and contemplations, which contaminate the soul. The Mishna Brura rules that even if a person has Torah and good deeds, failure to guard his eyes will subject him to the verdict of purgatory.

Lewd thoughts and unclean speech lead to violations of the holy covenant, since they defile the brain and the mouth. The brain was designed for contemplating Torah and Hashem, and the mouth was designed for speaking Torah and praying. A mouth that has been contaminated with unclean and lewd speech can't pray properly; such a mouth severs a person from holiness. Once severed from holiness, a person loses emuna and all his desire for prayer. Anyway, Hashem doesn't want to hear the prayers of a mouth that's used for lewd and forbidden speech.

Masturbation and spilling one's seed lead to a blemished psyche since the seed comes from the brain. One who spills seed in vain forfeits parts of his brain, which in turn causes the blemished psyche. As such, all emotional disturbances stem from a breach in one's personal holiness. The Zohar says emphatically he who spills seed outside the context of marital gratification and procreation squanders his brain and falls into all aspects of poverty - financial, emotional and spiritual. He falls into debt and loses his spiritual awareness. Since he loses emuna, he succumbs to the negative emotions of sadness, depression and anger, which themselves are emotional disturbances.

Failure to guard the holy covenant destroys personal holiness. Emuna is the main aspect of holiness. That's why emuna and promiscuity are mutually exclusive. When emuna is damaged, a person's entire life suffers; this is manifest in his health, his income and his marital peace, which all experience all types of difficulties. Such a person's world becomes darkness.

Promiscuity is the extreme opposite to Judaism. That's why the wicked Bilaam advised Balak to undermine the Israelites by way of harlotry. Hashem despises promiscuity. The goal of Judaism is to cling to Hashem; one's desire to cling to Hashem is directly proportionate to one's personal holiness. Since promiscuity is a love and yearning of animalistic acts that are the opposite of holiness, one who succumbs to promiscuity loses his love and yearning for Hashem, Heaven forbid. He loses all desire to learn Torah and to perform mitzvoth. He loses all taste for prayer and especially personal prayer, which are the main expressions of one's emuna.

The Zohar says that a person's principal test in the world is to overcome the lust for adultery. From a spiritual standpoint, adultery begins way before the forbidden act - as soon as a person looks at someone else's spouse or contemplates adultery in any way, the eyes and the mind become spiritually contaminated. Such contamination destroys the soul, Heaven forbid.

Our sages teach us that what the eye sees, the heart desires. Therefore, by guarding the sight of our eyes and by limiting our gaze to the permissible, we protect ourselves from falling into the trap of lustful desires. Lustful desires alone are enough to wreak havoc on the soul. Also, lustful desires are the spiritual opposite of the love of Hashem - one can't have both. A person can't have lustful desires and cling to Hashem simultaneously. Stop and think - is a lustful thought or desire worth being separated from Hashem? The lustful person fantasizes that all women are his. This way, says Rebbe Nachman (see Likutei Moharan I:54), his heart withers.

King David refers to several mutually-dependent things as "always". First, "I am always with You" (Psalm 73:23) - this refers to clinging to Hashem. Second, "My eyes are always cast to You" (ibid. 25:15) - this refers to guarding one's eyes. These two are mutually dependent. The prerequisite for clinging to Hashem is guarding one's eyes. The opposite is also true - forfeiting one means forfeiting the other.

One might guard his eyes on an external level but still harbor lewd images in his brain that impair his ability to cling to Hashem. Therefore, in order to cling to Hashem, one must also guard his eyes on an internal level; this depends on emuna. With emuna, a person can uphold the third "always": "I place Hashem before me always" (ibid. 16:8). In other words, with emuna, a person is able to see Hashem and His goodness in everything and in every situation.

The Land of Israel

To merit emuna fully, one must imbibe the holiness of the Land of Israel, which can only be obtained within the Land of Israel. Therefore, one who truly desires emuna should pray to Hashem for the privilege of coming to the Land of Israel, for there, one can nullify anger and melancholy. And, those who are already in Israel should pray to attain the holiness of the Land of Israel. A person can know if he or she has attained he level of Land of Israel holiness when they see that they are always happy and never angry. If not, they still have work to do in attaining the holiness of the Land of Israel.

"And you Shall Cling to Him"

The Torah commands us to cling to Torah scholars in order to learn from their personal example. Yet, the Torah issues this command in a seemingly odd way and says, "You shall cling to Him" (Deuteronomy 10:20), telling us to cling to Hashem. The Gemara asks a question: Cling to

Hashem? Hashem is like an all-consuming fire, so, who can cling to Him? Our sages answer that the Torah is telling us to cling to Torah scholars, for that way, we cling to Hashem. This concept is codified in the Rambam (Rambam, Hilchot De'ot, Ch.6).

A major tenet of our faith is the belief in our righteous scholars; this is also one of the forty-eight ways of attaining Torah excellence, as brought forth in the Mishna, Tractate Avot. Religious law requires us to cling to our wise men and to heed their words. A substantial portion of the Torah comes under the classification of "Oral Law," that which has been passed on from teacher to pupil in a generation after generation unbroken chain that dates back to Moses on Mount Sinai, who received the oral elaboration of the Torah directly from Hashem. Therefore, a person shouldn't think that it's sufficient to teach himself Torah - there's much room for error; one avoids error by clinging to a righteous scholar and learning from him.

In like manner, one cannot fully attain emuna without clinging to the righteous spiritual leaders of the generation, what we refer to as emunat chachamim, or belief in our sages. Without emunat chachamim, one cannot properly develop emuna in Hashem.

Two weeks before he departed from the physical world, Rebbe Nachman, in what is known as his will and testament, said (see Likutei Moharan II:8):

"One must therefore search for the true spiritual leader of the generation and seek to attain proximity to him. He has an aspect of a holy spirit that is tantamount to prophesy; for that reason, those who get close to him attain true emuna and holiness and become strengthened and rectified."

Rebbe Nachman isn't talking about clinging to the body of the tzaddik, but to his teachings, which are spiritual. Studying the works of the true tzaddikim is highly conducive to emuna, for the writings of a true tzaddik arouse one's heart to seek Hashem and to cling to Him. When a person receives an illumination from the tzaddik's writings, he is receiving an illumination from the tzaddik's soul; this is just like receiving an illumination from Moses, which a person's entire soul correction depends upon.

Consequently, a person must merit a huge portion of Divine mercy to find the true tzaddik. One does this by way of profuse and perseverant prayer.

We cannot find the true tzaddik by way of an intellectual or logical process, like going from place to place to look for him, for we are incapable of knowing who the true tzaddik is and are liable to make big mistakes such as comparing spiritual leaders or speaking slander about them, Heaven forbid.

A person who follows his own logic is vulnerable: he might end up believing in imposters while forsaking the truly righteous...

As such, Rebbe Nachman advises that we invest much effort into praying to find the true tzaddik and the right path to genuine emuna. In the meanwhile, one should seek peace and avoid dissension, never saying a bad word about a single person, much less a spiritual leader or a group of people. One must innocently search for the truth and Hashem will surely help. King Solomon says, "He who walks innocently, walks securely" (Proverbs 10:9).

On the other hand, if a person has ulterior motives in his search for a tzaddik, such as arrogance or the desire to cull people and/or groups, then his skewed motives will lead him down a skewed path, which ultimately leads to downfall on all levels.

With simple innocence and a desire for the truth, a person will surely find what he's looking for.

Rebbe Nachman of Breslev writes in Sefer HaMiddot (under the subject "tzaddik"):

- The main perfection of the soul is contingent on getting close to tzaddikim.
- The proximity of tzaddikim is beneficial in this world and in the next.
- The coming of Moshiach depends on getting close to the tzaddik.
- Those who are close to the tzaddik in their lifetime will be close to him after they die.
- That which you hear from the mouth of the tzaddik is more beneficial than that which you learn in books.
- It's good to invest a lot of time in order to merit one hour of proximity to the tzaddik.

For all the above-mentioned reasons, one must search for a genuine, righteous tzaddik and spiritual guide. By clinging to such a person and by learning his teachings - which is tantamount to clinging to his soul - one attains emuna.

Strengthening emuna

Rebbe Nathan of Breslev writes (Rebbe Nachman's Discourses, 222): "I heard that the Rebbe was once encouraging a man who was greatly confused about emuna. The Rebbe told him, 'It is written that all of creation came into being only because of people like you. G-d saw that there would be people who would cling to our Holy faith, suffering greatly because of the confusion and doubts that constantly plague them. He perceived that they would overcome these doubts and remain strong in their beliefs. It was because of this that G-d brought forth all creation.'"

Rebbe Natan adds, "This man was then greatly strengthened and unperturbed whenever he had these confusing thoughts. The Rebbe said many times that the creation was mainly for the sake of faith. Thus it is written, 'All His works are through emuna' (Psalms 33:4)."

Over two hundred years ago, Rebbe Nachman of Breslev warned of the great flood of atheism that will drown people in the spiritual and emotional perils that we're fighting against today. True to his words, the only way to save ourselves from modern society's perilous sea of denial and disbelief is to learn as much as we can about emuna, and to constantly reinforce it. More than anything, we should constantly pray to Hashem for more and more emuna and invest our principal efforts in attaining and strengthening emuna. **Our lives in this world and in the next depend on emuna.**

The only way of rescuing ourselves from the tsunami of heresy that's crashing down on all continents of the globe today is to learn extensively about emuna and to strengthen it constantly. This requires incessant prayer. Anyone who has compassion on him/herself should invest all their might in learning emuna.

Collection of Thoughts from "Sefer HaMidot" about Emuna

Factors detrimental to emuna

- Hardening one's heart
- Violating the laws of Torah
- Jealousy, anger, and covetousness
- Disdain of Torah scholars
- Dishonesty and flattery

Factors conducive to emuna

- Modesty and humility
- Tearful prayer
- Silence
- Charity
- Sleeping in holiness.

Chapter Six:

Emuna and Character

Sadness

Sadness is an emotion which directly results from the lack of emuna.

An important principle of emuna teaches that the Creator bestows His personal Divine Providence on each creation. The Creator provides each human - His most sophisticated creation - with a unique set of conditions which enable the individual to develop faith and to get to know Him. He tailors each set of conditions to each person; usually, a problem or deficiency is the catalyst designed to stimulate a person's spiritual development. Some people are afflicted with physical ailments while others suffer financial problems. Some people have grief from their children while others encounter marital difficulties. These tribulations motivate a person to seek Hashem; without them, he or she might never raise their voice in prayer.

With emuna, we never succumb to sadness or despair, for emuna teaches that the Creator does everything for our ultimate benefit. We learn that our difficulties in life are all for the best, to bring us closer to Him. But, without emuna, life presents plenty of reasons to be sad and depressed. Since a state of deficiency and imperfection are ingrained in creation, life is never exactly how we want it to be. Without emuna, we would be disappointed and saddened dozens of times every day, as soon as things don't go our way.

A weightlifter, gymnast or any other champion athlete uses the rigors of arduous training as a growth opportunity to attain excellence in his or her respective endeavor. A candidate for the Olympic boxing team doesn't cry when he gets punched in a workout; on the contrary, he uses his pain as a learning opportunity to better his performance. In like manner, the person with emuna isn't saddened by life's difficulties; he or she uses them as springboards for spiritual growth.

As soon as individuals without emuna don't get their own way, they start blaming themselves or those in their proximity. They succumb to sadness and depression. Even if they have a general belief in the Creator, they accuse Him of torturing or persecuting them for no reason.

One must strengthen himself in emuna, knowing that life's deficiencies are designed to trigger greater spiritual growth. With the spiritual awareness that life's difficulties are the Creator's way of bringing us closer to Him, we never sink into a state of sadness or despair. We utilize our difficult circumstances as platforms for prayer and penitence, ultimately getting closer to the Creator and rising above our difficulties.

Trials and tribulations make ideal spiritual vessels for getting close to the Creator. They resemble fire – when properly contained and harnessed, fire is a marvelous source of energy which does wonders such as cooking, heating, and healing. Likewise, trials and tribulations provide the spiritual energy which can propel a person closer to Him. What's more, those who have attained enhanced proximity to the Creator as a result of their tribulation-triggered prayers and emuna self-strengthening taste an indescribable sublime sweetness in life; they can virtually feel the Divine providence on their flesh.

There is no Deficiency

Sometimes, a person suffers from a spiritual deficiency like a bad habit or a lustful drive that's a direct hindrance in serving Hashem and getting close to Him. In such a case, one has an apparent "right" to be sad. He or she asks, "How can I be happy when I have this craving for certain things which are directly against Hashem's will?" One person feels compelled to steal while another craves the neighbor's wife. They feel sad and guilty that they can't overcome their lusts and bodily urges.

Here's news: with the principles of emuna in mind, we know that physical drives and appetites - like everything else in life - come from Hashem. This is what He wants? Why? That sounds outrageous! The explanation is that Hashem instills a particular lust or bodily drive in a person to direct that person to his or her needed soul correction. For example, overcoming the drive to violate the Ten-Commandment's prohibition against adultery is the very mission of a married person's soul on earth. With emuna, such an upright soul is happy for the opportunity to correct! What's more, the Kabbalists teach that when someone encounters a difficult challenge in life, such as overcoming a certain bad habit or detrimental character attribute, this is his soul correction. He must do everything in his power to refine himself and thereby rectify.

Meanwhile, if a person hasn't yet overcome his challenge, there's no reason to be disappointed or confused as long as he's making effort and learning how to overcome his negative habit or fault. Hashem gives us our faults, drives, and bad habits for our own good, to facilitate the correction of our souls. This is ample reason for rejoicing, not sadness!

If a person maintains composure, prays, and performs regular soul-searching, he or she will discover their apparent deficiencies are not deficiencies at all, but catalysts for personal growth and correction. Without emuna, life's difficulties and personal flaws are reasons for disorientation and despair. When we're sad, we don't accomplish anything, especially not a soul correction. Only emuna can save us from sadness and despair, the most devastating emotions, worse even than transgressions and bodily urges.

The Disadvantage is the Advantage

If we look at the Torah and at the annals of the Jewish People, we can see that on more than one occasion, the Creator chose people with apparent deficiencies as the catalysts for the nation's salvation:

Moses stuttered and grew up in the house of an infidel - Pharaoh, king of Egypt. Moses never received a formal religious education, yet he became the holiest of prophets of all time and God's chosen messenger to lead the Children of Israel out of Egypt.

Samson was lame, yet he became one of history's mightiest men who cast fear in the hearts of his enemies, even after his death!

According to various leading interpretations of scriptures, David was an outcast. His own father and brothers thought he was an illegitimate child. He was also short. Yet, he overcame the giant Goliath. He was also chosen to replace Saul - a man of perfect attributes - as the king of Israel and God's anointed.

A weak and insignificant woman - Yael, the wife of Hever the Kinnite - saved Israel from the hand of the mighty Sisera.

Abaye - one of the greatest scholars in Talmudic history - was an orphan. His father died before he was born and his mother died in childbirth. Such dire disadvantage didn't prevent him from becoming one of history's leading wise men.

The Maggid of Mezeritch - was the tzaddik of his generation despite the fact that he was lame in both legs. The bulk of the Baal Shem Tov's teachings and the great Chassidic masters such as the Noam Elimelech, The Ba'al HaTanya, Rebbe Aaron of Karlin, Rebbe Levi Yitzchak of Berditchev, Rebbe Zusha of Annipoli and many more come to us by way of the Maggid.

The list of seemingly disadvantaged people who rose to greatness is long and exhaustive, but the point is clear.

Disadvantages don't prevent a person from attaining greatness. On the contrary, they are often the springboard to greatness. Disadvantaged people who live with emuna don't fall into despair; they live in humility and turn to Hashem for help. They readily know the important lesson that everyone needs to know, namely, that they are dependent on Hashem. As such, Hashem helps them and they ascend to heights that defy people's preconceptions. Without their disadvantage, they might have become merely mediocre at best. As such, the disadvantages are truly advantages.

The same goes with a person with emuna who is in trouble. When others persecute and humiliate him, he flees to

Hashem. He doesn't succumb to sadness and depression because he lives with the emuna that Hashem will help him in every situation. With this type of individual as well, his tribulations catapult him higher.

Positive Thinking

The battleground where the evil inclination attacks the good inclination is the human mind, where one's thoughts are. At close inspection, we see that our good thoughts come from the good inclination and our negative thoughts come from the evil inclination.

Therefore, **the primary challenge of a person** is whether he or she will succumb to negative thoughts and believe in them, or strengthen themselves with emuna, replacing feelings of sadness and depression with optimism and happiness while clinging to Hashem. In the latter case, problems always turn themselves around, for the individual successfully and courageously withstood the test of faith. Now, he or she has earned a noble vessel of abundance.

Let's take the example of a person who's been unsuccessful over a long period of time in finding his or her soulmate. This is no easy trial; the Evil Inclination (EI) pounces on opportunities like this to infuse despair and depression into a person's heart and to destroy their emuna altogether. The EI says, "With all of your hangups, who'll want you?" Or, "With the high cost of living today, how will you ever be able to support a wife!" The EI, like a nagging fly in the ear, gives a person 350 reasons why he'll never marry in order to destroy his emuna and to knock him down into depression. Certainly, all these negative thoughts are devoid of emuna. Hashem can give a person his soulmate any time He deems fit.

The first thing a single person must do is to thank Hashem for being single until now, for that has been His will and all for the best, of course. He shouldn't blame himself or anyone else. Once he strengthens himself in emuna, he can begin to pray properly for a soulmate.

A person with emuna turns to Hashem in prayer, as follows: "Master of the World, You alone know which of my misdeeds might have delayed my finding a soulmate until now. Please forgive me for them and help me correct what needs correcting; You Yourself know that a person can't truly correct his or her soul without being married. For that reason, please help me find my partner in life."

A person with emuna in Hashem turns only to Him and solves all his problems with prayer!

It's Either Emuna or Heresy

Additional Advaice for Attaining Emuna

Evil Inclination and Heresy say:	Good Inclination and Emuna say:
I'll never solve my problem.	If the Creator wants, He can solve my problem this very minute!
The Creator forgot all about me.	The Creator forgets no one. He loves each of His creations, including me. His Divine Providence is for the very best.
The Creator doesn't want to help me.	The Creator created me as an act of Divine compassion; within this particular predicament is the spark of salvation.

I don't know how to pray. I've got no will to pray. I find prayer belabored and difficult.	I'll ask the Creator to help me pray, to teach me how to pray, to open my mouth in prayer
I'm a loser. I never succeed.	Success is from the Creator. If I turn to Him sincerely, He'll certainly help me succeed.
Nothing ever goes my way.	Everything goes my way; my setbacks are from the Creator, so I can realize my nothingness and turn to Him for help.
Somebody gave me an evil eye.	There is no one but the Creator; no one can do me harm against His will. From this moment on, I'll try harder to look at others favorably, so they'll look at me favorably.
Everything is dependent on my own efforts.	My efforts mean nothing; as soon as the right time comes, my soulmate will find me! All I have to do is pray...
I'm lazy.	I'm lazy because I don't believe in myself. I tortured myself and fell into depression. I'll ask the Creator to help me believe in myself so I'll be happy and energetic. He will surely have pity on me and help me.
I blew it; the solution to my problem slipped through my fingers.	Even if I missed the train, the Creator will send me another train. Whatever happened is what He wanted!

There's no correction for my soul.	The Creator can remedy any situation and correct my soul as well.

Notice in the above table, the Evil Inclination speaks all the time about "I" and "me" and the Good Inclination speaks about the Creator. The Evil Inclination inflates a person with egotism, despair, and heresy, while the Good Inclination gives the person emuna, encouragement, and optimism.

Use the above table to insert your own thoughts on whatever challenge you're facing at the moment and see which the dominant force in your life is right now. Don't forget that there's a war in your mind going on between emuna and heresy, and between the good inclination and the evil inclination. Awareness of this basic and vital fact will help you prevail, with emuna, optimism and positivity gaining the upper hand.

As we see, the EI injects heresy into a person. Consequently, anyone who lives in emuna immobilizes the Evil Inclination.

Self-Persecution

Self-persecution is a prime cause of sadness and depression. Self-persecution is another expression of deficient emuna, when one blames himself for his failures. One may ask, "How can I be happy when I fail?" The answer is simple and it's also the cure for self-persecution: With emuna, a person addresses a setback with emuna, knowing that anything that happens in his life is exactly **what Hashem wants and all for the best**!

One must internalize the belief that prayer is the solution to any problem. We must ask the Creator for the power of prayer and to give us sufficient prayers in quality and quantity until we see salvation with our own eyes.

We must adopt two mindsets: before the fact, we have free choice; after the fact, we have the free choice to look at the outcome with emuna, knowing that this is what the Creator wanted and thanking Him for it, or to stick our heads in the mud of failure, depression and self-persecution.

Let's take an example: A women is married for eight years already and she hasn't yet been blessed with children. Without emuna, she starts persecuting herself in all sorts of ways, such as: "I'm not normal; I'm not deserving of children; Hashem doesn't want anything to do with me; I was born with bad fortune..." and so on. These thoughts are the sole result of insufficient emuna, since she thinks child-bearing is dependent on her, when actually she has little say in the matter. Children, like everything else in life, come from Hashem only.

The childless woman would therefore be best advised to turn to Hashem in prayer, like this: "Heavenly Father, You can help me. Show me why I don't have children and what's lacking in me. If I lack emuna, give me emuna! If I haven't prayed enough, help me pray more! Teach me how to ask for what I need; I know that everything You do is for the best and that You want our prayers just like You wanted the prayers of our forefathers. Ultimately, I believe You will make me a mother too."

Here's an important rule: Most people are sad and depressed because they feel that they are failures, and they lack hope. This is the product of negative thoughts about themselves, which is the result of self-persecution. Self-persecution results from a lack of emuna.

Emuna says, "Hashem can help me this very minute; and, even if He decides not to help me, it's still for the best." Emuna and sadness are mutually exclusive.

To break the cycle of sadness, one must stop persecuting oneself. In order to put an end to self-persecution, one needs emuna. In order to obtain emuna, one must talk to the Creator in extensive personal prayer and ask for emuna. As such, talking to Him in personal prayer can literally uplift a person from the depths of sadness and depression.

Self-persecution begins as soon as a person says, "I didn't succeed." This is a faulty way to think. The right way is to say, "Hashem doesn't want me to succeed right now, and this is surely for the best, because He wants me to learn something or to strengthen something. He probably wants me to strengthen my emuna; I'll do just that and ask Him to help me!"

By focusing on Hashem rather than on oneself, a person breaks the cycle of self-persecution. As the say in Hebrew, he stops "chasing himself". The awareness that every occurrence in life is from Heaven and for the ultimate good is the basis of emuna and the key to a happy mood, no matter what. Consequently, following a setback, a person should think, "OK, I didn't succeed this time; obviously, this is for my eternal benefit. I probably didn't pray enough (or maybe I forgot to pray completely and ask for Hashem's help), so if I would have succeeded, I'd have probably become bloated with arrogance. So now, I'll strengthen myself in prayer - this itself is an eternal triumph."

What's the Complaint About?

Rebbe Nachman of Breslev teaches that a sad and bitter person is in effect making the statement that he or she is dissatisfied with the way the Creator runs the world. No other feeling in the world so negates emuna.

The reason a person complains when life doesn't proceed according to plan is because he doesn't accept what happens to him with emuna. A person with emuna harbors no complaints; he never falls into depression because he believes that Hashem is doing everything for his perpetual benefit. Emuna in simple terms is the belief that everything that happens in my life comes from Hashem, and He does nothing but good.

Growth Power

Emuna is growth power. It's the moving force which helps a person achieve personal gain more than anything else in the universe. Emuna gives a person the will to live and the power not only to withstand tough times, but to gain by them. Emuna resembles the deep roots of a tree which enable it to withstand wind, storm, and drought.

The power of emuna is vast. A person with emuna fears nothing. He or she retains composure under stress and meets challenges with a smile. With emuna, one is confident that Hashem listens to every prayer and never forsakes us. Knowing we can always turn to Him, in any circumstance, we should always be happy.

A person who always has someone to turn to never loses hope. What's more, when the "someone" is Hashem and one prays to Him at every opportunity, not only does he never lose hope but he's always happy. He resembles a seed that's planted in moist, fertile ground that grows into a beautiful, vibrant fruit-bearing tree that no wind or extreme weather can knock down.

In summary, sadness is merely a lack of emuna. The Creator looks at a person and asks, "If you believe in Me, why are you sad? I can help you in any situation, anytime, so start smiling and turn to Me!"

We should all constantly ask Hashem for emuna - specifically, for the emuna that everything He does is for our ultimate benefit and for the very best. We must pray for the emuna that He alone knows what's best for us, and even if He doesn't answer our prayers, it's because He either wants us to pray more or that He has different and better plans for us.

Self-Strengthening

Self-strengthening - known in Hebrew as hit'chazkut - is a vital element for a healthy soul. Most people have never heard of such a trait because it's emuna-oriented. Self-strengthening is the ability to interpret whatever happens in life for the very best, and to use everything in life as a springboard to further growth.

The Torah shows us many examples of self-strengthening, how our ancestors turned hopeless situations into total triumphs. Had they not withstood such difficult tests in life, they would not have risen to greatness.

Let's take Joseph for example: as a lad of seventeen, he was daddy's spoiled son, always dressed impeccably and looking like he just walked out of a men's hairdressing salon. Suddenly, the wheel of fortune did a "180" on him. With no physical or emotional preparation, he faced a certain death in a pit of snakes and scorpions. He was pulled out of the pit, sold as a slave and exiled from his father and his homeland. In Egypt, his master's wife tried to seduce him; when he refused, she had him thrown into prison for over a decade, with no hope of ever being released, much less a free man again.

Surely, Joseph would have preferred to remain in his father's domain, continue learning, marry a nice girl and build a nice home. Hashem, though, had different plans; Joseph accepted the His will lovingly and with emuna. Eventually, everything turned around again for the very best and Joseph became the Viceroy of Egypt.

Against all Odds

The Torah doesn't tell mere stories; whenever it tells us about the life of a certain person, there is an important lesson to be learned. Therefore, when we read about Joseph, we should imagine ourselves in his place - how would we feel? How would we react?

Joseph had no idea how long he'd be forced to remain in prison. Perhaps he'd have to spend his whole life away from his family, devoid of a single friend or person who cared whether he was alive or dead. Life became a sudden dead-end, with no chance of better conditions, much less career advancement or aspiration fulfillment. Marriage and children became nothing more than a rosy dream - a fantasy. He couldn't even serve the Creator as he wished. Together, we have a formula for frustration and bitterness, if not loss of sanity altogether.

Were it not for Joseph's self-strengthening and simple emuna that everything is for the best - against all logic and the horrendous circumstances at hand - he would have become a broken shell of a man. Blaming his brothers for tormenting him and selling him into slavery, his heart would have overflowed with an acid sea of hate, revenge and self-pity. He would have cried day and night.

That and more: without emuna, Joseph would have doubted Hashem, feeling animosity toward Him as well. "What did I do to deserve this? I have been trying to do Your will my entire life; is this the way You reward those who are faithful to You? How do You expect me to serve you when I'm surrounded in a filthy incarceration surrounded by idols and idolaters? You obviously hate me; You want me to die a miserable death after unspeakable suffering. I'm sick of this! I'll terminate my own life and put an end to this nightmare..."

Maybe Joseph would have begun to persecute himself like many others do in similar situations, when things don't go the way they planned.

But no! Joseph strengthened himself. He put logic and intellect aside and clung to emuna. He told himself continuously, "This is all from Hashem and it's all for the best, whether or not I understand how at the moment. Hashem loves me always!" So Joseph danced in prison, maintaining a happy and optimistic outlook. He thanked Hashem for everything and he used every available moment to speak to Him in personal prayer.

The Torah teaches that Joseph became successful in prison. Ancient biblical commentators write that Joseph sang and danced in prison. He also encouraged other prisoners. By virtue of his positive attitude and his self-strengthening, he climbed to success. **He believed that everything was for the best!**

In Our Ancestor's Footsteps

We all have deficiencies which we allow to impair our joy in life. But, let's once more remind ourselves of Joseph and ponder his circumstance as a prisoner with no trial, no sentence and no release date. The ancient Egyptians never heard of human rights. Therefore, Joseph had no logical hope of ever becoming anything other than a prisoner.

Therefore:

A person who has not yet found his or her soul-mate and thinks that this is a legitimate reason not to be happy must remember that there were no matchmakers bringing marriage proposals to prison for Joseph, for maybe he'd spend the rest of his life there - **yet he was always happy**.

A person who has not yet been blessed with children might think that this is a legitimate reason not to be happy; Joseph, as a prisoner in jail, had no hope of ever being a parent - **yet he was always happy**.

A person with no home of his own, someone in severe financial trouble or a person who has been unfairly sent to prison might think that this is a legitimate reason not to be happy; Joseph had no home, no income and he was unjustly imprisoned without even a trial - **yet he was always happy**.

A person in a difficult marriage who thinks that his tribulations are unbearable, who thinks that he or she won't be able to stand another day with their spouse and are sure that their circumstance more than justifies a lack of joy must remember that Joseph had many "partners in life" whom he couldn't avoid - thieves, murderers and rapists - whom he had to cope with - **yet he was always happy**.

An elderly person with no loved ones who feels lonely should remember how lonely Joseph was, with no letters, no visitors and no hope of ever seeing his family again - **yet he was always happy**.

If every person in any difficult circumstance would believe that this is what Hashem wants and it's all for the best, he or she would be unconditionally happy! It doesn't matter if a person lacks a soul-mate, children, his own home, a satisfying job, or money in the bank; it doesn't matter if he or she has the meanest spouse in the world. Usually things aren't as extreme as that, but one's lack of emuna and disgruntlement blow the negative way out of proportion.

The War Against Negative Thoughts

Maybe the reader sighs and asks, "How can I compare myself to Joseph? He was righteous - it was easier for him than it is for me." That's not true. Joseph also had to battle negative thoughts. He had to contend with contemplations that he may never marry, may never be a free man and that no one remembered him or cared about him. His life was a potential waste, entrenched in a swamp of lowlifes and idolatry, with no chance of serving Hashem. He had more than enough reasons to persecute himself and to harbor malice toward Hashem.

Let's not forget that Joseph's tribulations were a lot more arduous than ours. According to nature or logic, Joseph had zero hope and nothing to look forward to. Who has use for a life like that? What encouragement can you give a person like that? What ray of hope does he have? Especially, after years had transpired, he could have certainly fallen into despair seeing that his prayers had not been answered. Just imagine the depth of depression that Joseph could have succumbed to.

But Joseph stood up and fought against negative thoughts. He overcame! He yelled out to Hashem and begged for emuna that everything is for the best. He cast his intellect aside and decided that he doesn't understand a thing; he only believes that everything is for the best. Perhaps he surmised that his soul correction and mission on earth was to believe in the Creator in the worst possible circumstances. He continued to sing, dance and thank Hashem. He thought for a moment and said to himself, "Joseph, there's one of two choices: either you believe in the Creator or you don't believe in Him. If you believe that everything is from Him, then believe that it's all for the best! Be happy, dance and thank Hashem."

When Joseph's intellect told him that he's totally justified to be depressed, he said to himself: "Maybe you're right; maybe I do have legitimate reasons to feel sad. But these legitimate reasons will bring me down and I'll lose everything. As soon as I become sad, Hashem will leave me, Heaven forbid - I'll forfeit my emuna and whatever spirituality I've managed to obtain. Then, the real troubles will set in. So rather than being logical and justified, I'd prefer to be smart. I won't let the evil inclination lead me to depression."

Learn from Joseph; don't be "logical" or "justified". Be smart! Cling to emuna and you'll see big miracles and salvations!

A winner chooses emuna, for by choosing emuna, he merits Divine providence. By believing that everything is good, Hashem ultimately shows us that everything is truly good and we see phenomenal salvations!

I Don't Understand a Thing

The Evil Inclination attacked Joseph and said, "You're finished, pal. Look where you are - in a filthy dungeon, and for posterity! You'll never get out of here. Forget about ever getting married..."

Joseph reacted with another dance and song. "I don't understand a thing. What do I care? Whatever the Creator wants, that's what will be. It's all for the best. If I never get married, that's the best thing in the world for me. I thank the Creator for everything! I don't understand, I only believe! But one thing I do know - a person must be happy and dance his whole life long."

A person has the free choice every moment of being happy or sad. Without emuna, he cannot possibly be happy.

The Evil Inclination was like a fly buzzing in Joseph's ear: "You'll never have children...you'll never have a cent to your name...look at the lowlifes who you must spend the rest of your life with...you'll never see your family again...all this is happening to you because you're a sinner...it's all your fault...throw in the towel, Joseph - your life's over!

Joseph's answer to the hounding negative thoughts was another song and dance. He'd simply thank the Creator, reminding himself that everything is from Him and all for the best. "Thank You, Master of the World, for the emuna You have given me."

Joy Sets You Free

No matter what trouble befalls a person, he or she must remind themselves that everything is from the Creator and all for the best. Only then, will a person find a way out of his personal prison, whatever it is.

If a person isn't happy with his situation in life, if he doesn't dance and sing in his own personal prison, he'll never find a way out of it!

Only a happy person can pray properly. A person who lacks the desire to pray has not yet obtained the awareness of emuna that everything is from the Creator and all for the very best. As soon as a person believes that everything is for the best, he doesn't stop praying.

Happy End

What happened in the end with Joseph? He married a beautiful woman and had two very successful sons. He became rich - not just "rich" but fabulously wealthy. He rose to great power as the viceroy of Egypt. He attained fantastic intellectual prowess. This was all by virtue of his emuna.

Without emuna, Joseph would have been another clinically depressed statistic. He wouldn't have merited the holy spirit that enabled him to interpret the dreams of the two incarcerated Egyptian ministers. He certainly would not have had the confidence to stand before Pharaoh in the Royal Court and interpret his dream. He would have been another forgotten prisoner who ended his life in prison.

The Torah teaches us the annals of the great tzaddikim so that we'll learn from them. If we each take a good look at ourselves, we'll come to the conclusion that our worst troubles don't reach a tenth of what Joseph endured. If Joseph would have reacted to his life's tribulations like most people do, he wouldn't have earned the title of "Joseph the Righteous." He would have been Joseph the Complainer or just another emotionally sick person.

Joseph attained everything by way of his emuna. The same can hold true for all of us. By way of emuna, a person can uplift himself from the deepest depths to the loftiest heights. Joseph rose from a lowly slave and prisoner to the all-powerful viceroy of Egypt. From a disparaged and hated slave, he became the nationally-loved leader whom everyone admired.

A person should not entertain the fantasy that if he or she believes for a week or a month, everything will turn around for the best. Emuna must be permanent, with no limits, for salvation will come exactly when Hashem wants it to.

The Way of the Righteous

Despite his many tribulations, King David - like Joseph - was always happy, singing and dancing. He wrote the Book of Psalms, history's greatest best-seller. King David had every reason to be sad and depressed. His own son rebelled against him. His closest advisors betrayed him. His father-in-law tried to kill him. He had enemies lurking on every border. But, as he was always happy, he showed that he was a true son of the King worthy of being king.

The great tzaddikim attained what they did by virtue of their self-strengthening, always reinforcing their belief that everything Hashem does in the world is for the very best. They were full aware that Hashem had a master plan for them.

Sure, they would have preferred to sit in a tranquil atmosphere and learn Torah, with no outside interference or hardships. But, when things did not materialize according to their best-case scenario, the nullified their will to Hashem's will and accepted lovingly everything Hashem had in store for them. Since they realized that this was the way to get close to Hashem, they merited great ascent.

Joseph and David successfully and joyfully weathered unprecedented tribulations with complete emuna. No wonder that Hashem chose their descendants to be the two Messiahs - Moshiach ben Yosef and Moshiach ben David - may they come soon, amen!

Good Versus Bad

One of the ways that the evil inclination bombards a person with negative thoughts is by focusing on that person's problems, faults and deficiencies. The EI conceals a person's good points. That's how it traps a person in its net of sadness and depression. Everyone has loads of good points; there's not a single soul on earth who hasn't done good things. If he would focus on his good points, he'd strengthen himself. He'd be able to stay happy in any circumstance.

Let's illustrate this critically important point with the following parable:

A man owns a fantastically busy gas station right at the entrance to the beltway. His eight gas pumps pump out gasoline non-stop around the clock. He makes millions of dollars. A person approaches the owner and tells him, "I don't see any school buses filling up in your station. You're probably losing thousands of dollars!"

The owner smiles and says, "Do you think that worries me? In one hour, I do more business than all the county school buses can bring me. Do you think I have a second to worry about such trivia?"

The same goes for all of us. Rather than concerning ourselves with what we might be losing - wasting our emotional strength in vain - let's look at the millions we can earn every moment by serving Hashem with joy in prayer and self-reinforcement, strengthening ourselves in emuna and in positive aspirations. Every tiny good point of doing Hashem's will is worth a fortune greater than millions, for this is the purpose of all of creation. This is the key to true joy. During a person's daily session of personal prayer and self-assessment, he can rectify what needs correcting rather than being sad about it.

Be smart - don't look at your bad points at all. Amplify and focus on your good points and rejoice in them every day. Devote a daily hour to personal prayer and self-assessment and confine those aspects of your character and your life that need improvement to that time slot, praying to Hashem to help you rectify. The rest of the day, be happy and look only at your good points.

Anger

Anger is a difficult and very detrimental character trait that destroys not only the life of the angry person but the lives of everyone who comes in contact with him.

The Many Forms and Levels of Anger

Anger ranges from the quiet fuming embers in the heart to outward rage and expressions of violence. Anger can be unfounded, based on an imagined reason, or apparently justified. Since our sages condemn the anger of the apparently justified type, all other forms of anger should certainly be avoided.

Everyone desires to break away from the chains of anger, but few really succeed. The key to removing anger from our lives is emuna.

"Anger management" and such partial solutions as self-control exercises fail to uproot anger. Only emuna can completely dislodge anger from a person's heart. People with high levels of emuna are not affected by anger.

Since a person comes to this earth for the purpose of fulfilling his or her designated mission, it's virtually impossible to avoid challenging situations which stimulate feelings of anger. The Creator pits us against all types of people and events which are not to our liking; with emuna, we realize everything is from Him and for the best. Without emuna, we're dangerously susceptible to anger.

By living our emuna, we avoid anger. Even when others treat us unfairly, insult us, or cause us extreme injustice, by focusing on the Creator and remembering that everything He does is for our ultimate benefit, we don't succumb to anger.

Even when things don't go the way we'd like them to, or when we're disappointed in ourselves or in our shortcomings, with emuna, we're not upset; we realize that overcoming life's difficulties and our own shortcomings are the very reason we're alive on this earth, so we don't get angry. Instead, we simply roll up our sleeves, and get to work!

When we observe life's difficulties as personal messages from Above, not only do we avoid anger, but we achieve a high level of gratification. Nothing is more satisfying than receiving a message from Hashem, understanding it, and taking necessary action on it.

Spiritual Awareness: Wisdom and Understandinbg

In order to uproot anger from our lives, we must profusely ask Hashem to help us achieve wisdom and understanding on a spiritual level. This is the spiritual awareness we ask for every weekday in the Chonen Hadaat prayer of the Shmona Esrei. Spiritual awareness is the cognizance that Hashem alone runs the world and does everything for a specific purpose. Consequently, nothing in the world is random or coincidental.

King Solomon said (Ecclesiastes, 7:10), "Anger rests in the bosom of fools." Foolishness is ignorance, and ignorance is the opposite of awareness. As such, the more a person is spiritually cognizant of the Creator, the less he or she is subject to anger. Children, for example, easily become upset when they don't get their way, because they haven't yet developed spiritual awareness. Maturity therefore is not so much a function of chronological age as it is of spiritual awareness.

A person with highly developed spiritual awareness and strong emuna won't be upset even when subjected to extreme insult or humiliation, because he or she realizes the trial or tribulation is coming from Hashem to strengthen him and thereby aid him in performing his task in life. On the contrary, this person is happy!

We can conclude from all of the above that even if anger were not so destructive, a person with emuna and good sense would never become angry.

Having Mercy on the Soul

Anger has more of a negative effect on the body and the soul than all other biblical transgressions combined. Even if a person has learned scriptures extensively and done many good works, he forfeits all his hard-earned spiritual growth through succumbing to anger. Anger resembles a spiritual acid which literally corrodes a soul. Anger is a "false god" which chases away a soul's righteousness.

Angry people consequently lose all connection with Hashem. When a person gets angry, his or her soul departs; dark-side forces of evil instantly fill the void created by the soul's exit and gain control of the angry person. One must work very hard to escape such a spiritual abyss. Teshuva is impossible without learning emuna and overcoming anger. One must uproot anger to regain the holiness of the soul and rectify it.

The Explanation to Life's Riddles

We often hear inexplicable and unexpected phenomena such as:

The couple who had a great marriage, and now suddenly, the wife demands a divorce;

The two partners who built a thriving business, and now one is demanding the other buy out or sell out;

A person was making a nice living, and suddenly he or she can't make ends meet for no apparent reason;

A formerly level-headed person suddenly begins acting like a wild man.

The list is long. One master key unlocks all of the above riddles - anger. By becoming angry and losing his or her righteous soul, the person's life took a sudden turn for the worst. The wife no longer wants to live with a husband whose actions are governed by the dark side.

Abundance eludes such a person, as do sanity and reason as well.

Nothing in the world is worth losing the purity of our souls. Anger is worse than the allegorical person who sells his soul for some desire - for with anger; one gets nothing in return. On the contrary, even this world becomes a living purgatory. Why? A soul that lacks purity is susceptible to all sorts of ills, damages and maladies. A weak soul is prone to fear, anxiety and sadness constantly.

A Proper Reckoning

With the above in mind, each person must evaluate himself even before he encounters a test of anger. Stop and think if there's anything in the world that is worth getting angry about and paying the price of forfeiting the holiness of our souls. Is it worth losing your soulmate, your income, your health and all the merit of your good deeds? For sure, not!

One must consequently do everything to uproot the heresy and foolishness that cause him to become angry. We should all beg Hashem to help us to avoid anger at all costs, no matter what. Even if people are insulting us or being rude to us; even if our children are behaving in total insolence and not listening to us; even if we're 100% right and the other party is completely wrong; even if someone is willfully and maliciously trying to damage us, we must not let anger rob us of our souls! Why add more damages and destruction to whatever we already must cope with? Anger makes no sense, ever.

Now, we can clearly understand what King Solomon said, that "Anger rests in the bosom of fools." Only a fool is willing to forfeit the purity of his soul together with the accompanying damages.

The losses of anger are tremendous while the benefits are nil! Nothing in the world is worth losing one's soul over.

Peace with the Creator

The Creator's system of Divine providence is individually tailor-made, designed to help each person accomplish his or her task and mission in life. Sometimes, Hashem sends people different catalysts to trigger such actions as penitence, character improvement or a strengthening of faith. These catalysts are not always pleasant to us, but they are always geared for our ultimate benefit.

A person who understands otherwise is a person who thinks he's smarter than Hashem. Such an individual wants everything his way, easy and pleasurable, ignoring the fact that there are so many facets of himself that need strengthening, rectification or improvement. He prefers to play or relax and is in a deep spiritual slumber his whole life long.

Self-rectification and improvement - like any other worthwhile accomplishment - require dedication and hard work, whereas a picnic requires neither. Life is no picnic, but a picnic can't correct a soul. As such, anger is frequently the result of moral and spiritual laziness, when a person isn't willing to rise to the challenges that the Creator presents him with for his own welfare.

With emuna, we can truly be at peace with the Creator, knowing that even our greatest challenges, tribulations and difficulties in life are all from Him, for our ultimate good and for the purpose of making us better people and bringing us closer to Him.

Not only should we avoid anger at all costs, we should subjugate our will to Hashem's will. That way, we can better interpret Hashem's subtle messages that come to each of us by way of the various events and stimuli all around us, thus enabling us to capably and efficiently fulfill our personal mission in life.

Golden Rule

The following principles may sound harsh, but the more you think about them, the more you'll realize that they're the solid-gold truth:

1. **The angry person is actually angry at the Creator!**
2. **The angry person is angry with Hashem! With emuna, we know that everything is Hashem's will. So, if anyone is angry, they're angry at Hashem for not doing their will!**

Jealousy

With emuna, a person knows that he or she has a unique soul with its own special task on earth. The Creator, by way of His compassionate individual Divine Providence, gives each soul the qualities and conditions it requires to achieve its rectification, according to the root of that soul and its previous incarnations. Our sages said, "Just as their faces are different, their opinions are different." Each person has his or her individual path. There are no two people on the same path, so every individual must pursue his own path with emuna. With this in mind, the strong believer never falls into the pit of jealousy nor looks at others in envy.

Living Life's Purpose

Jealousy is an indication that a person hasn't yet started living a purposeful life. Another person's fame, fortune, or success doesn't help any of us fulfill our mission in life; therefore, when we gaze at other people's gifts in life, we fail to develop our own gifts in life, the needed tools in accomplishing what we need to do in this world. Why be jealous of someone else's car, house or spouse? One gains nothing but misery; that's why jealousy is always a bad deal and a lack of emuna.

If a person has a physical handicap, he should believe that this is a state of perfection for him, for the Creator knows that the only way he can accomplish his mission in life is by being handicapped. In that respect, a handicap - observed through eyes of emuna - is not a handicap.

Look at Helen Keller, for example. For her, blindness was not a handicap - it was a critical tool for her mission in life. One person's handicap is therefore another person's springboard to greatness. If Helen Keller would have been miserably bitter and jealous of those who see, she certainly would not have accomplished her mission in life.

A person with emuna looks at what he or she should be doing in the world. In regard to their life's mission, they'll find that their particular physical limitation does not hinder them from performing their task in life. The great virtuoso violinist Yitzchak Pearlman had polio as a child and is crippled in the legs; his crippled legs never got in the way of becoming one of the world's finest musicians. If he had healthy legs, he might have channeled his efforts into football with no success. By the same token, Stevie Wonder and Ray Charles were blind; both were not destined to be airline pilots, but their blindness didn't get in the way of their making millions of people happy with their music.

A person with emuna looks at life's purpose, realizing that his or her handicap does not impair their fulfilling of their mission on earth. Indeed, such people are frequently great achievers.

For example, Hashem might decide that a person must be extremely ugly to perform his mission on earth. The Gemara tells such a story:

Rebbe Yehoshua was extremely ugly. Caesar's daughter once chided him and asked, "How is such magnificent wisdom in such an ugly vessel?"

Rebbe Yehoshua smiled, then asked Caesar's daughter how her father stores his fine wines. "In simple ceramic jugs," she answered. He laughed and said that it's ridiculous that Caesar, the richest man in the world, should store his wine in simple earthenware jugs. She agreed and transferred her father's best wine to solid gold vessels.

A day or so later, Caesar asked for a glass of his favorite Cabernet. The wine was completely sour. Caesar summoned his royal wine master and demanded an explanation. "Your Majesty," shrugged the wine master, "the princess ordered me to transfer all the Cabernet into golden vessels!"

Caesar sent for his daughter and demanded her explanation. "It's not my fault, father," she cried, "Rebbe Yehoshua ben Chananya told me to do it!"

Caesar's guards seized Rebbe Yehoshua ben Chananya and brought him to the royal court. Undaunted, Rebbe Yehoshua said, "Your daughter doesn't like ugly vessels, Your Majesty; but, wisdom and fine wine are similar, they are both preserved in ugly vessels. If I were handsome, then I'd be haughty. The Torah must be in a humble vessel."

Rebbe Yehoshua ben Chananya conveyed an important message - just as wine is best preserved in a simple earthenware vessel, so is Torah best preserved in a simple, not-so-beautiful individual. Such a person is far from pride, arrogance, and vanity. Gold - indicative of pride - sours fine wine. Rebbe Yehoshua ben Chananya was a man of complete emuna - he knew that his ugliness was by no means a deficiency, but an important quality necessary in accomplishing his mission on earth.

In light of the above, one person's deficiency is a valuable tool in another person's soul correction. If Rebbe Yehoshua ben Chananya would have been jealous of beautiful people, and if he would have wasted his time in pursuit of physical perfection, he would have become a bitter and frustrated individual that missed the opportunity of becoming one of the greatest minds of all time. When one pursues his or her true purpose in life, there's no room for jealousy!

Focus on Your Own Task

With Hashem's magnificent Divine providence, each one of us receives the tools, talents, aptitudes and conditions that are most conducive to performing our individual specific mission in life.

Focus on your task in life. Use your own tools to the hilt. If you were born short, don't be jealous of the players in the NBA - it's not your job to play professional basketball! If you're near-sighted, then you probably weren't destined to be an airline pilot either. Yet, wearing thick glasses doesn't hinder your excellence in a myriad of other endeavors. Take a good look at what you do best and develop the special tools which the Creator gave you. If you're jealous of someone else, then you're not concentrating on your own task and not properly utilizing the wonderful tools that Hashem gave you. Get back to focusing on your individual mission!

Every time we detect jealousy within ourselves, we must beg Hashem to give us emuna. One of the greatest barometers of emuna is being content with one's own lot in life, and the content person is never jealous of anyone else. A person with emuna knows that his own set of circumstances in life is for him a best-case scenario. We all must withstand life's tests and tribulations, but we must remember that they too are tailor-made for each of us to accomplish our own purpose in life, and to stimulate us to prayer and to teshuva.

The Test of Poverty

People often ask why Hashem makes a person poor. The poor person most likely needs a soul-correction that necessitates humility, emuna, trust in Hashem and constant prayer. Poverty is the exact climate that helps certain people get close to Hashem and to acquire many wonderful blessings like righteous children, which are countless times more valuable than material wealth. What's more, if they were rich, they'd probably never pray, for they'd likely put their trust in their assets and not in the Creator.

The test of poverty is not easy; but, if a person is poor, then it's a clear sign that poverty is his or her personal path to getting close to the Creator. With eyes of emuna, such a person isn't jealous of someone else's wealth, nor does he or she resort to transgressions in trying to attain more money. With emuna, the poor person knows his current situation is for his ultimate good.

Once again, as soon as the poor person becomes jealous of the rich neighbor, he is not concentrating on his own mission in life. If the poor were rich, they'd likely feel an abyss of spiritual emptiness, for they'd have much less incentive to strengthen themselves in emuna, to pray, and to trust in Hashem. One who feels deficiency when poor will continue to feel deficiency even if he acquires money; in reality, the only deficiency he has is emuna.

The Test of Wealth

The challenge of a rich person is to develop generosity, humility, and trust in the Creator despite his or her wealth and power. As such, wealth is a more difficult test than poverty. It's much easier for a poor person to cast his or her hope on Hashem than it is for a rich person. It's not easy for a rich person to avoid the pitfalls of pride and stinginess, as Hashem commands him to.

The test of wealth is much more difficult than the test of poverty. The wealthy must realize that the Creator gave them money and power for a purpose other than feeding their own bodily appetites. He expects them to overcome natural human egotism, feelings of power and grandeur, and stinginess in order to perform acts of charity and loving-kindness; it is no simple task. The rich are expected to support such lofty causes as spiritual growth and outreach, and not use the Creator's gifts for their own selfish pleasures.

Our sages teach that the more money and assets a person has, the more worries he has as well. The rich person must know that Hashem bestowed him with wealth in order to do many worthwhile things such as helping the poor, supporting Torah learning and spreading emuna. This way, the money brings blessings to his life rather than worry, for he sees himself as an emissary of Hashem in doing good with his assets.

Oftentimes, rich people obtained money illegally in a former life; in this life, they have the opportunity to correct this by distributing sums to the needy. Chances are they are simply returning to a needy person what they took from him unjustly in a former life. Therefore, a rich person should get used to giving as much and as often as possible.

Hashem Decides

A person has free choice in spiritual endeavors only. All the material aspects in his life are the products of Divine decree, in accordance with that person's individual needs and mission in life.

A person with complete emuna is therefore not envious of a single soul on earth. One who lacks emuna though, thinks that other people attained what they did with their own efforts, good luck, cunning or ability. He becomes jealous because his measure of success falls short of the other person's. This is a grave error, for Hashem was the One Who gave the other person everything he has, including his success.

Even though success appears to be the result of diligence and hard work, know full well that it too comes from Hashem. Since a particular person has such a great desire to succeed, Hashem grants him success. In fact, that same person might have succeeded just as well with less effort on his own part. Therefore, a person who is boastful and smug about his success in material endeavors is sorely out of line, for the Creator is responsible, not him.

He Succeeds in Everything He Does

Rabbi Yosef Chaim of Baghdad tells the story of the rich person who was envied by the whole town. The rich person feared that someone would give him an evil eye, so he decided to make a ridiculous investment that would cause him subsequent losses so that others wouldn't be jealous of him anymore. No matter how he invested his money, he still made a windfall. The rich man complained to his rabbi; the rabbi replied, "Success or failure is not up to you. Hashem decides!"

The opposite also holds true. Our great Spanish sage the Ibn Ezra tried everything to make money, but no matter what he did, he failed. "If I'm to be poor all my life, why work? I might as well learn Torah!" The Ibn Ezra dedicated his life to Torah and was destined to write one of history's most significant commentaries on the Torah. Had he spent his life in commerce, subsequent generations wouldn't have benefited from the depth of his wisdom.

We Know Nothing

Why look at others in envy? Despite the fact that you might be jealous of other people, you may be much closer to your soul correction than they are to theirs.

We don't know what Hashem knows. Therefore, we can't assess another person's situation because we know basically nothing about their task in life. When we don't look at others, we don't fall prey to jealousy.

The meaning of "happy with our lot in life", which is the true barometer of emuna, means that we're happy with every single aspect of our lives, in other words, our individual "lot", or portion. Only then, can we avoid jealousy and be truly happy while joyfully fulfilling our mission on earth.

Stinginess

Stinginess is a terrible trait and a sign of cruelty. The stingy person's love of money blinds him from seeing the needs of his fellow man, even those closest to him such as his wife and children. Therefore, a stingy person is disdained by others and seldom has peace at home.

There are several types of misers:

1. Stingy with outsiders but generous with his own family;
2. Stingy with his own family and generous with outsiders - these are the types that give charity for prestige and publicity;
3. Stingy with everyone but lavish with himself;
4. Stingy with everyone including himself - these are the types that hoard their money and end up losing it or leaving it to others.

It's Mine!

Stinginess stems from heresy, when one believes that his own prowess earned him his money. Such a person tends to hoard wealth, for he doesn't realize that Hashem gave him his money. And, if Hashem wants him to have money, then he'll have it. Therefore, when he spends his money on worthwhile things, the money will be replenished.

What's more, if the Creator decides that such-and-such an amount of money are part of a person's assets, then no one can touch a cent of that money. On the other hand, if Hashem doesn't want him to have money, then all the wheeling and dealing in the world won't bring him money. Even if a person has an army of Brinks, armed guards and massive safes protecting his money, if Hashem decides to take it away from him, nothing will help.

The Good Husband

One of the most tragic examples of stinginess is that of the stingy husband. Stinginess is a double expression of cruelty and insensitivity; the stingy husband is cruel to his wife and children and insensitive to their needs and feelings. Every household expenditure triggers his wrath.

There's no greater sorrow to a wife than a stingy husband. According to Kabbala, the health of a wife's soul depends on the abundance that her husband showers upon her. When the husband is poor and lacks the means to provide his wife with plenty, she is saddened. But, when he has the means, and still doesn't give to her, she withers like a plant that's not watered. Even worse, when he says no to her needs, yet turns around and buys whatever amenities he desires for himself, she becomes his bitter enemy.

The Gemara in tractate Bava Metzia 59a teaches that whoever honors his wife gets rich. If a man were smart, he'd cherish his wife, buy her whatever he can, and never criticize her about her expenditures. Just as honoring his wife brings him riches, being angry at her causes him to lose money.

Our sages also teach (Hulin 84b) that a man should forever eat and drink less than what he can afford, dress according to what he can afford, and honor his wife **more** than what he can afford. This is the only mitzvah in the Torah that requires a person to spend more than what he has. Even for a mitzvah as important as honoring the Sabbath, the Gemara says to avoid buying lavish food and drink if it means borrowing from others (Pesachim 112a)!

Hashem is very concerned about a wife's dignity; therefore, a husband should honor her the best way he can. If he can't afford to buy what his wife wants, then he should make a concerted effort to pray and ask Hashem to help him meet his wife's needs and to make her happy. If a man prays for his wife's happiness like he would pray for his own health, then Hashem will surely give him the ways and means to satisfy her.

If a wife makes a request from a husband, and he doesn't have the means to fulfill that request, he should never say no. Instead, he should promise her that with Hashem's help, he'll make every effort to fulfill her request as soon as he possibly can. The husband should complement his own efforts with prayer - the more the better. When Hashem sees that a person is sincere in his desire to honor his wife, Hashem will answer his prayers.

A Difficult Departure

A person with emuna is not stingy, for he trusts in Hashem and not in his money. He knows that a person and his money don't stay together for posterity. Ultimately, one difficultly departs from the other. One of two things happens to money: **Either the money is taken away from the person, or the person is taken away from the money.**

Therefore, one can't depend on money. We all know stories of rich people who ended up dying as paupers; after spending a lifetime accumulating money, they lost everything. On the other hand, there are many cases of rich people who became so sick they couldn't enjoy their money, and ultimately left this world and their money. A popular expression laughs at those who sacrifice their health in search of money, then end up sacrificing their money in search of health. Either way, the money doesn't last.

Full Expense Account

A person with emuna believes that Hashem will fulfill all the basic needs he or she requires in life - food, clothes, shelter, and the like. With emuna, we realize that as long as Hashem wants us to continue living on this earth, He will pick up the tab for every needed expense. The Creator is the boss that provides a complete expense account.

Hashem Enjoys when You're Happy

A person with emuna believes that He Who provides for all his needs today shall continue to provide tomorrow. Therefore, he's not afraid to use the money that Hashem gives him, especially in the fulfillment of His commandments. With emuna, a person realizes that Hashem gave him the means to provide his children with a good education and to buy his wife a new outfit for the upcoming holiday or family celebration; He doesn't send money to hoard in the bank. With emuna, one isn't afraid to put his hand in his pocket for a necessary expenditure - especially for such noble endeavors as charity and supporting worthy causes.

Without emuna, a person suffers every time he spends a cent. Remember - if the Creator sees that his children suffer every time they spend a cent, He is also disappointed. An ancient adage says, "A person with bread in his basket who asks what there will be to eat tomorrow is a person with no emuna" (Sota 48b).

Hashem derives tremendous gratification when a person enjoys the money He gives him. This is like a loving father who gives his cherished son money to live at a better standard of living with no deficiencies. If the son uses the money wisely, renting an apartment in a better neighborhood, buying healthy food and good clothes and shoes for his own family and sharing the money with his brothers, then the father is delighted. He'll be happy to give the son more money in the future.

But, when the father in our example sees that the son continues to live in poverty despite the money, the father is saddened. "What did I give him money for..." the father asks himself, "so that he can hoard it under the floorboards?"

The same goes for our loving Father in Heaven, the Creator. He gives money to people so that they can fulfill their needs and do charitable deeds for their fellow human. This is His will and His gratification, that a person should use his money happily. There are, although, those who are destined by Divine decree to live in poverty, for that too is the Creator's will. Poverty is the best thing for certain souls, for reasons beyond our scope of elaboration here. Those who have money, yet live stingily and unhappily, cause Hashem much sorrow.

Recognized Expenses

When a person spends money to do Hashem's will, including honoring his wife and providing for his children, he reveals his level of trust; in other words, he trusts in Hashem and not in his money. He knows that by doing Hashem's will, he won't lack a thing.

A person who gives money to charity is in effect giving a loan to Hashem. Hashem is then "indebted" to return the loan in full. Indeed, the Creator always gives back much more.

For that reason, those who give a tithe to charity ultimately get rich. In a measure-for-measure manner, a person who has compassion on those less fortunate invokes Hashem's infinite compassion on him.

In short, he who happily spends money to do Hashem's will is a person with true faith in Hashem.

A Loyal Trustee

With emuna, we understand that our money is basically not ours at all, but Hashem's. Hashem lets us invest the money He gives us in a way that earns dividends. For example, when we convert our money into mitzvahs and Torah learning, then the money becomes elevated from a material state to a spiritual state. Hashem considers that a wonderful use of the money and is happy to give us more money since we've acted like a loyal trustee that knows how to invest properly.

Hashem gets no satisfaction from the stingy person that hoards money and fails to put it to use; He is also disappointed when someone squanders money on frills or uses money to violate the Torah's commandments.

A poor person once came to the famed 18th century Chassidic master, Rebbe Avraham Yehoshua Heschel of Afta, known affectionately as "The Afta Rov". The poor man needed a dowry to marry off his lovely daughter who had come of age but didn't have a cent to his name. He asked the Rebbe for help; the Rebbe wrote a personal note, sealed it in an envelope, and told the poor man to take it to a certain rich man in the big city.

The poor man arrived at the rich man's mansion and presented the Rebbe's letter to him. The rich man read the letter, frowned, snarled, and then ripped the letter up. "Who does that Rebbe think he is! What gall! I barely ever heard of him, and he has the nerve to send you here and demand three thousand rubles! Since when does he have the right to put his hand in my pocket?!? Where does he get off thinking that I have to listen to him?"

Humiliated and degraded, the poor man left the rich man's mansion empty-handed. He returned to Afta and told the Rebbe about his unsuccessful journey to the big city. The Rebbe sighed deeply and said, "Go see Avremel - he's a pupil of mine that lives in a thatch-roofed cabin on the edge of town. Tell him that I said to give you five-hundred rubles." Five hundred was much less than three thousand, but to Avremel - a pious but poor Talmudic scholar - five hundred rubles was like five million rubles to the rich man.

The poor man found Avremel's cabin and relayed the rebbe's request. Avremel quickly put on his frayed gabardine and said happily, "Certainly my friend. You sit here and rest from your journey. My wife will give you food and drink. I'll be back in an hour or two." Avremel exchanged a few quiet words with his wife. Smiling, she took all her jewelry and silver ornaments and put them in a cloth rucksack. She blessed her husband with success and he left he house in the direction of the town center.

Avremel pawned his wife's jewelry, his Chanukah candelabra, his silver heirloom Kiddush cup, his silver snuff box and his wife's silver candlesticks. All in all, he put together a sum of 320 rubles. He then ran from merchant to merchant, telling them that he needed an urgent sum for a poor man to marry off his daughter. In an hour, he raised the additional 180 rubles. With joy in his heart, he raced home to present the poor man with the 500 rubles, the exact sum that the Rebbe told him to give.

Everyone was delighted. The poor man blessed and profusely thanked Avremel and his wife. Encouraged, he was soon able to raise the rest of the money that he needed to marry off his daughter honorably. And, Avremel and his wife praised Hashem for enabling them to perform such a lofty mitzvah.

During the subsequent months, Avremel's luck took a sharp turn for the better. Inexplicably, good investments were literally forced on him. He began earning more money than he ever dreamed of, even though he barely picked his head up from his Talmudic studies. Before long, he became one of the richest men in the area.

The rich man from the big city wasn't so fortunate - his dealings plummeted, until he lost nearly everything he owned. Intuitively, his wife made the connection between her husband's misfortune and his refusal to heed the Rebbe from Afta. She urged her husband to go immediately to Afta and beg the Rebbe's forgiveness. So he did...

The former rich man was ushered in to the Rebbe. "Rebbe, please forgive me for my insolence!" the man cried pitifully.

"What insolence?" asked the Rebbe.

"The fact that I ridiculed the Rebbe's word, and refused to help the poor man as the Rebbe requested."

"Aha," nodded the rebbe. "There's nothing to forgive. You were given a task to do and you failed."

"My task?" asked the man. "What task?"

"Let me explain," said the Rebbe. "My soul was destined to descend to this world as a rich man. I appealed before the Heavenly throne that riches will only distract me from devoting my life to Torah learning and the service of Hashem. My appeal was accepted on condition that I find another soul that would be willing to be a trustee over my riches. I appointed you. Your riches were actually mine, given to you for safe-keeping. So, when I asked that you give the poor man the three thousand rubles to comfortably marry off his daughter, I was asking for my own money. Your refusal showed that you were no longer a reliable trustee for my money, so you lost it. My pupil Avremel became the trustee instead of you."

"Rebbe, please take pity on me," cried the former rich man. "Please arrange for me a minimal stipend so that my wife and I won't starve to death!"

Avremel was more than happy to obey the Rebbe's request to send a monthly allotment to the former rich man from the big city. "After all," Avremel told himself, "The money's not mine - I'm only a trustee anyway!"

Humility

True humility is not parading around and declaring, "I'm a nothing." True humility means knowing your virtues and knowing that they are all gifts from Hashem. True humility is also knowing your shortcomings. A person who sees his own faults as well as his futility and limited ability knows just how much he is dependent on Hashem.

Success is a reason to rejoice, for Hashem helped that person be successful. Indeed, it's vital that everyone must be aware of his or her virtues and successes, while thanking Hashem for granting them those virtues and successes. Despite success, one must always ask Hashem for continued assistance, for perpetual prayer and dependence on Him lead to true humility. Yet, if a person fails, he shouldn't be disappointed; he should realize that Hashem is showing him where he stands without Divine help. As such, failure and setbacks should be catalysts to trigger more prayer and more dependence on Hashem rather than on "the might of my right hand".

Here's an important principle: the arrogant person severs himself from Hashem for he only sees his egotistical self. He becomes over-inflated with pride when "he succeeds", but becomes bitterly depressed when he fails, for he attributes both success and failure to himself. On the other hand, the humble person connects both success and failure to Hashem: when he succeeds, he thanks Him; when he fails, he puts more effort into praying.

Know full well! Hashem does not torture a person; He doesn't ask anything that a person is not capable of doing. Hashem knows that we are human and not angels. The only thing He asks when a person transgresses is, "Why didn't you ask for my help? Why did you think that you were capable of overcoming your evil inclination on your own?"

No matter if a person commits the worst sin, he should know that teshuva doesn't mean self-persecution or depression; it means confession, remorse, apology and a resolve to do better. Real teshuva can only be accomplished with joy. One should therefore never forget Hashem! He should say to himself, "I'm powerless without Him. Hashem wanted to show me that I need His help. He loves me and He wants me to be close to Him. I tried on my own, but I fell on my face. But now that I've had my setback, what does He want from me? Does He want me to be sad or to persecute myself? For sure, not! He wants me to live my life with Him. He wants me to be happy and to pray more. He wants me to repent because He's a loving Father and He wants me to succeed!"

After the above bit of self-strengthening and encouragement, he should say: "Thank You, Master of the World, for showing me that I am powerless without you. From now on, help me remember You always and to seek Your help, so that I won't do anything without prayer."

A person's mind functions most efficiently when he is in a happy mode. Happiness is therefore a prerequisite for meaningful self-assessment and penitence. Sadness and self-persecution are conducive to neither and serve no purpose. Prayer, on the other hand, illuminates a person with the light of emuna and he therefore escapes the darkness in his life, replacing it with awe of and love for the Creator.

Rebbe Nachman of Breslev tells a fable about a king who had an only son. The king wanted to crown his son the prince in his own lifetime, so he made a royal celebration.

All the nobility of the kingdom shared the king's joy and even the general populace was invited to the palace to witness and rejoice in the coronation.

When everyone was exceedingly happy, the king took the prince aside and said: "My son, I am a skilled astrologer; I see in the stars that you are destined to lose your kingship. Make sure to be strong and not be sad. If you remain joyful, I too will be joyful. But, if you succumb to sadness and depression, I will still be joyful because it shows that you didn't deserve to be king anyway. But, if you remain joyful, I will be exceedingly joyful."

Rebbe Nachman's fable shows us the intrinsic value of maintaining a positive outlook despite the peripheral hardships. It also reveals the secret of true humility. The king symbolizes Hashem - He knows that we, His children, have setbacks in life, and difficult ones at that. Yet, He wants us to remain joyful. He wants us to avoid sadness and depression at all costs. Just as He commanded us not to sin, if we do sin, He commands us not to be sad. In joy, we pick ourselves up, rebuild and rectify.

Every person must know: **Hashem loves you!** He rejoices in you! He loves when you're a successful prince or princess, and He also rejoices in you when you fall, as long as you don't fall into sadness.

Why does Hashem love a person who maintains a positive outlook even after a setback? Such a person has two feet on the ground; he knows who he is and he doesn't fool himself with fantasies. He doesn't consider himself holy and pious. He knows that he is a mere human with fallacies and that he is prone to sin. He therefore is not surprised when he does sin. On the contrary - when he acts in a righteous manner, he is amazed. He thanks Hashem for His helping him overcome his evil inclination.

As in Rebbe Nachman's allegory, Hashem desires to "crown His son in His lifetime" - He wants a person to succeed with His help. The sign that a person is worthy of success is when he remains joyful and optimistic even after a setback. A person must know that his success - his "kingship" - is none other than a gift from his Father the Creator. It doesn't belong to him. He therefore rejoices when he is successful and is just as happy when not. The level of true humility is evident in a person who remains happy even when success is taken away from him.

True happiness is the sign of "spiritual nobility" - a true son or daughter of the King, and the product of emuna and humility. True happiness is unconditional and independent of any outside variable. The happy person is not happy because he has a certain something; he is happy in any event.

A person must know that he is the son or daughter of the King and succeeds only because the King wants him or her to succeed. The evil inclination constantly lies in ambush, waiting to knock a person down. Without the King's help, the son or daughter cannot possibly succeed. The humble son or daughter therefore isn't disappointed when he or she doesn't succeed; they know that this is only natural, considering their limited ability, innate character flaws such as egotism and cruelty and their inclination toward evil.

Maybe you want to ask why Hashem in certain cases doesn't help people. Why does He let them fall? Hashem refrains from helping them in order to show them their true dimensions, that they cannot succeed without Him. Rather than persecuting and blaming themselves, they must humbly appeal to the Creator and seek His help to improve and rectify as needed. On the other hand, when they do succeed, they must not attribute their success to themselves but profusely thank the Creator for His help.

Hashem refrains from helping a person when that person's ego becomes inflated and he or she forgets that they're dependent on the Creator's help.

The challenge after a setback is to avoid falling into the pitfalls of sadness and depression. A happy person is happy no matter what. He knows that Hashem wants him to be happy even when things don't go his way, for this is true humility.

Failure is the outcome of forgetting Hashem and that success comes from Him. As soon as he attributes success to himself, he is already on the way down. The more he forgets the Creator, the harder he falls.

A person who strengthens himself in joy after a setback rectifies the cause of his fall. He forgot that his prior success came from Hashem, so he fell. Now, when he is happy instead of sad, Hashem sees that he understands the nature of his fall and deserves to have his former level of success restored.

King David fell one time in his entire life and never forgot it his entire life. He understood that if a person takes his mind off Hashem for a split second, he is liable to fall. That's why King David was so humble, praying to the Creator his entire life long. Despite his many tribulations, he was always happy and truly deserving of being a great king.

King David had every reason to be sad and depressed. His own son rebelled against him. His closest advisors betrayed him. His father-in-law tried to kill him. He had enemies lurking on every border. But, as he was always happy, he showed that he was a true son of the King worthy of being king.

As a young boy, King David was a shepherd. All his life, he could have cared less whether he was a shepherd or a king. He was happy either way, for his inner joy wasn't contingent on any external variable.

The same goes for anyone who desires to sincerely serve Hashem. A "fair-weather friend" is one who serves Hashem on condition that he gets what he wants but walks away from Him in anger and in sadness as soon as things go otherwise. Such a person never grows or improves and is far away from true happiness. The joy of a truly happy person is unconditional; he serves Hashem in any situation. When things go his way, he is especially agile in serving Him. And, when things don't go his way, he serves Hashem the best he can and prays for happiness and His help.

In light of the above, a person's main teshuva should be for forgetting Hashem, for had he remembered Him, he surely would not have sinned. Arrogance is the product of forgetting Hashem. Conversely, humility depends on remembering Him always.

A person who remembers Hashem can rectify with joy rather than persecuting himself. No matter what, he has someone to turn to, a powerful Father in Heaven who will always have mercy on him and help him as long as he sincerely seeks Him. With such a positive outlook, teshuva and self-rectification are not only easy, but a pleasure. Without joy, all the confessions and apologies in the world are worthless, mere expressions of arrogance, when a person cries that he's not an angel devoid of an evil inclination. The arrogant person cries because he's not the Messiah; some even cry because they're not the Creator Himself...

Summary

We learned in this chapter how difficult negative character traits are and that they stem from a lack of emuna. On the other hand, we learned how wonderful positive character traits are. In effect, we can write an entire volume on each individual trait, but we trust that Hashem will help the reader understand within the scope of this book that emuna is the key of ridding oneself of negative character attributes and attaining positive character attributes.

As food for thought and further self-improvement, here are a few words on how emuna affects those attributes that we didn't elaborate on:

Arrogance - the believer has no arrogance, for he knows that all his successes are gifts from Hashem.

Gluttony - a believer isn't constantly craving food, for he knows that Hashem sustains him, not the food.

Trust - emuna enables a person to trust in Hashem, to believe that He constantly watches over him and therefore he is in good hands.

Compliance - a compliant person gives in to others because he knows that Hashem wants him to. He is therefore successful always, for Hashem is with him.

Joy - the believer is always happy, for emuna means that there is no bad in the world; everything is good and all for the best.

Flattery - the believer is far away from flattery, for he knows that everyone is a mere puppet with Hashem pulling the strings. He therefore fears no one and doesn't need to flatter anyone, for he knows that Hashem alone will determine what will be in his life.

Honor - a person with emuna isn't chasing after honor and prestige, for he knows that honor and prestige belong to the Creator.

Slander - the believer doesn't talk about other people for he knows that as a mere mortal, he is incapable of passing judgment on anyone; he cannot determine who is upright and who is not. He knows that there's an omniscient Creator whose task it is to judge all of creation and he is not so presumptuous as to think that he can do the Creator's job.

Argumentative - a person with emuna steers clear of arguments and strife, for he knows that everything that happens to him comes from Hashem. He therefore doesn't come into conflict with people; he turns to Hashem and thereby avoids all strife and arguments.

Patience - a person with emuna has patience for everyone and everything, for he knows that everything in life goes according to Hashem's timetable, both spiritual matters and material.

Developing Proper Character Traits

We'll now discuss a practical approach to character improvement.

Intellect is not sufficient in ridding oneself of negative character traits. One must internalize what the intellect knows into the **heart.** This is what the Torah commands us when it says, "And you shall know today and you shall internalize it in your heart" (Deuteronomy 4:39); when the knowledge of good is internalized in the heart, a person can rectify any given negative character trait.

Here's proof: there are many highly intelligent people with terrible character traits. Why? Their hearts are still contaminated. On the other hand, there are many simple people with impeccable character, for their hearts are pure.

The way to internalize in the heart what the brain knows is to learn and review what one learns all about a given character trait, then to pray for Hashem's help in internalizing and implementing what we learn. Prayer drives things that the brain understands deep into the heart. This is called complete awareness. A person who behaves with such complete awareness has good character.

According to everything we have learned, the source of all good character traits is emuna. Therefore, to rectify any negative character trait, one must first learn emuna, particularly how emuna affects that particular trait. He must assess himself daily and pray for Hashem's guidance and assistance. He must thank Him for every little success and for every time he succeeds in avoiding temptation. If he fails, he must pray for Hashem to help him overcome his deficiencies and rectify, for in most cases, setbacks indicate a prior lack of prayer. If he transgresses, especially from the result of a negative character trait, he should implement the four-step process of penitence - confession, expression of remorse, apologize and resolve to seek Hashem's help in improving. One cannot rid himself of a negative trait without profuse prayer.

A person who walks the above path and implements the advice of this book and others like it, praying daily and asking Hashem to help him internalize what he learned, will surely succeed in rectifying his character and in living a happy, sweet life.

Strong Self-Composure

Many people complain that even after reading books and listening to lessons, even praying profusely, they don't succeed in changing themselves for the better. For example, one person complained that he heard a CD lesson about anger, doing his best to internalize the teachings and praying to implement them, yet he still loses his temper. What can he do?

What's happening here? What's the problem? Why doesn't a person succeed in improving himself?

Rebbe Nachman of Breslev provides the answer. He says, "People are far away from the Creator because they lack **self-composure**. Therefore, a person must compose himself, stop and think: what is the purpose of lust and bodily appetites and all the amenities of this world? Once he asks himself, **he will surely return to the Creator**."

If we take a deep look at Rebbe Nachman's answer, we'll see that the root of a person's problems is that he's chasing things that won't bring him genuine happiness, as if he's a chinchilla on a wheel, for he lacks self-composure. He never stops to think!

What does Rebbe Nachman of Breslev mean by a lack of self-composure? In his own words, "One must take stock of what he's doing in the world, whether or not it's worthwhile to spend his life acting like he does. **Since he lacks self-composure, he lacks spiritual awareness.** Even if he does pause to think sometimes, it doesn't last for long. And his bit of self-composure is not reinforced with conviction and inner strength, realizing that this world is but folly."

We hereby learn a deep principle: spiritual awareness depends on self-composure. Without self-composure, a person functions on bodily instincts like an animal. He is bewildered, unaware of what's happening to him in his life and why. Sometimes he thinks one way and then overnight changes his opinion - or even his spouse - for no valid reason. The proof is that the next day, he regrets what did the day before. He lacked self-composure and lacked clarity.

Even when a person lacks clarity, with self-composure, he is aware that he lacks clarity and that he must clarify the truth before he makes a decision and takes action.

Let's go back to our example of the young man who prayed to overcome anger. Anyone who prays to overcome a negative character trait - or prays for anything else, for that matter - must first compose himself. Once he pondered the truth and clarified it in his mind, his self-composure leads to inner strength and strong conviction. The stronger his conviction, the more powerful his prayers become. Ultimately, nothing can sway him from the truth. Now he's ready to pray. His three key terms are self-composure, inner strength and conviction. For example, once he has composed himself, realizing that anger destroys his entire life having learned the causes and damages of anger, his awareness of the truth strengthens him and gives him conviction. His prayers become so much more effective as well as his efforts to rid himself of this detrimental trait.

On the other hand, without self-composure, he is confused, easily swayed and too weak to tackle the challenge of character improvement, which is by no means an easy task. The slightest test of character will knock him down.

The fruits of self-composure, inner strength and conviction are truth and spiritual awareness, the weapons that disarm the evil inclination.

Imagine a person who builds a wall to keep enemies away. If the wall has no breaches, it can prevent infiltration attempts. But, if the wall is breached in several places, despite the fact that it is mostly thick and formidable, it's virtually worthless in keeping the enemy from penetrating the city.

The intellect is a person's wall. When a person fortifies his intellect with self-composure, he can internalize in his heart what his brain knows. This way, there are no breaches in his "wall". But, when he lacks self-composure - even if he prays - his wall is breached; he acts according to impulse and instinct and he continues to make the same mistakes, succumbing to anger, getting entangled in arguments and the like.

Suppose a person wants to overcome anger. He prays, but if he's honest with himself, he'll realize that his conviction to avoid anger is not yet strong enough. He has not yet reached the point of inner strength and conviction where he tells himself that he'll do anything in his power to avoid anger. He'll admit to himself that certain situations are still capable of igniting his fuse. He might even justify getting angry in those situations. As such, no prayer in the world will help him overcome anger until he firmly establishes in his mind and heart that he must never get angry, otherwise he risks weakening his connection to the Creator. He therefore won't pray for help in overcoming anger in those situations where anger is justified in his mind.

On the other hand, if he thoroughly composes himself, pondering anger, its ramifications and the Creator's will, he'll arrive at the truth. Let him ask himself: is there any situation where anger is justifiable? In marriage? In child education? Maybe it's okay to get angry in the course of making a living... This way, he should establish the truth until it's crystal clear in his mind.

With in-depth self-composure, a person will discover that there is no situation in the world that justifies anger. Every time he becomes angry, he commits a severe transgression, for anger is a breach of emuna in the Creator and tantamount to idolatry. The losses of anger are many and prodigious. Once again, with self-composure and the inner strength and conviction that result from self-assessment and clarifying the truth, there will be no situation where he succumbs to anger.

One should pray profusely, seeking Hashem's help in strengthening his character: "Master of the World, have mercy on me. Help me realize that anger is forbidden at all costs and totally against Your will. Let me internalize this fact in my heart, so that my heart will not tempt me to get angry in certain situations. Let it be clear in my mind that anger is a transgression. If I get angry, it means that I'm sinning – there's no way of circumventing this fact. Enable me to stand strong with firm conviction never to get angry."

In a person's daily self-assessment, he should evaluate how his behavior has been during the last 24 hours since yesterday's self-assessment session. If his behavior has not been up to par, then he should pray for the Creator's help during the coming 24 hours. He should see if there is a pattern to his setbacks, such as repeated anger at his children or at his spouse, praying for extra special help in whatever problematic area he has where he is prone to setbacks. He should especially observe the situations where the evil inclination succeeds in knocking him down.

Most importantly, a person should be honest with himself and admit his setbacks rather than justifying them or rationalizing them, for these self-indulging thought processes distance him from the truth. Honesty is the basis of self-assessment.

To stand firm in the face of life's challenges, a person must have self-composure, inner strength and conviction. Self- composure leads to truth clarification, and clarity of truth leads to inner strength and conviction. Prayer that results from the three assets of self-composure, inner strength and conviction is the way to overcome any type of character flaw, including lust and bad habits. Such self-rectification brings a person close to Hashem.

Chapter Seven:

The Virtues of Emuna

The virtues of emuna are beyond description, for emuna is the essence of mankind's potential for greatness. Rebbe Nachman of Breslev says that by way of emuna, man attains perfection of character. Emuna is the moral and spiritual leg that the human soul stands on. In brief, emuna is the sum of Divine will.

Emuna is the conduit of Divine blessings and abundance. A person with emuna is capable of invoking every blessing imaginable.

Emuna is so strong that it leads a person to the level of strong desire, where he or she yearns for the Creator and serves Him with all their heart.

Emuna leads to patience and to every other desirable character trait. It uproots undesirable character traits. With emuna, a person believes in Divine providence, that everything that happens to him is for the very best. This prevents a host of negative emotions.

Emuna is the basis of marital bliss and therefore a vital factor in building a stable family unit. Emuna contributes to the emotional health of the children and of all of society.

Emuna has many additional virtues. Rebbe Nachman writes that emuna brings blessings to a person, sharpens his mind, gives him spiritual awareness, cancels harsh decrees, leads to self-composure and atones for all of one's sins. Emuna also leads to one's personal redemption.

Rebbe Nachman also teaches us that the perpetuation of exile and Diaspora stems from a lack of emuna. As such, we learn that the Geula - the full redemption of our people - depends on emuna (see Likutei Moharan I:7).

The Purpose of the Soul's Descent to the Physical World

The human soul is a tiny spark of the Divine. Before it descended to this world, it saw Divine illumination and basked in it. Apparently, there is no greater proximity to Hashem. But, in actuality, it was far from Him because **it didn't know** Hashem. Sure, the soul was well-aware of Hashem's light and its indescribable sublime pleasure, but it knew nothing of the Hashem's ways, will and attributes.

The following analogy will facilitate our understanding: Imagine someone standing in front of you who shines forth with the most beautiful and dazzling lights imaginable, making a Fourth-of-July fireworks spectacle look like a bore. You have the urge to approach him and to learn what his powers are, to learn how those breathtaking lights shine from him. You long to talk to this amazing person and are not satisfied with merely enjoying his lights without getting to know him.

In the Heavenly realm, there are no obstacles and no evil inclination or temptation, only dazzling illumination. The soul needs no help, solutions or salvation. Its faith, patience, morals and resolve are not tested. The quality and attributes of any soul only become apparent when challenged down here below in the physical world.

Hashem created the world in order to reveal His mercy. Without creation, there was no one on whom He could bestow His mercy (see Likutei Moharan I:64).

The soul therefore descends to the material world in order to become familiar with the Creator's infinite mercy, for down here, we need the His mercy every second of the day our entire lives. As such, Divine will and the purpose of creation are fulfilled.

Pleased to Meet You!

Let's clarify the concept above with the following anecdote:

One of Rebbe Natan's students complained: "I'm sorry I didn't have the privilege of knowing Rebbe Nachman of Breslev personally."

Rebbe Natan answered sternly, "And who has the audacity to think that they 'knew' Rebbe Nachman? Yosef Frunick?"

Yosef Frunick was a simpleton who operated a ferry on the river. All day long, he'd transfer people from one side of the river to the other. Rebbe Nachman of Breslev used Yosef Frunick's services frequently. Yosef therefore enjoyed boasting, "O-ho, I used to spend a lot of time with Rebbe Nachman - I knew him well!"

Rebbe Natan of Breslev - Rebbe Nachman's prime disciple - desired to stress that a physical knowledge of someone or something is meaningless. Yosef Frunick knew what Rebbe Nachman looked like, but he hadn't the slightest idea about Rebbe Nachman's enormous spiritual stature. To begin to know Rebbe Nachman of Breslev, explained Rebbe Natan, one must learn and practice his teachings. Therefore, a disciple in a latter generation can know a wise man better than a contemporary acquaintance who saw him in the flesh.

Yosef Frunick not only saw Rebbe Nachman of Breslev; he actually touched him several times while assisting him on and off the ferry. Yet, physical proximity has nothing to do with spiritual awareness. In effect, the simple and crass ferryman was as far removed from the wise man as east is from west. He had no idea of Rebbe Nachman's holiness, his wisdom, his teachings, his spiritual prowess, his capabilities, and the breadth of his righteous soul. He simply helped him cross the river.

The same principle applies to the knowledge of the Creator: The soul in the upper worlds takes pleasure in the Divine light without knowing anything about the Creator. It therefore resembles the ferryman who boasted he knew Rebbe Nachman of Breslev, when in reality he knew nothing more than the color of Rebbe Nachman's beard.

Rebbe Nachman himself defines proximity as spiritual awareness when he writes, "By virtue of spiritual awareness - the knowledge of the Creator - one attains oneness with Him" (see Likutei Moharan I:21). Therefore, by seeking a connection with the Creator in the physical world, one can actually get to know Him better down here than the mere proximity to Him "upstairs" in the spiritual world. It may not be apparent, but the Creator's presence is everywhere; the advantage of the material world is it enables spiritual gain, whereas the spiritual world does not. This is an apparent contradiction, but a cardinal principle of spirituality.

In the material world, we sorely need the Creator's constant assistance, especially to successfully weather the trials and tribulations of this world. This is the environment where our souls can really tell Him, "It's a pleasure to meet You!"

She Says – But I Know

There's a well-known story about the Rebbe Levi Yitzchak of Berditchev. He grew up in a family of Misnagedim, those who opposed the Chassidic movement, which was still in its early years:

Despite his father's objection, Rebbe Levi Yitzchak had a burning desire to taste the sweet light of Chassidic thought and practice. Therefore, after his wedding, he spent three years studying in holiness under the tutelage of the Maggid of Mezeritch, who was the prime disciple and the successor of the Baal Shem Tov.

Before he left home, Rebbe Levi Yitzchak succeeded in placating his wife and receiving her permission but his father roared in anger: "You just got married! How do you leave a young wife alone on her own with no income to fend for herself?" He tried to stop his son, but to no avail. When he saw Levi Yitzchak's insistence and dedication, he let him go. The father consoled himself in the likely prospect that his son would return as an ordained rabbi and certified religious court judge, with high status and good income potential.

Three years later, Levi Yitzchak returned home. His father received him with untold excitement. After he rested from his journey, his father asked him, "Dearest son! Please tell us about what you learned. Which Torah areas have you specialized in? Have you received your ordinations as rabbi and rabbinical court judge? Do you have a new title? What nuances have you garnered from your teacher?"

Levi Yitzchak responded, "Dear father, for three years, I worked day and night to attain spiritual awareness.

I learned one thing - there is a Creator who rules and directs the universe - Hashem, He is G-d!"

"What?!" thundered the father. "That's all you learned in three long years away from home? That's so simple - every imbecile knows that..."

The father summoned their simple housemaid and asked her, "Tell us, please: who runs the world and created every living thing?"

"The Creator," she answered, "He controls Heaven and earth."

"And who is the healer of all flesh?" he asked.

"The Creator," she responded.

"And who sustains all of creation?" he asked once more.

"The Creator," answered the housemaid.

Straining to restrain his anger, the father looked at Levi Yitzchak and said, "You see? The simple housemaid knows everything you learned! Why did it take you so long?"

Levi Yitzchak answered, "Dear father, **she says so, but I know so!"**

The same holds true for the soul in the upper realm before it descends to this world. It has its limited simplistic knowledge of Hashem's goodness and magnitude, but this knowledge is theoretical at best, for it has never been tested. Once the soul enters a physical body in the material world, it undergoes test after test of emuna. This gives it both its practical knowledge and its deep internalization of Hashem and His mercy. This knowledge is no longer academic or theoretical.

A person should therefore welcome the tests of faith in this world, for otherwise, he'll never attain emuna or any semblance of spiritual awareness. Without the "combat experience" in the challenges of this world, the soul is like a basic trainee who has never been tested under fire. Down here, we fulfill our mission of getting to know Hashem, for that is our entire objective.

By the Sweat of Your Brow

No one likes to feel like a beggar. We receive gratification by knowing that we earned what we have. For that reason, the soul actually desires to descend to the "war zone" of the material world in order to rightfully earn a lofty place in close proximity to the Eternal One where it can bask in Divine light. As long as the untried and unproven soul derives unearned pleasure in the spiritual world, it is sorely embarrassed in front of those souls who have rightfully earned their places. Since our loving and merciful Creator wants the soul to have complete pleasure, He gives it the opportunity to achieve the status it desires.

Concealment

When the soul descends to this world, it falls into an abyss of spiritual darkness, where Divine light is hidden within layer after layer of concealment. A thinking person may ask, "How can the soul possibly find the Creator and get close to Him in an environment where everything seems to hide or deny His very existence?" We see with our own eyes few people - even so-called "religious" people - succeed in cutting through the layers of darkness and concealment to reveal the Creator's splendid illumination.

Let's answer our above question by examining the various layers of concealment, as follows:

First concealment - nature: The laws of nature appear absolute, and therefore conceal the reality of Hashem. We would think that if He wanted to make His presence apparent through the material world, He'd perform many more miracles so everyone would make no mistake about His existence and reign.

Second concealment - humans: Human beings are obstructions in the way of realizing the reality of Hashem; since they have free choice, they are able to do for the most part what they want when they want. When they lie or steal, a bolt of lightning doesn't appear from the sky to kill them. When they help a blind or crippled person cross the street, an angel doesn't dive down to earth in order to put a $100,000 check in their pocket. On the surface of things, Hashem doesn't seem to react to their good or evil, so, where is He? Even worse, since most people have no idea what emuna is, their speech and outlook reflect heresy and agnosticism. Why doesn't the Creator make it easier to believe in Him?

Third concealment - the body: The physical body which hosts the soul is the coarsest form of material matter, with needs, drives, and lusts that pull in the exact opposite direction of spirituality and Godliness. The body strongly gravitates toward physical amenities and further conceals the Divine light from the soul. Why must the body be so crass? Couldn't the Creator have created a more spiritually-refined and receptive body, so it would be easier to recognize Him?

Fourth concealment - trials and tribulations: Life in this world conceals the presence of the Creator in many ways. The biblical word for "world," olam, also means concealment. The trials and tribulations of daily life - financial difficulties, sickness, crime, international strife, emotional pressures, and many more - all conceal the Creator's loving-kindness. Terror, fatal accidents, crippled children, and other apparent injustices and human suffering render emuna nearly impossible. Where is He?

Why couldn't Hashem make life easier for us? What does He care if we all have nice penthouses on the riviera with an ocean view and a Maserati parked downstairs? What's wrong with everyone being rich, with no discrimination, wars or suffering? Why can't it be paradise down here?

Fifth concealment - fulfilling the Creator's will and commandments: This is the most difficult concealment, for the Creator's commands are within themselves concealment. They are often not clear enough, to the extent that experts even argue about the proper way to observe and fulfill them. Each person claims to know what the truth is. Man becomes confused; what is he supposed to do, when one "great spiritual leader" says one thing, and another "great spiritual leader" says the opposite?

Why wasn't the Creator clearer in His directives? Why is the Torah so cryptic and open to so many interpretations? Why doesn't Hashem shine the light of truth on anyone who earnestly learns His commandments?

Do you feel like screaming? Doesn't all this sound unfair? Everything seems to work against us in our search for Hashem and emuna. Doors of difficulties shut in our faces and the entire world seems to be pitted against us to prevent us from feeling His presence in our lives. We're bombarded with agnostic and atheistic stimuli from morning until night. We turn to Him for consolation, and even He seems to push us away. If the purpose of the soul's descent to the material world is to get to know the Creator, then why is it such a difficult task? Couldn't life be made easier? It looks like the soul is fighting a losing battle. Why is the body always resisting the soul and pulling in its own direction? What's a person supposed to do?

Revelation

Heaven forbid, there's no mistake or oversight down here. The constant struggle of life in this material world is exactly what drives a person to seek the Creator, if he only desires.

As soon as we realize our futility against all the forces in the world that work against us, we become modest. Awareness of human limitation and fallibility is an important prerequisite for emuna, when a person realizes that he or she is incapable of navigating the troubled waters of this world without Hashem's help. Consequently, we turn to Him, and develop a strong desire to feel His comforting influence in our lives and to get close to Him and to get to know Him.

But, one requires much self-strengthening to remember Hashem during times of extreme suffering and difficulty. Why? At these times, one's spiritual awareness is taken away; he or she is left with no other choice but to cry out to Hashem.

Know full well that if a person had an easy life with no challenges or difficulties, he or she would never get close to Hashem! There would be no purpose in the soul's descent to the physical world; let it remain up by the Heavenly Throne, learning Torah and basking in Divine light.

The whole purpose of concealment is for a person to know that he or she needs Hashem every moment of their lives, not just in overcoming difficulties and bad habits, but in learning Torah and praying as well. One needs Hashem's guidance constantly to remain on the path of truth. That's what King David meant when he said to Hashem such things as, "Guide me on the path of Your truth", "Teach me Your ways", "Help me understand and retain Your Torah", "Guide me in the path of Your commandments", "Turn my heart to Your laws", and many other similar passages as we see throughout the Book of Psalms.

Consequently, concealment - like everything else Hashem does - is all for the best, for it brings a person to need Hashem and to seek Him. We all need Hashem to override nature and to help us rid ourselves of lust and bad habits. We need Hashem to help us overcome obstacles and to guide us amidst this confusing world on the path of truth.

We see with our own eyes how people with easy lives are far from Hashem. Sure, at close inspection, we'd find that they need Hashem too because their lives are surely empty and tasteless without Hashem's light. As such, there are those who have everything, but they taste nothing but boredom and emptiness.

Therefore, people must wake up and observe that life is slipping through their fingers. Even if they live in comfort and relative ease, they should realize that only a strong connection with Hashem can give them gratification of the soul.

Why wait for times of trouble? The more we truly seek Hashem, the more we improve the quality of our lives. Even if we don't suffer from any earth-shaking difficulties, we should nevertheless turn to Him on a regular basis, for we must realize that the whole purpose of our lives is to get to know Hashem and to get close to Him.

Slowly but Surely

Despite the above explanation, some people still ask, "If the Creator wants me to get closer to Him, why doesn't He simply reveal Himself to me?"

Let's answer with an analogy: Imagine that the electric company wants to save money, so they close down their transformers and relay stations, and send a direct cable from their main generator to your house. When you'd turn on the switch to your 100-watt bulb in the living room, 50,000 watts of power would come through the cable. The bulb would burst to smithereens in a split second. Even worse, the cables in your walls would explode, and the whole house could catch fire. For that reason, the electricity can't reach your home without a series of transformers, circuit breakers, and relays which reduce the core power of the generated electricity to a measure which you can safely use.

By the same token, Hashem's Divine light is infinite and unlimited. For our own benefit, He doesn't give us an illumination which is too strong for our souls to handle, otherwise we'd "burn out" - die, become insane, or lose our faith altogether. This is exactly what happened with Rebbe Akiva and his friends, as the Gemara tells us in tractate Chagiga. They exposed themselves to the upper realms and a prodigious amount of Divine light - one died, one lost his mind, one become a heretic and only Rebbe Akiva emerged in peace, unscathed. The other three were not suitable vessels for such a level of Divine light.

Our difficulties in life serve as shades to diminish exposure to a measure of Divine light that we cannot yet handle. Rebbe Akiva was worthy, since he was a man of humble beginnings, a poor agricultural laborer and the son of converts. Despite his rise to lofty spiritual heights, he retained his humility. He prayed profusely, leaving trails of tears behind him. His difficult life prepared him as a worthy vessel for such Divine light that other Tannaic sages could not cope with.

Knowing that our difficulties in life are the vehicles which actually strengthen our souls and bring us closer to the Creator, we become girded with the strength to handle any situation. What could be a bigger encouragement than knowing that the Creator wants to bring us closer to Him? So, when we look at the difficulties of our lives through eyes of emuna, we instantly become both stronger and happier.

Once more, don't be jealous of someone who has an easy life - it's not a prize. People who haven't been tested are very limited in their capability to grasp emuna or to get close to Hashem, like Rebbe Akiva did.

We now realize that people with easy lives, who lack the benefits of life's difficulties, forfeit the spiritual advantages that those difficulties offer, particularly in learning our own futility, attaining emuna and getting close to Hashem. Spiritual gain is much harder to attain without life's hard times.

Looking for the Light

Each of life's difficulties that we endure and overcome with the help of prayer grants us additional knowledge of Hashem. Life's darkness and difficulty come from a lack of spiritual awareness. So, in order to cut through the concealment, we seek spiritual awareness, which is none other than Divine illumination. Again, the difficulty is the catalyst in our spiritual growth; without it, we'd still be on the lower level and further away from Hashem.

When we "look for the light," in other words, when we search for the Divine message within tribulations and realize that He uses them to stimulate our personal and spiritual growth, despair becomes hope. Life's overwhelming situations become challenges which we're equipped to meet when we look for the light within the darkness. This enables us to rectify what we must and to find our own individual path in the world.

My Soul Thirsts for Hashem

Life's trying times are what cause the soul to yearn for its Creator. Since the soul is spiritual, it thirsts for Godliness. Nothing can satiate it other than Hashem's Divine light, as King David wrote (Psalms 42:3), "My soul thirsts for Hashem, for the living God."

The soul derives virtually no gratification from material amenities. A long list of celebrities had everything a person could dream of - money, vacation homes, swimming pools and tennis courts in their back yards, fame, and literally anything that money could buy - yet many of them became insane or committed suicide. They had everything but they had nothing.

When the soul feels darkness, it becomes restless. The feeling of unrest, emptiness, and a squirming sensation in the abdomen indicates the soul's longing for Hashem. By searching for Hashem's light, the soul attains proximity to Hashem. Hashem illuminates the soul's darkness, thus helping the soul to overcome its difficulties. As a result, the soul gets to know, love, and appreciate Hashem more and more.

Endless Difficulties

The more a person has problems, the more he or she is likely to seek Hashem, just as a person in darkness seeks the light. Even if a person seeks Hashem just for the sake of relief, and not for the loftier motive of adding Godliness to his or her life, they still discover Hashem's infinite mercy and compassion.

The Gemara says (tractate Nedarim 81a), "Beware of the sons of the poor, for they shall become the scholars of Torah." The struggles of lads from impoverished families stimulate them from a young age to seek Hashem; they subsequently develop a strong measure of emuna and thirst for Torah.

King David suffered untold difficulties from a tender age and thereby sought Hashem constantly, ultimately reaching the level of a prophet and Hashem's anointed. He composed The Book of Psalms, the world's foremost collection of personal prayers. Our sages teach us that our ancestral mothers Sarah, Rebecca, and Rachel were barren because Hashem wanted to extract their prayers. If they would have had children with no difficulty, they'd certainly have prayed much less, both in quantity and in intensity. If we examine the lives of the great tzaddikim, we find almost always that their lives were an ongoing saga of one difficulty after another.

Life's difficulties are a clear sign that Hashem wants to bring us closer to Him.

Obstacles Fuel Desire

Rebbe Nachman of Breslev writes (Likutei Moharan I:66), "The degree of longing is enhanced by the obstacles that stand in the way of the goal, for when a person is prevented from attaining his wish, then his desire is greatly enhanced."

With the above principle in mind, we can view the difficulties, troubles, trials, and tribulations of life in a positive light. As soon as we encounter difficulty, we should arouse our desire and longing for Hashem, for the very purpose of trying situations is to bring us closer to Hashem.

Jeremiah the prophet says (Jeremiah 30:7), "It will be a time of trouble for Jacob, but from it shall he be saved." In other words, the same dire situation that Hashem saves Israel from is the catalyst that drives the Jewish people closer to Hashem. The serious trouble stimulates them to pray from the depths of their souls and to seek Hashem. As such, the trouble is ultimately a gem of untold value. Hashem says (Ezekiel 33:11), "I do not desire the death of the wicked, but that he should return from his evil ways and live."

Hashem doesn't want us to suffer; He wants us to live upright lives and to be happy. Life's difficulties are wake-up calls to initiate soul-searching on two levels, namely, to prod us to seek Hashem and to stimulate teshuva and character development. If we were always successful, we would most certainly become smug and arrogant, never seeking Hashem, and never correcting a single character flaw. That's what the Torah means when it says, "And Jeshurun waxed fat - and kicked" (Deuteronomy 32:15). When a person "kicks" - in other words, when he gets arrogant - the Divine Presence leaves him. So, even if he had everything, he'd really have nothing.

Joy of Living

Life is joy and happiness. Only a happy person can be called "alive". Practically speaking, "life" and "happiness" are synonymous, since life indicates a joyful state (just as conversely, death indicates a forlorn state). Many people have beating hearts and functioning lungs, but they lack the joy of living, for they lack emuna. Rebbe Nachman of Breslev teaches that without emuna, life isn't worth living; the smallest difficulties in life sink the non-believer into sadness, depression, and despair. Without emuna, a person suffers from worry, stress, confusion, and self-persecution.

Rebbe Nachman explains that the non-believers are incapable of understanding or effectively coping with situations that don't go according to their plans or wishes. They feel helpless at the hands of "fate" and "nature" that torture them with no rhyme or reason. On the other hand, people with emuna seldom lose composure, since they realize how life's trying times are for their ultimate best. Consequently, they live joyful and sweet lives, in this world and in the next.

Agnostics and atheists have no life in this world or in the next. If you check closely, you'll find that beneath the veneer of an artificial smile, you'll find them to be anxious, worried, and stress-ridden. Their lives are full of inexplicable difficulties, day-to-day struggles of survival or a never-ending chase for material amenities that almost always elude them. The believer, in contrast, understands what he or she is doing in the world and how life's challenges are milestones for personal and spiritual growth designed to accomplish a clearly defined goal.

To taste the joy of life, one needs emuna. Knowing that everything in our lives is an eternal gift from our loving Father in Heaven for the very best provides the joy of life that fuels inner strength. With emuna, a person is also able to put the difficulties of this life in proper proportion, especially when looking at the ultimate goal of eternal bliss in the next life.

The War Against Amalek

Amalek is the symbol of evil and a nickname for the Yetzer Hara, or evil inclination. His main weapon is the venom of doubt; he injects doubts of emuna within a person's mind and heart. In fact, the Hebrew numerical equivalent of Amalek, 240, is also the numerical equivalent of the Hebrew word for "doubt", safek. Two facts characterize the evil inclination:

1. The evil inclination comes to a person who has doubts in emuna. But, when a person is strong in emuna, knowing that Hashem is always with him, the evil inclination cannot touch him.
2. As soon as a person begins to doubt Hashem, he or she encounters immediate difficulties that are designed to make them cry out and seek Hashem again.

The Torah relates (Exodus, chapter 17) that the Children of Israel defeated the Amalekites only by virtue of emuna. When Moses' hands were extended to the Heavens in prayer, Israel held the upper hand. When Moses' hands fell, Amalek gained the upper hand. The Mishna in tractate Rosh Hashanah asks hypothetically, "Do the hands of Moses win or lose a war?" The Mishna answers its own question and says, "As long as Israel cast their eyes skyward and subjugated their hearts to their Father in Heaven, they overcame their enemy - if not, they fell." We therefore conclude that Amalek wins when a person forgets Hashem, Heaven forbid.

Uplifting our Eyes

Consequently, Amalek - the evil inclination - strives to destroy a person's emuna, so that he or she won't look skyward. With emuna, a person is protected against the evil inclination. When the wall of emuna crumbles - Heaven forbid - a person is exposed and defenseless. By uplifting our eyes and remembering Hashem, Amalek is disarmed.

Whenever a person suffers, he or she simply can look skyward, call out to Hashem in personal prayer, and ask for help. No prayer goes unanswered, for Hashem is near to those who call Him in earnest. What's more, the Gemara in tractate Kiddushin says that no one is capable of overcoming the evil inclination without Hashem's help. Hashem helps those who turn to Him, for, "Hashem is close to those who call Him, to those who call Him in truth" (Psalm 145:18).

Emuna, whose practical manifestation is prayer, is the only surefire weapon against the evil inclination. For this reason, we should all strive to constantly enhance our emuna and powers of prayer.

The Purpose of Torah and Mitzvoth

All our endeavors in learning Torah, praying and performing the mitzvoth are geared to reveal Hashem's monarchy in the world and to bring a person to emuna and to recognition of Hashem's Divine providence, with no dictates from nature at all.

The entire purpose of Torah is to bring us to emuna, as King David says in Psalm 119:86, "All Your mitzvoth are emuna."

Rebbe Nachman of Breslev writes that the epitome of Divine service is to attain emuna, "To merit in knowing the Creator, for this is the main purpose - His will is that we get to know Him. Any other intent in Divine service is not befitting, for we must fulfill Divine will." Deep spiritual knowledge is insufficient if a person lacks simple emuna, for the purpose of everything is to attain emuna. One cannot understand the Torah properly without emuna.

Rerbbe Nachman writes: "**The purpose of everything is to serve Hashem walk and in the way of Hashem for His Name's sake, for it is His desire that we get to know Him. It is not befitting that a person have any other intent in his service of Hashem, other than doing Hashem's will**" (Likutei Moharan II:37).

A Person's Spiritual Level

The Gemara in tractate Pesachim 50a tells about Rav Yosef the son of Rabbi Yehoshua ben Levi who became so sick the he reached the state of clinical death. By Hashem's grace, Rav Yosef recuperated after his soul had entered the threshold of the world to come. His father asked him, "What did you see in the spiritual world?"

Rav Yosef answered, "I saw an upside-down world; the high were low and the low were high."

Rabbi Yehoshua ben Levi commented, "My son, you saw a clear world," in other words, an accurate picture.

Let's elaborate on the above simple but very profound thought: Many people in this world enjoy wealth, prestige and are considered "high society." But, in the spiritual world, they're on the bottom rung. The opposite also holds true; certain people in this world are humiliated, ridiculed, or persecuted, yet in the next world they enjoy a high level of status. A person's spiritual level is determined by the extent to which he or she has developed their emuna and successfully passed life's many tests of faith during their term in the material world.

Emuna is the root and foundation of life. The prophet (Habbakuk 2:4) said, "And the righteous will live by emuna." With emuna, a person is assured a good, gratifying and meaningful life in this world and in the next. As emuna increases, so does one's spiritual status.

Greatness and Insignificance

The prophet says (Samuel I, 16:7), "For a person sees the eyes and Hashem sees the heart." In other words, we lack the tools to judge the true status of another person. People tend to evaluate the worth of others according to money, wisdom, beauty, or pedigree; such yardsticks are both deceiving and inaccurate. They often show a great person as insignificant, or an insignificant person as great.

An illiterate person could feasibly be a greater individual than a doctor or university professor, especially if the former has strong cognizance of his mission in the world and the latter does not. One who possesses a strong cognizance of Hashem far surpasses the person that has no idea who created the world and for what purpose, even if the former is a street cleaner and the latter is a nuclear physicist. Isaiah the prophet teaches (Isaiah 1:3) that a person who has no awareness of Hashem is on a lower spiritual level than an ox, when he chastises Israel for forsaking emuna: "An ox knows its Creator and a donkey its Master's trough; Israel knew not, for they failed to observe." In other words, the ox and the donkey are aware that Hashem sustains them, but he who blindly seeks a life of physical amenities never finds Hashem.

Rebbe Nachman writes: "The main aspect of a human is his spiritual awareness. One who lacks spiritual awareness lacks the essence of humanity and cannot be called human at all; he only resembles a human. Moses had mercy - he engaged in settling the world, so that the world would be settled by humans, in other words, those with spiritual awareness" (Likutei Moharan II:7).

Emuna - the Best Merchandise

In light of everything we've discussed in this chapter, a person would be smart to invest the bulk of his or her efforts in attaining and developing emuna. Emuna is the world's most important commodity.

The Gemara teaches (tractate Shabbat 31a) that the first question a person is asked when he or she leaves the material world is, "Did you negotiate in faith?". The basic interpretation of this question is whether a person dealt fairly and honestly in commerce. But, on the allusive level, the person is being asked whether he or she negotiated to acquire the commodity of faith - **emuna** - by learning emuna, talking emuna, practicing emuna, and striving for emuna.

The Zohar teaches that Hashem manipulates entire worlds so that two people will come together and discuss emuna.

Emuna is the key to true happiness and success in this world, as well as the only guarantee of success in the next world. This chapter has briefly touched on the benefits of emuna, but essentially, there're no limits to its virtues. Happy is the person that obtains true and lasting emuna.

A Concluding Word

Now that we've learned the best advice that life has to offer - emuna - we must emphasize that the implementation of all the lessons in this book are based on one main premise, the knowledge that everything that happens in life is for the very best. Without earnest daily personal prayer and self-assessment, one cannot attain this awareness. To attain the cognizance that everything is for the best, one must confess to Hashem daily. Without the daily hour of personal prayer that includes self-assessment - judging oneself and one's actions during the previous 24 hours since his last personal prayer session - he or she won't have the capability of receiving the greatest gift there is, the cognizance that everything is for the best. Rebbe Nachman of Breslev writes that when a person knows that everything in life is for the very best, he or she lives a life of paradise like in the world to come (Likutei Moharan I:4).

Everyone should therefore pray profusely to merit a daily hour of personal prayer, and that way, he or she will become a true believer. There will be no stern judgments on them and they will merit the blessing, "A faithful person shall abound with blessings", amen!

Completed, with praise and thanks to Hashem

Did you enjoy this book?

Help partner in printing and distributing

the new enlarged edition of

The Garden of Emuna

For information call:

972-52-2240696

Made in the USA
Middletown, DE
22 August 2024

59615080R00263